MW00855752

The Power of Godliness

The Power
of Godliness

Mormon Liturgy and Cosmology

JONATHAN A. STAPLEY

OXFORD
UNIVERSITY PRESS

Oxford University Press is a department of the University of Oxford. It furthers
the University's objective of excellence in research, scholarship, and education
by publishing worldwide. Oxford is a registered trade mark of Oxford University
Press in the UK and certain other countries.

Published in the United States of America by Oxford University Press
198 Madison Avenue, New York, NY 10016, United States of America.

© Oxford University Press 2018

All rights reserved. No part of this publication may be reproduced, stored in
a retrieval system, or transmitted, in any form or by any means, without the
prior permission in writing of Oxford University Press, or as expressly permitted
by law, by license, or under terms agreed with the appropriate reproduction
rights organization. Inquiries concerning reproduction outside the scope of the
above should be sent to the Rights Department, Oxford University Press, at the
address above.

You must not circulate this work in any other form
and you must impose this same condition on any acquirer.

CIP data is on file at the Library of Congress
ISBN 978–0–19–084443–1

3 5 7 9 8 6 4

Printed by Sheridan Books, Inc., United States of America

To Kathryn, with whom the cosmos is as enjoyable as it is interesting.

Contents

Acknowledgments

BOTH THIS WORK and I have been enriched by generous associations with scholars focused on Mormons and Mormonism. It is a field rich in documentary resources and passionate practitioners. My fellow contributors to the *By Common Consent* and *Juvenile Instructor* websites have been particularly encouraging. Colleagues have often shared references that have expanded my views and understanding. Ardis Parshall was particularly helpful in sharing material and friendship. Gary Bergera and Brett Dowdle pointed me to several important items key to the chapter on baby blessings. The staff of the Church History Library of the Church of Jesus Christ of Latter-day Saints were incredibly helpful in making available materials germane to this project. Their work to preserve and make materials of historical interest available is simply extraordinary.

Mark Ashurst-McGee, Samuel Brown, Kathleen Flake, Lisa Olsen Tait, Ryan Tobler, and John Turner reviewed sections of this book. Matthew Bowman, Terryl Givens, Amanda Hendrix-Komoto, Ellen Henneman, Michael MacKay, Quincy D. Newell, Joseph Stuart, William V. Smith, and Stephen Taysom reviewed chapters (sometimes multiple). All offered helpful questions, comments, and criticisms, for which I am grateful. Kristine Wright is a longtime friend and collaborator without whom I would not have been in a position to write this book. She also read and responded to several chapters. I must thank and credit Jill Mulvay Derr for inspiring me generally and to start this project particularly; her regular encouragement and critique were essential. Of course, misinterpretations and errors are solely mine. Jana Riess was a skillful and efficient editor who helped me clarify my natively turbid and obscure prose.

My family has been a constant support as I research and write. My parents, Ron and Julie, are generous with their interest and encouragement. Kathryn, my wife, is patient and gracious. She is the person to whom I owe the greatest debt for my time on this project and on religious history more broadly. Thank you.

Abbreviations

BYOF   Brigham Young Office Files, 1832–1878, CR 1234 1, Church History Library, The Church of Jesus Christ of Latter-day Saints, Salt Lake City, Utah.

CD   *Collected Discourses*, 5 vols., ed. Brian H. Stuy (Sandy, UT: B.H.S. Publishing, 1987).

CHL   Church History Library, The Church of Jesus Christ of Latter-day Saints, Salt Lake City, Utah.

FFY   *The First Fifty Years of Relief Society: Key Documents in Latter-day Saint Women's History*, ed. Jill Mulvay Derr, Carol Cornwall Madsen, Kate Holbrook, and Matthew J. Grow (Salt Lake City: Church Historian's Press, 2016).

FHL   Family History Library, The Church of Jesus Christ of Latter-day Saints, Salt Lake City, Utah.

FPL   First Presidency letterpress copybooks, Church History Library, The Church of Jesus Christ of Latter-day Saints, Salt Lake City, Utah.

JD   *Journal of Discourses*, 26 vols. (London and Liverpool: LDS Booksellers Depot, 1854–1886).

JH   Journal History of the Church 1896–2001 July, CR 100 137, Church History Library, The Church of Jesus Christ of Latter-day Saints, Salt Lake City, Utah.

JSP D1   *Documents*, Vol. 1: *July 1828–June 1831*, ed. Michael Hubbard MacKay, Gerrit J. Dirkmaat, Grant Underwood, Robert J. Woodford, and William G. Hartley, in *The Joseph Smith Papers* (Salt Lake City: Church Historian's Press, 2013).

JSP D2   *Documents*, Vol. 2: *July 1831–January 1833*, ed. Matthew C. Godfrey, Mark Ashurst-McGee, Grant Underwood, Robert J. Woodford, and William G. Hartley, in *The Joseph Smith Papers* (Salt Lake City: Church Historian's Press, 2013).

JSP H1   *Histories*, Vol. 1: *Joseph Smith Histories, 1832–1844*, ed. Karen Lynn Davidson, David J. Whittaker, Mark Ashurst-McGee, and Richard L. Jensen, in *The Joseph Smith Papers* (Salt Lake City: Church Historian's Press, 2012).

JSP H2   *Histories*, Vol. 2: *Assigned Historical Writings, 1831–1847*, ed. Karen Lynn Davidson, Richard L. Jensen, and David J. Whittaker, in *The Joseph Smith Papers* (Salt Lake City: Church Historian's Press, 2012).

JSP J1   *Journals*, Vol. 1: *1832–1839*, ed. Dean C. Jessee, Mark Ashurst-McGee, and Richard L. Jensen, in *The Joseph Smith Papers* (Salt Lake City: Church Historian's Press, 2008).

JSP J2   *Journals*, Vol. 2: *December 1841–April 1843*, ed. Andrew H. Hedges, Alex D. Smith, and Richard Lloyd Anderson, in *The Joseph Smith Papers* (Salt Lake City: Church Historian's Press, 2011).

JSP J3   *Journals*, Vol. 3: *May 1843–June 1844*, ed. Andrew H. Hedges, Alex D. Smith, and Brent M. Rogers, in *The Joseph Smith Papers* (Salt Lake City: Church Historian's Press, 2015).

JSP W   Joseph Smith Papers Website, http://www.josephsmithpapers.org

JWML   Special Collections, J. Willard Marriott Library, University of Utah, Salt Lake City, Utah.

LTPSC   Tom Perry Special Collections, Harold B. Lee Library, Brigham Young University, Provo, Utah.

MCL   Special Collections and Archives, Merrill-Cazier Library, Utah State University, Logan, Utah.

Introduction

We have the ancient order
To us by prophets given,
And here we have the pattern
As things exist in heav'n.[1]

ELIZA R. SNOW, 1857

ON FEBRUARY 17, 1847, Brigham Young lay sick in his bed, tottering in and out of consciousness. Outside, his people swarmed throughout the refugee camp in the Omaha Nation Territory. The bulk of the Latter-day Saints had followed Young and the other twelve apostles after Joseph Smith was killed almost three years earlier. They only had enough time to finish their temple on the Mississippi River before fleeing west. Everything they had worked so hard to build slipped from them, and they needed a new home. While other church leaders addressed a meeting of Young's expanding kin, Young had a dream in which Joseph Smith appeared to him. This vision was so important to him that as soon as he was able, he wrote down a description of it in his own hand.

After writing of his joy at being with his friend and prophet again, Young described asking for help to better understand the meaning of the rituals he had performed in the Nauvoo Temple. In response, Smith laid out a panoramic vision of human history from before the creation to the final hour. Young observed: "Our Father in he[a]ven organized the human famely, but they are all disorganized and in grate confusion." Smith showed him "the patern how they they ware [*sic*] in the begining." This pattern, Young wrote, "I cannot describe but saw it and where the Preasthood had ben taken from the Earth and how it must be joined to gether so there would be a perfect chane from Father Adam to his latest posterity."[2] This vision of organizing the human family into one salvific whole drove Joseph Smith, Brigham Young, and subsequent Mormon leaders. And their rituals were their tools.

A church's liturgy is its ritualized system of worship—the services and patterns in which believers regularly participate. While the term often refers to a specific formal ritual like the Roman Catholic Mass, church liturgy is also used to celebrate major life events—birth, coming of age, marriage, death. In Mormonism, the temple liturgy is only the most obvious ordering of the cosmos, and it is the foundation of the faith's most notorious practices. Mormon liturgy, however, constitutes a much larger and more complex set of rituals and ritualized acts of worship than the specific rites of initiation, instruction, and sealing that are localized within the temple walls. In exploring Mormonism's liturgy more broadly, not only do nuances of belief and practice become evident, but we see how the ordering of heaven and earth is not a mere philosophical or theological exercise. Rather, liturgy informs and reinforces believers' behavior. Moreover, by exploring Mormonism's liturgical history, we find a more complete religious world, incorporating women, men, and children of diverse races and sexualities all participating in the construction of the Mormon universe.

This book argues that a fundamental force in the development and interpretation of Mormonism's liturgy and cosmology has been the religion's conceptions of priesthood. Brigham Young's vision was an inflection point in the developmental curve of these conceptions. It was a time when a temple-based priesthood cosmology saturated discourse and conversation, and strongly influenced the organizational decisions of the Saints as they wended their way across the plains. As was common in Mormon communities sixty years later, the women of the rural Panguitch Stake in southern Utah blessed pregnant women for their safe deliveries and used Young's same visionary imagery. They pronounced blessings on the mother and the unborn child. The women proclaimed that the child would "be brought forth in perfection with-out spot or blemish that every spot or limb may be perfect," and "be lovely in its disposition, peaceful, and happy filled with wisdom, intelligence and faith from the womb." The women also declared that the child was to be "one of the noble spirits that has been held in reserve to be born in the priesthood."[3]

Understanding what those women meant over one hundred years ago when they stated that the child be "born in the priesthood" and what priesthood Brigham Young saw that must "be joined to gether" to make the human family whole is a principal aim of this volume. More broadly, this book uses liturgy to elucidate the cosmologies and authorities that order and structure Mormon life and opens new possibilities for understanding the lived experiences of women and men in the Mormon past and Mormon present. In many ways this book begins to address the question of what work these rituals and ritualized acts actually did in the communities that performed them. By tracing the development of the rituals and attempting to ascertain the work they have accomplished, the Mormon universe, with its complex priesthoods, authorities, and powers, becomes comprehensible.

Structure of the Volume

After this introduction's brief overview of Mormonism's liturgical terrain from Joseph Smith's earliest revelations to the present, each subsequent chapter traces a ritual or liturgy along that topology, revealing different aspects of Mormonism's lived religion and cosmology. In each case issues of authority and gender interplay with priesthood, a dynamic that is most explicit in chapter 1, which explores ordination and priesthoods. "Priesthood" is a word with dramatically shifting definitions throughout Mormon history, and it is also an area of intense social interest today. In some historical uses priesthood required the inclusion of women to be cohesive, while in others, female exclusion was deemed necessary. Chapter 1 outlines this evolution, following changes in ordination patterns and detailing the complex rise of a priesthood ecclesiastical bureaucracy that was cosmologically and discursively male. This chapter lays the foundation and analytical framework for the balance of the book as well as introducing important context for Mormon polygamy and the church's racially exclusive practices.

One of the most significant and misunderstood features of Mormonism's priesthood cosmology is the creation of eternal kinship relations through temple sealing rituals. Chapter 2 deals with Joseph Smith's revelation of these "priesthood" relationships, investigates what they have meant over time, and chronicles the efforts of church leaders to faithfully manage their creation. Perhaps no ritual deals so intimately with the self-identities of Latter-day Saints as the temple sealing. The cosmic and eternal relationships of spouses, parents, and children reify the aspirations of millions while also at times contradicting them, as when church policies prohibit sealings in some cases of remarriage. Meanwhile, leaders continually struggle to maintain the connections with the past. Nineteenth-century Mormons were notorious for their polygamy, but while the gendered asymmetries of their marriage practices certainly directed Mormon life in profound ways, sealings more broadly ordered their existence. The imprint of the resulting cosmologies endured long after the church abandoned polygamy at the turn of the twentieth century, and nowhere is this more explicit than in twentieth-century sealing practice. In many ways it is helpful to view the twentieth-century church as struggling to embrace its past while fashioning a new present.

Chapter 3, which focuses on baby blessings, explores one of the earliest and least studied rituals in Mormonism. Mormons have always been staunch advocates of believer's baptism, but Joseph Smith revealed that church elders were authorized to take very young children, lay hands on them, and "bless" them in the name of Jesus Christ. This observance quickly began to function as a naming ritual, but, more critically, it also functioned to demarcate the boundaries of communal salvation. Over time baby blessings incorporated the expansive cosmologies of later Saints and eventually became a performative duty of Mormon fathers. As such, this ritual is an incredibly useful tool for understanding the construction of a Mormon fatherhood that is now completely entangled with the Mormon ecclesiastical priesthood. As the Latter-day Saints experienced all of the transitions from the Zionist period of the early 1830s through the adoption of the Nauvoo Temple cosmology and into the eras of polygamy and post-polygamy, the baby blessing ritual demonstrated that the liturgy was flexible and adaptable, and not just prescriptive. Whether used to announce a child's heirship in the Zion community or to declare his or her place in the material network of heaven, a baby blessing has always been an exercise in building the salvific community. Furthermore, as the designated performer of the baby blessing came to be the father instead of a local church leader, the ritual also revealed a shift in Mormons' understanding of who the builders of that community were. Latter-day Saint liturgy simultaneously ordered Mormons' lives and was adapted by Mormons to better fill their changing needs.

One of the most important issues to church leaders throughout Mormon history has been that of authority, particularly who has the proper authority to perform church rituals. Perhaps no liturgy complicates Mormon authority better than healing, as it has been the single most diverse liturgy—not only in terms of the rituals performed, but also in terms of the identities of the ritual performers. Both men and women, church members and officers, have performed healing rituals with authority, but after the first generation of church leaders died, an ecclesiastical priesthood bureaucracy arose as a principle of church and cosmological order. In chapter 4 I review the history of Mormon healing and the regular participation of women in the liturgy. Female ritual healing was a celebrated feature of Mormonism for a century and is an extraordinarily rich practice that challenges many core axioms of modern Mormonism. In particular, the details of ritual administrators, ritual form, and ritual justification all interacted with broader conceptions of authority, power, and priesthood in and out of the church. The context of both the rise of female healing and its decline is important to our understanding of the formalization of liturgy more broadly in the church as well as the church's creation of a core set of priesthood "ordinances," or necessary (and often salvific) rituals.

Last, chapter 5 approaches the practices of folk Christianity in Mormonism—activities often maligned as "magic." This chapter explores the overlooked context of the transatlantic dispersion of "cunning-folk" practice. Early Mormon leaders were tremendously tolerant of folk ritual, believing as they did in supernatural power and an open heaven. And while some aspects of this culture were formally incorporated into church belief and activities, more commonly, church leaders equipped believers with the tools of liturgy to reach their desired ends. Like women's performance of healing rituals, the incorporation of cunning-folk practice into the church shows important tensions between lay members and priesthood officers in the area of authority as well as the ultimate dominance of the ecclesiastical priesthood. However, as folk ritual often related to healing, cunning-folk practice is also an important context for the popular use of complementary and alternative medical therapies among Mormons today.

Each liturgy explored in these chapters has its own particular trajectory while also sharing a broader history. Before exploring them in detail, this introduction reviews the contours of that shared history, from the beginning of the church in 1830 to the present. This backdrop enables more relevant and contrasting analyses.

The History and Topology of Mormon Liturgy

On Sunday, December 14, 1834, Joseph Smith preached a three-hour sermon "during which he exposed the Methodist Dicipline in its black deformity and called upon the Elders in the power of the spirit of God to expose the creeds & confessions of men."[4] The Methodist *Discipline* was a rule book that in several hundred pages delineated proper Methodist Episcopal policies, beliefs, liturgies, and church regulations. It is easy to find portions of the *Discipline* with which Smith would have strongly disagreed—the retention of infant baptism, for example. At the same time, early Mormonism was saturated with the language and polity of Methodism, whether governance by conferences (general or otherwise) or rule by bishops. When Joseph Smith met Methodist circuit rider Peter Cartwright in the early 1840s, Smith purportedly told him, "We Latter-day Saints are Methodists, as far as they have gone, only we have advanced further."[5] Smith's earlier comments had not been nearly so conciliatory.

A recurring injunction of the *Discipline* is that believers must follow its rules, forms, and practices. Like the traditional Christian creeds, which infuriated Mormons and other anticreedal denominations,[6] the *Discipline* represented a sort of stasis—a stricture on the possibilities of Smith's revelation, even if the precise content was largely unobjectionable. An important contrast to the *Discipline* is the Doctrine and Covenants, a compilation of Smith's revelations, including a catechism used for training evangelists, that was just being prepared for publication when Smith uttered his December 14 sermon. Smith's revelations were heavy on exhortation and extremely light on polity. Baptism as a requirement was mentioned repeatedly; however, the only part of the liturgy to be documented was the short twenty-five-word baptismal prayer. The Methodist baptismal prayer was only nineteen words long, all of which were incorporated into the Mormon prayer. However, the *Discipline*'s ritual of baptism also included the recitation of nearly seven hundred additional words. The Methodist baptism ceremony was largely prescribed and maintained its continuity over decades. In contrast, over its first decades, Mormon baptism was comparatively chaotic and multidimensional.[7]

During the first five years of Mormonism, Smith revealed a series of rituals largely inspired by Book of Mormon and New Testament precedents: baptism, the Lord's Supper, confirmation, ordination, baby blessing, healing blessings, patriarchal blessings, sealing up to eternal life, and foot washing. Some of these, like the Lord's Supper, remained fairly static in Mormon practice; but others, like foot washing, evolved with successive iterations of liturgy in expansive ways. In 1835 church leaders edited, updated, and harmonized key early revelations to conform to the cosmos as they had grown to see it. Joseph Smith's revelations as published in 1835 included the word of the Lord on church order, visions of heaven, and calls to church office. There are also key revelatory texts on ecclesiology, liturgy, and cosmology. And while this publication crystallized Smith's early revelations in a way that prevented further textual evolution, he also began to deprecate the completed text in favor of his living oracle. Instead of a systematic written liturgy, Smith introduced ritual concepts and people learned to participate in them through proximate example and oral instruction. Each ritual was thus performative in the sense that church members and leaders learned it together. Informal instruction allowed ritual to bend to the needs of the community.

At the end of 1835, a year after preaching against the Methodist *Discipline*, Joseph Smith introduced the beginnings of the Kirtland Temple liturgy, with its ceremonial washings, anointings, exclamations, and sealings.[8] Although these rituals were new among the Latter-day Saints, Smith also took rituals that had been in circulation previously and recast them with an expanded meaning in the new context of the temple. He drew from the consecration of priests in the Hebrew Bible, for example, to introduce consecrated oil to the Saints. Other traditional church liturgies such as ordination and healing were informed and expanded by temple practice. The cleansing of the feet, which had been a ritual used by evangelists to indict individuals and communities, was recast for the School of the Prophets (a sort of seminary for early Mormon evangelists) as a ritual cleansing from the world. This valence was amplified in the Kirtland Temple liturgy and it became the culminating ritual of the temple. Conversely, church leaders took consecrated oil from the temple and adapted temple anointings for use in healing. Anointing ultimately became the normative ritual of the healing liturgy.[9]

A similar reformulation occurred seven years later when Smith introduced the Nauvoo Temple liturgy, with its initiations, dramatic ritual, prayers, and sealings. The Nauvoo Temple introduced a radically expanded cosmology, which will be described in chapters 1 and 2, and the entirety of Mormonism realigned itself to accommodate. But just as the Kirtland Temple had adapted existing rituals for its liturgy, the Nauvoo Temple liturgy was an expansion of extant rituals in the church—namely, sealings and the Kirtland Temple liturgy.[10] And also like their Kirtland antecedents, the Nauvoo Temple rituals were similarly used for healing and blessing outside the temple walls. The liturgy was at once concentrated in the temple and centrifugally dispersed in all directions, wherever the Saints found themselves.

Smith was killed less than a year after revealing the complete Nauvoo Temple liturgy, when only a few close associates had participated in all the ceremonies. The remaining members and church leaders struggled to establish a succeeding church organization, but also to take the unsystematized revelations Smith had left behind and communicate them—first to each other, and then to the generations and waves of converts that followed. The Nauvoo Temple liturgy included themes intimately associated with death and resurrection, and almost immediately after they encountered it, Mormons developed deathbed rituals and funerary rites that incorporated elements from it.[11] Over the next decades, dedicatory rituals for homes as well as buildings became common.

In 1877, the Saints dedicated the St. George Temple that Brigham Young had urged them to complete. During the inter-temple period between 1846 and 1877 Mormons were without a temple and they consequently performed the temple rituals for the living in various locations including the temporary Endowment House. During this period, officiators performed proxy baptism and proxy marriage sealings for the dead. Though Young passed away shortly after the St George Temple's dedication, he presided there over the first child-to-parent sealings since the Saints had occupied the Nauvoo Temple thirty-one years earlier. He also oversaw the performance of the complete proxy liturgy for the first time in the church's history. Young then worked with Wilford Woodruff to systematize temple practice and create the first written texts for most of the temple rituals.[12]

The inter-temple period was one of ritual innovation outside of the temple as well, with Mormons by 1880 developing other rituals such as grave dedication[13] and a specific blessing for expectant mothers.[14] This was the height of ritual diversity in Mormonism.

In 1890 Wilford Woodruff announced the manifesto that began the process of ending lived polygamy in the church. Four years later he announced a revelation that also ended the practice of ritual adoption—the sealing of church members as children to those other than their own parents. The former shift is well recognized as a transition point in the development of the Mormon religion, and justifiably so. It came in response to real existential peril for the church. But, as chapter 2 will describe, the latter is perhaps the next most significant event in the foundation of modern Mormonism and is perhaps even more cosmologically momentous.

Within a decade of the Manifesto, the first generation of Mormons, and many of the second, were dead, and younger leaders populated the governing quorums. Joseph F. Smith occupied an important and unparalleled position during the first decades of the twentieth century, participating in the highest quorums of the church. As a member of the Smith family who had spent his childhood in Nauvoo, he was a living receptacle of liturgical history, connected to a time when no written liturgical histories or instructions existed. And as leaders modernized church bureaucracy and liturgy, he wielded tremendous influence over the patterns, forms, and rituals of church life.

It was Joseph F. Smith who initiated the progressive Priesthood Reform movement, which centralized curriculum, employed scientific management techniques, and began a formal process of priesthood progression from deacons through teachers, priests, and elders.[15] While Joseph F. Smith did introduce some novel changes to church liturgy and cosmology, as discussed in chapter 1, he also was very conservative. When younger church leaders questioned practices such as baptism for health, he maintained and defended them as venerable aspects of the Latter-day Saint tradition.

The process initiated in Joseph F. Smith's administration at the turn of the twentieth century culminated in a complete reformation of all church liturgy under his successor, Heber J. Grant. Anthon Lund was Smith's trusted lieutenant and a traditionalist, but as soon as he passed away in 1921, Grant directed a complete retooling of Mormon liturgy that successfully formalized it. Working with Apostle George F. Richards over a period of several years, Grant approved the reformation of the temple liturgy, including the creation of the first written text of all the rituals, changes in liturgical vestments, revisions to the endowment drama, and the removal of healers from the temple.[16] The First Presidency during this time also abolished baptism for health and dedicatory last rites from the formal church liturgy altogether.[17] The modern and codified liturgy that resulted from this process created an impressive level of uniformity across the growing church and successfully trained many subsequent generations in ritual practice.

Priesthood Correlation arose in the latter half of the twentieth century as a continued progressive reform of church bureaucracy, finance, and liturgy. Priesthood organizational charts and lines of authority became paramount as the governing priesthood ecclesiology came to oversee every aspect of the church and its auxiliaries. For example, Relief Society leaders gave up control of their magazine, their properties and finances, and their curriculum. The Correlation Committee rewrote church manuals and handbooks for all church governance, both quorum and auxiliary leadership, as well as curricula. Correlation reforms also included the introduction of the first liturgical texts for use by all priesthood officers and the elevation of home dedication from an informal observance to the formal liturgy of the church.

Conclusion

Many parties have an interest in defining priesthood for today's Mormonism. This volume does not propose a normative definition for believers. It does, however, use liturgy to explore Mormonism's priesthood cosmologies, the adapting framework of authority which supports it, and the over 180 years of lived religion within it. The integration of the experiences, beliefs, and cosmologies of Mormons into broader narratives requires vigilance against the pernicious specter of presentism. The ways that early Mormon women and men experienced the liturgy of the church have shifted to such an extent that many of the beliefs and practices of early Mormonism are now foreign to academics and believers alike. To bridge the chasms that divide us from the past, we must excavate pieces of the lives that remain buried in documents and archives. Only when we have integrated the experiences, beliefs, and practices of women and men of all sorts into our narratives will we begin to approach a faithful understanding of Mormonism, let alone understand its broader relevance in history. It is my hope that this volume provides a set of tools and frameworks that allow for more responsible and better analyses of Mormonism in the past and present.

I

Priesthood Ordination

We ordain you to be an Elder in the Church of the Latter-Day Saints and one of the 70 to go into all the world to preach the gospel to every creature. You shall have the powers blessings and previleges of this ministry, equal to any of your brethren. You shall go forth, but shall return to the embraces of your family, and they shall have much peace with you. Amen.[1]

Ordination of Wilkins Jenkins Salisbury, 1835

ON DECEMBER 6, 1897, Osmer Flake was twenty-nine years old and married with three young children. "I must leave all that I hold dear on earth except the Gospel," he wrote, "and go into an unbelieving cold world and preach to an unbelieving nation and depend wholy on the Lord to feed and provide for me the necessaries of life." From his small hometown in west-central Arizona, he was to take the train and make his way through New Mexico and Colorado, eventually arriving in Salt Lake City. At his departure, his three-year-old son Louie clung to him and wept. His wife Elsie could not speak and simply kissed him goodbye.

Over the next few days, Flake continued to record his experiences. Once in Salt Lake City, like all new missionaries, he presented himself at the Historian's Office to deliver his genealogy. Since he had already been to the temple for his marriage to Elsie, he did not need to stop there.[2] The following day, however, he walked to the Salt Lake Temple Annex, where he met nineteen other men to be formally commissioned for their labors.[3]

Two members of the Quorum of the Twelve Apostles and two members of the First Council of the Seventy waited for them. Flake observed that of the twenty men going on missions, not a single "seventy"—a priesthood office designated at the time for evangelism—was among them. And like the others, he sat down to allow one of the church leaders—in his case, Apostle George Teasdale—to ordain him. Teasdale laid his hands on Flake's head and ordained him to the office of seventy in the name of Jesus Christ and set him apart for his mission to the southern states.[4]

Photograph of the Salt Lake City Temple Annex, where church leaders ordained and set-apart missionaries at the turn of the nineteenth century. By Charles R. Savage. MSS P 24 Item 489, L. Tom Perry Special Collection, Provo, Utah.

When Joseph Smith published his list of core Mormon beliefs in 1842, he declared: "We believe that a man must be called of God by 'prophesy, and by laying on of hands' by those who are in authority to preach the gospel and administer in the ordinances thereof."[5] Osmer Flake's ordination as a seventy was this belief in practice, but it also occurred during an important nexus of change in the development of ordination practice and priesthood cosmology. While the question of what "the ordinances" of Mormonism are is reserved for a later chapter, this chapter analyzes what priesthood has meant to Mormons.

Today, the Mormon priesthood vestments of men's business attire—in lieu of chasubles, dalmatics, and stoles—are a quotidian veneer overlying one of Mormonism's most distinctive claims: a priesthood that orders heaven and earth. How Mormons have conceptualized this priesthood is far more complicated than is evident from contemporary discourse, catechism, or shirt color. In the first years of the church, ordination by the laying on of hands was a ritual that authorized priesthood officers to govern the church, evangelize, and administer church liturgies. Moreover, Joseph Smith consistently sought to create rituals and ecclesiastical structures to channel the power of God in the lives of believers. Priesthood ordination and the temple liturgies are examples of these structures. The expanded temple liturgy and cosmology Smith revealed in the early 1840s entailed the creation of a material heaven, comprising eternal sealed relationships between believers, both male and female. Those who participated in these relationships called this material heaven the priesthood. This expanded priest-hood was not ecclesiastical in nature; instead, it constituted the very structure of the cosmos. With time, Latter-day Saints moved away from the use of priest-hood language to describe the temple cosmology, and at the turn of the twentieth century—precisely the moment Flake received his ordination as a seventy—they began to describe a new priesthood cosmology based on the expansion of priest-hood ecclesiology. In conjunction with this shift, church leaders and members began to grapple with the relationships of women to the church and the priest-hood. Ultimately, instead of viewing priesthood as channeling the power of God, church leaders began to describe the priesthood *as* the power of God. As the ecclesiastical priesthood had been reserved for men in the church, the place of women in this new priesthood cosmology was not obvious to church members and leaders. More recently, church leaders have developed a new framework of authority in the church that allows women to exercise priesthood authority with-out being ordained to priesthood office.

Three primary loci have anchored Mormon conceptions of priesthood: author-ity, godly power, and liturgy. By analyzing these in the rise of church ecclesiastical structure, the discourse regarding God's power, and liturgical history, we can see how Mormon beliefs and teachings have expanded from the church's beginning with a small group of family and friends in rural New York to its current state with a membership of millions of believers wrestling with ideas of race and gen-der. This chapter documents the shifting Mormon lexicon to contextualize the Mormon past and historicize its present.

The Open Heaven and the Church

On the morning of April 6, 1830, a group of men and women met in the modest home of the Whitmer family in Fayette, New York. As they gathered to formalize their association, they focused their attention on two young men: Joseph Smith and Oliver Cowdery. For months Smith and Cowdery had worked together to transcribe and then publish the Book of Mormon. They had produced written revelations—manuscripts that captured the voice of the Lord speaking to their immediate context. And that morning they laid their hands on each other to establish the ecclesiastical structure of a new church, ordaining one another as its first elders. The previous summer Cowdery had produced a revelatory text that outlined an ecclesiology for believers.[6] After being ordained, Smith dictated a document that built off of Cowdery's, and the members of this new church accepted it as their Articles and Covenants.[7]

Despite centuries of cessationism, Christians had frequently defied orthodoxy in their lived religion. The intimate band gathered in the Whitmer home were among those who yearned for a religion that did not cease with the compilation of the Bible.[8] And if an angel visiting Joseph Smith and directing him to ancient plates did not sufficiently rend the veil of divine silence, the words that Smith revealed from those plates most certainly did. The Bible records Jesus giving his disciples power to heal the sick and cast out devils (Mark 3:14–15, Luke 9:1–2, Matthew 10:1), but when he returned from the dead and commissioned the disciples to go out into the world to preach, he indicated an expansion of God's power. Those who believed and were baptized would also have miracles follow them (Mark 16:15–18; see also 1 Corinthians 12). If miracles ever ceased, the final narrators of the Book of Mormon claimed, it was due to a lack of faith and because of widespread iniquity.[9] If there were no miracles, there was no salvation. This belief in the manifestation of God's power in believers' lives was the inverse of orthodox cessationism. Early Mormons believed that God was the same yesterday, today, and forever, and they expected to experience the biblical miracles anew.[10]

With its apparent purpose of rending history away from Protestant quietude,[11] it is no surprise that the "power of God" figures more prominently in the Book of Mormon than in any other Mormon scripture. The text is saturated with references—testaments to God's intervention in the world of the faithful. The litany includes the power by which Christ was conceived[12] and the power by which the plates were translated and subsequently shown to the witnesses.[13] Prophets broke down the prisons that held them by the power of God.[14] The Book of Mormon was preserved to show God's power to the inhabitants of the Americas.[15] The gentiles were led to discover the Americas and preserved by the power of God,[16] and individuals were convicted of their sins and overwhelmed by the same power.[17] Miracles were simply the manifestation of the power of God.[18]

Culminating the volume, the prophet-scribe Moroni tied this power of God to faith, promising, "Christ hath said: If ye will have faith in me ye shall have power to do whatsoever thing is expedient in me." He emphatically predicated miracles and angelic ministrations upon faith in Jesus Christ.[19]

Jesus framed miracles in terms of faith, and drawing from both the New Testament and the Book of Mormon, Joseph Smith frequently taught that faith was a prime variable in accessing the power of God.[20] The Lectures on Faith, the first catechism of the church, was used to train evangelizing elders. The Lectures evoked Hebrews 10:3 in teaching that even the greatest of all miracles—the creation—was realized by faith.[21] But miracles were elusive, and Smith consistently sought a means for his people to manifest the power of God. In principle, every believer could see angels, be miraculously healed, and receive revelations. In practice, Joseph Smith created ecclesiastical and liturgical structures to mediate the open heaven.

The Book of Mormon was the basis for Cowdery's and Smith's new ecclesiology. At the apex of the volume is an account of the visit of the resurrected

Christ to the Nephites, ancient Christians in the Americas. The text records how Jesus bestowed the authority to baptize on twelve of these men and gave them the words of a baptismal prayer.[22] But it was Moroni, the volume's guardian, who created the foundation of Mormon worship, ending his work with general instructions on church structure and liturgy, alongside his anticessationist warnings. He wrote that Jesus had also laid hands on the twelve men he had authorized to perform baptisms and had bestowed upon them the authority to lay hands on others to impart the Holy Ghost.[23] In the text, Moroni clarified that these twelve were called "elders of the church." He then included instruction on the qualities of baptismal candidates, outlined the regular worship of the church, and provided the ritual texts for ordaining church officers, namely, priests and teachers, and for administering the sacrament of the Lord's Supper.[24] With time these offices and authorities became the priesthood of the LDS Church.

Similar to Moroni, Smith and Cowdery emphasized anticessationism, ecclesiastical structure, and liturgy. God acted and interacted, but did so through the structures of the church. In his revelation of the "Prophesy of Enoch," written during the winter of 1830 to 1831, Smith detailed the "High Priesthood," an institution not yet established in the church. Those who were ordained to that order "should have power by faith" to work great miracles.[25] The first High Priesthood ordinations in June 1831 constituted the first "endowment of power" in the church.[26] Still contingent on faith, priesthood was to be one way to channel the power of God.

Priesthood officers were often the administrators of church liturgy. When Parley Pratt remembered the "Day of Power" in the 1839 summer during which Joseph Smith rose from his own sickbed to heal scores of people on the shores of the Mississippi, he wrote that "Brother Joseph, while in the Spirit, rebuked the Elders who would continue to lay hands on the sick from day to day without the power to heal them. Said he: 'It is time that such things ended. *Let the Elders either obtain the power of God to heal the sick, or let them cease to minister the forms without the power.*'"[27] Performance of the ritual forms, however, was not limited to the church elders. Affirming a practice that had existed in the church for years, Smith declared that women were to cast out devils, work miracles, and heal by laying on hands.[28] He sought to have all the Saints filled with the power of God,[29] and understood that the healing liturgy and exorcism rituals were not the only avenues to access it. Earlier, in the first year of the church, alluding to the resurrected Jesus's instructions to his disciples in Jerusalem, Joseph Smith revealed the voice of the Lord and dictated that in Kirtland, Ohio some were to be "endowed with power from on high."[30] First associated with the ordinations to the High Priesthood in 1831, eventually the idea expanded with revelations detailing the purpose of a "House of the Lord"—what Mormons at the end of the decade called a temple.

Jesus commanded his disciples: "Tarry ye in the city of Jerusalem, until ye be endued"—or clothed—"with power from on high" (Luke 24:49). The realization of this endowment was the Day of Pentecost. Before the completion of the House of the Lord in Kirtland, Smith exhorted the recently established Quorum of the Twelve: "You need an endowment brethren in order that you may be prepared and able to overcome all things, and those that reject your testimony will be damned. The sick will be healed the lame made to walk the deaf to hear and the blind to see through your instrumentality; But let me tell you that you will not have power after the endowment to heal those who have not faith, nor to benifit them."[31] Despite their holding ecclesiastical priesthood office, Smith directed the Mormon evangelists to tarry in Kirtland until they were filled with the power of God—until they were endowed. In preparation for this endowment of power, Smith revealed a set of preparatory rituals administered outside of the House of the Lord. In the months before the building was ready, church leaders washed all priesthood officers with water, anointed them with oil, and perfumed them with scented alcohol.[32] In the days after the first dedication ceremonies for the House of the Lord, these officers then gathered within it for an all-night solemn assembly, during which church leaders washed their feet, administered the Lord's Supper, and many experienced great outpourings of pentecostal power— prophecy, glossolalia, visions, and angelic visitation. Smith's diarist declared: "It was a penticost and enduement indeed, long to be remembered."[33] The evangelists were thus prepared to go preach the gospel.

The concept of an "endowment of power" expanded further in Nauvoo in association with the temple liturgy. There, Smith revealed an expanded set of rituals to be performed in the temple, comprising an initiation of washing, anointing, and clothing in priestly vestments, as well as an interactive dramatic ritual endowment. Both men and women equally received this endowment and participated in the comprehensive temple liturgy.[34] From this point forward, all church members were to be endowed with power.

Expanding Ecclesiastical Structure

Since the early twentieth century, Mormons have placed extraordinary emphasis on a divine vision Joseph Smith received as a young boy at the dawn of the Restoration,[35] although this event was clearly in the Evangelical tradition of visions at the time.[36] Instead when early Mormon evangelists proselytized, their primary message was that an angel had interrupted the Reformation—that the days of miracles had not ceased. This shattering of heaven's silence was cacophonous, and Joseph Smith sought to harmonize the outpourings of God's power ecclesiastically in the revelation of priesthood bureaucracy.[37]

When Oliver Cowdery revealed his early version of the Articles and Covenants in the summer of 1829, he hewed carefully to the structures and liturgy described in the Book of Mormon. When Joseph Smith revealed the version of this document accepted by the church in 1830, he was not so constrained. His revelation included the office of deacon, a position found in the New Testament but absent from the Book of Mormon. It also included the ritual of baby blessing—a dry christening of sorts that was not common to any church traditions familiar to Smith. From that point until his death fourteen years later, Joseph Smith never stopped his revelation of church structure and ritual.

Within five years of Cowdery's and Smith's ordinations in April 1830, the first four offices of the church—deacon, teacher, priest, and elder—had dramatically expanded to include the offices of (in order of their revelations) bishop, high priest, patriarch, apostle, and seventy. Moreover, the church and these offices were to be governed through a rapidly growing system of quorums, presidencies, and councils. In April 1835, Smith received a revelation that church leaders then combined with the edited texts of a few earlier unpublished revelations to outline a new organizational structure for these offices. Smith's revelation introduced the idea of a "Melchizedek Priesthood" and an "Aaronic Priesthood," between which the various offices were divided. The Aaronic Priesthood, Smith revealed, comprised the offices of deacon, teacher, priest, and bishop, with the Melchizedek Priesthood encompassing the ranks of elder, high priest, patriarch, apostle, and seventy. This priesthood division instantly normalized the discourse of church leaders and lay members. Texts of revelations that had previously referred to the High Priesthood (the office of high priest) were harmonized with the newer revelations in ways that allowed readers to impute the new Melchizedek Priesthood organization to the earlier references to the High Priesthood.[38]

Throughout this period, and despite the changes in organization, the ritual of ordination remained relatively static. Ordination followed a process outlined in the Book of Mormon, which indicated that after praying, the administrator of the ordination was to place his hands upon the candidate and declare: "In the name of Jesus Christ I ordain you to be a priest to preach repentance and remission of sins through Jesus Christ, by the endurance of faith on his name to the end, Amen."[39] Like the other rituals adapted from the Book of Mormon—namely, baptism, confirmation, and the sacrament of the Lord's Supper—ordination in early Mormonism invoked the authority of Jesus but made no other authority explicit. Clearly, certain ritual performances were reserved to the specific church offices. For example, according to the Articles and Covenants, priests could baptize and administer the Lord's Supper, but teachers and deacons could not.[40] As directed by a revelation[41] church leaders used the Book of Mormon text as a pattern, generally accompanied by extemporaneous blessings on the candidate, to ordain all church officers—including women, as will be discussed later in chapter 4.[42]

With the publication of the revelation compilation describing the new Melchizedek–Aaronic Priesthood organization in the 1835 Doctrine and Covenants, the concepts became canonical. Moreover, because the 1835 edition crystallized and stabilized Smith's revelation texts, they have been extremely influential over successive generations of Latter-day Saints. However, Joseph Smith had not finished his revelation. He had introduced the idea of a lineal priesthood with the ordination of his father as patriarch. While other men were ordained as patriarchs during Joseph Smith's lifetime, Joseph Smith Sr. remained the chief patriarch in the church, and his office was intended to pass onto his posterity at his death.[43] In an 1838 revelation, Joseph Smith revealed that he too held his office—colloquially known as church president—by virtue of a lineal priesthood.[44] This concept—along with ritual adoption, salvation for the dead, and persevering relationships—swirled into a new cosmology associated with the liturgy of the Nauvoo Temple.

The Cosmological Priesthood

Joseph Smith's revelation of the Nauvoo Temple liturgy in 1842 and 1843 required an expanded cosmology in which kinship, priesthood, government, and heaven all became synonymous. This heaven was not a future reward for the faithful or the elect; it was a material heaven on earth, constructed welding link by welding link on the anvil of the temple altar. Ann Taves has used the Catholic Eucharist analogically to understand Smith's golden plates, but her analogy is far more potent when used in relation to Mormon temple sealings.[45] The sacramentalism of the Mormon liturgy that so irritated the Protestant Atlantic faltered at the threshold of the temple, and, as the priest who holds the host at the altar to materialize the flesh of Christ, the Mormon priest materialized heaven at his altar, sealing wife to husband and child to parent. Where these linkages did not exist, there was simply no heaven[46]; where they did exist, so did heaven. And this heaven persevered.[47]

Those who participated in this temple liturgy during Joseph Smith's lifetime commonly referred to themselves, as well as this material network of heaven, as the "priesthood." As part of the temple liturgy, both male and female participants dressed in priesthood robes, shared priesthood symbols, and looked forward to the promise of the "fullness of the priesthood"—the assumption of the status of king and priest, or queen and priestess, for eternity.[48] Brigham Young even described those who went to the temple in 1846 as receiving the "keys of the

Nauvoo Temple Architectural Drawing, ca. 1841. The temple was finished in 1846. By William Weeks. LDS Church History Library, Salt Lake City, Utah.

Priesthood."[49] To distinguish it from the older ecclesiastical priesthood offices, I refer to this temple priesthood—this material network of heaven—as the "cosmological priesthood."

Understanding early Mormon sealings as materializing heaven and the discursive use of priesthood to describe that network renders Nauvoo's complex sealing practices relatively comprehensible. Joseph Smith and subsequently Brigham Young were intent on creating a durable network on which generations of church members and ultimately the entire human family were to rely as a framework in which to be integrated. At the time of the introduction of the Nauvoo Temple liturgy this network was necessarily unrealized. It was still conceptual. As Smith and other Latter-day Saints began performing sealing rituals, they undertook the process of rendering the conceptual into the actual and material. But whereas sealings between a monogamous husband and wife persevered within this cosmology, they did nothing to create a broader heaven that integrated their community into one whole. The immediate need to nucleate heaven seems to have driven Nauvoo's most complex sacerdotal relationships.

In the summer of 1842, Joseph Smith sought marriage to Sarah Whitney, the daughter of his close friends and fellow church leaders Elizabeth and Newel Whitney. On July 24 Smith dictated a revelation that the family kept but never published. In this text Smith revealed the basis not only for the proposed plural marriage, but also for his entire temple liturgy. Perhaps peculiarly, the revelation was directed to Newel Whitney, who was promised "immortality and eternal life" for himself and for all his "house both old and young because of the lineage of my Preasthood saith the Lord[.] it shall be upon you and upon your Children after you from generation to generation."[50] By having his daughter sealed to Smith, the voice of the Lord declared, Whitney was to become part of the structure of heaven—a priesthood that was also lineal, passing from parents to children, both male and female. Smith's revelation to the Whitney family appears steeped in an explicitly patriarchal culture that is foreign to modern readers, but it is also clear that the promise that Newel Whitney would enjoy an assured position in the priesthood cosmology with the capacity to extend that position to others was not some reward for offering his daughter on the altar of polygamy (though it may very well have felt that way to the Whitneys). Instead, the promises extended in the revelation were a natural consequence of the Whitneys' resulting sealed position in the burgeoning network of heaven.

For heaven to be materialized, Smith needed to be connected to other believers in Nauvoo, not just his own immediate family. The connection between Smith and the Whitneys was real, but it was also indirect. Earlier in the revelation of polygamy, Smith had married women who were already married. Regardless of debates over whether polyandrous sealings in Nauvoo were for "eternity only" or whether Joseph Smith engaged in sexual congress with any of his wives, Smith's sealings bridged the gap that divided Mormons from each other in the cosmological priesthood network. Some early plural wives may have viewed themselves as sealed to each other, as well as to their husband.[51] And while some have hypothesized that Smith's early polyandrous marriages may have been shared marriages or polyamoric in nature,[52] it is evident that in accepting a heteronormative cosmology and recognizing that child-to-parent sealings were strictly reserved to the completed temple,[53] the only way for Smith to be directly connected to other married Mormons was through polyandrous sealing.

Once the temple was finished and child-to-parent sealings became available, Brigham Young expanded the range of sealings available to include adoption— the practice of sealing biologically unrelated people in child-to-parent relationships.[54] While Young tied up some of polyandry's loose ends in the temple, and the practice of polygyny expanded, adoption provided a new way to connect married couples, bridging the gaps that existed between the Saints. Married as well as single men and women were adopted to couples in the temple, and adoption practice and theology served as an important nexus in organizing migration to the Great Basin. With sealings reserved for people who had accepted the message of the Restoration in mortality, adoption was critical in tying the first generation of Mormon converts together into a single family. Moreover, adoption demonstrated that Young and other members of the Quorum of the Twelve could be viewed as viable alternatives to the Smith family in organizing this cosmological priesthood. The imperative to be connected to the heavenly priesthood network trumped biology, just as it trumped the proto-Victorian household.

Within this context, Brigham Young's justification for excluding black people from the temple liturgy (the cosmological priesthood) and the ecclesiastical priesthood becomes at least coherent, however repugnant. Historians frequently describe the exclusion of black people in Mormonism before 1978 as a "priesthood ban," but it was far more than a ban on the ecclesiastical priesthood of the church. Despite Joseph Smith establishing a precedent of priesthood ordination for black men, after leaving Nauvoo and over a protracted period, Brigham Young formulated a policy that prohibited all black people, both men and women, from participation in the temple liturgy. This prohibition consequently barred black men from ecclesiastical priesthood office.[55]

Young formulated his justification from the common Christian beliefs that black people were descendants of Cain and/or Ham—ideas that had been used to justify and sustain chattel slavery for generations. Young transformed these ideas into the cosmology of the Nauvoo Temple and in doing so crafted a new Genesis narrative. In a February 13, 1849, meeting, Apostle Lorenzo Snow "presented the

case of the African Race for a chance of redemption & unlock the door to them."
Church minutes record Young's response: he "explained it very lucidly that the
curse remains on them bec[ause] Cain cut off the lives of Abel to hedge up his
way & take the lead but the L[or]d has given them blackness, so as to give the
children of Abel an opportunity to keep his place with his desc[endant]s in the
et[erna]l worlds."[56] Though the longhand minutes of the meeting are somewhat
disjointed, the narrative that Young repeated frequently throughout his life was
clear: Cain's murder of Abel was an attempt to eliminate Abel's posterity—his
kingdom in the cosmological priesthood.

As we saw at the beginning of this book, two years before this 1849 meeting
Brigham Young had a near-death experience in which he had a vision in which
Joseph Smith appeared to him. During this vision Young asked to know more
about principles related to adoption sealings, and Smith showed him the organization of the human family before the world was created. A primary implication
of the vision was that the human family was intended to be ordered in mortality.[57]
Young concluded that the network that Smith revealed as part of the temple cosmology was to be somehow patterned on a premortal template. Consequently,
Young taught that Cain's murder was not mere fratricide. It was a strike against
the material network of heaven, a fracturing of the cosmos. Abel was supposed
to be a node in the heavenly network, with vast numbers of descendants and kin.
According to this view, black men and women, the purported descendants of
Cain, were not to be integrated into the cosmological priesthood until Abel's posterity was somehow restored—until the breach created by his death was healed.
If Abel couldn't have a kingdom, neither could Cain. Because of the tight association between the cosmological priesthood and the ecclesiastical priesthood of
the church, one manifestation of this fractured human network was the ecclesiastical priesthood restriction. Focusing on this restriction, however, obfuscates the
reality that black Mormon women and men were not to be integrated into the
material family of God.

Jane Manning James was a black church member who had lived with Joseph
Smith in Nauvoo, emigrated to Salt Lake, and remained faithful.[58] During her
life she repeatedly petitioned the First Presidency to participate in the temple
liturgy, and in 1894 the First Presidency decided to use an ad hoc temple ritual
to seal James as a servant to Joseph Smith. This decision was not because Wilford
Woodruff, who followed Young and Taylor as president of the church, or other
church leaders viewed black people as eternal servants, but because this relationship was the only way they could conceive to link her to Joseph Smith without
integrating her into the priesthood family.

It is no coincidence that Manning's extraordinary sealing occurred mere
weeks after Woodruff's revelation ending the practice of temple adoption (see

chapter 2). After years of struggling over how to surmount the biological chasms reified in child-to-parent sealing practice, in which only those who had accepted the restored gospel during their lives could be sealed as parents, Woodruff transformed the temple liturgy and opened up sealing to all those who had died.[59] "There will be very few, if any," he explained, "who will not accept the Gospel" in eternity.[60] This sweeping change transformed the very fabric of the cosmological priesthood, expanded heaven and for many healed the broken human family. It was in this context that Woodruff approached the case of Jane Manning James. However, the fracture that cleaved black men and women from integration into the human family remained in place. Brigham Young's exclusionary narrative triumphed over Woodruff's revelatory universalism, and the structural consequences persisted for nearly a century.

After Young's death in 1877, the cosmological priesthood as a means to comprehend the temple liturgy and the organizational fabric of heaven rapidly diminished. This left an explicative vacuum in which some traditional usages of the term "priesthood" in the Mormon lexicon grew incongruous with newer catechismal definitions of the word, rooted in a more expansive reading of the priesthood ecclesiastical structure of the church. For example, Young's Genesis narrative remained the de facto explanation of the temple and priesthood restrictions on black people for several decades after he passed away. In the early twentieth century, church leaders moved away from describing temple sealing in terms of priesthood and priesthood inheritance. There was an associated decline in the cosmological priesthood as a means of comprehending the temple.[61] Outside of this context, Young's racial narrative made little sense, and it eventually became irreconcilable to church members and leaders, who found other explanations, like premortal valiancy, to have greater explanatory power.[62] The incomprehensibility of Young's narrative resulted in a focus on the exclusion of black men from the ecclesiastical priesthood and deemphasized the broader temple restrictions on both black women and men.

A similar shift can be seen in how Young and twentieth-century church leaders regarded the miracle of creation. Young had emphasized that "priesthood" was the organizational medium for heaven and, ideally, earth. The Nauvoo Temple cosmology influenced his understanding of this organization during the trek west and his teachings in Utah.[63] Young taught that priesthood "is the law by which the worlds are, were, and will continue for ever and ever," and that "it is that system which brings worlds into existence and peoples them, gives them their revolutions." However, he also emphasized that the priesthood was "a perfect system of government," and that the creation had been effected through God and the angels' knowledge of chemistry.[64] While he constantly referred to "the power of God," he never associated it with priesthood. In the late nineteenth and particularly the twentieth centuries, however, church leaders grew to view priesthood instead as the power of God—the power used in the creation—and to teach that this priesthood was coterminous with the ecclesiastical priesthood of the church. Moreover, after the official end of polygamy as an organizational force in Mormonism, the priesthood ecclesiology of the church became the primary means by which to direct and order the lives of church members.

Ordination, Church Authority, and the Power of God

At the end of the nineteenth century, in place of the cosmological priesthood of the temple, some church leaders began to articulate their understanding of priesthood by reinterpreting the priesthood ecclesiastical texts crystallized and published in the 1835 canon. Because of the relatively late introduction of the concept of a bifurcated priesthood—the Melchizedek and the Aaronic—early revelations dealing with priesthood were open to new readings over time.[65] Some individuals began to view the terms "ordain," "confer," and "set apart" as having new and important distinctions.[66] Whereas the traditional ordination ritual based on the example in the Book of Mormon simply ordained an individual to a particular office, some began to believe that as offices were understood to be part of either the Aaronic or Melchizedek Priesthoods, people needed to receive the priesthood *before* holding a particular office. Thus, some Mormons taught that one should be "ordained" to either the Aaronic or the Melchizedek Priesthood and then "set apart" to a particular office, whether deacon, priest, or elder.[67] Others viewed the bifurcated priesthood as necessitating a "conferral" of those priesthoods before a person could be "ordained" to a particular office.[68] Citing the ordination texts in the Book of Mormon and Doctrine and Covenants, Church President John Taylor wrote in 1887 that such distinctions were innovations that were both "wrong" and "improper."[69] In 1901 Church President Lorenzo Snow told a stake president that "one should not confer the entire priesthood then ordain to office within." Instead, perhaps alluding to the temple, he argued that one obtains the priesthood "by degrees of office and does not hold all of that priesthood until he has been ordained to the highest degree."[70] Snow may have been reacting to published statements by his counselor in the First Presidency, Joseph F. Smith, who taught precisely that priesthood must be conferred upon an individual before that individual could be ordained to an office.

In 1899 and 1901, Smith published in the general church periodicals an innovative reading of Sections 2 and 107 of the Doctrine and Covenants that argued explicitly for an initial conferral of priesthood and subsequent ordination to office.[71] In 1902, with Smith as the new church president, the First Presidency and Quorum of the Twelve discussed the diversity in ordination forms that had resulted from Smith's advocacy. Perhaps indicating the difficulty of changing traditional practice, the council remained divided on the issue, despite Smith arguing emphatically for his new approach.[72] Writing to British Mission officials in 1911, Apostle Rudger Clawson acknowledged the two separate forms of ordination but noted that the preference was for the older, traditional form to be used.[73] Still, the conflict was not resolved; two years later Smith reaffirmed his position with the Quorum of the Twelve but, in the face of widespread traditional practice, conceded that God would still honor the action if a man did otherwise in ignorance.[74] At some point during his tenure as church president, he also changed the proxy ordination ritual of the temple to conform with his views to confer the priesthood first and then ordain the deceased man to priesthood office.

Smith died in 1918, and the following year the church published a compilation of his teachings titled *Gospel Doctrine*, which became a popular reference work. Several church leaders objected to the mode of ordaining put forth in this volume on the basis that it was "opposed to the Book of Mormon and to the practice under all foregoing Presidents."[75] A second edition was published within the year that included an addendum comprising a First Presidency letter addressing Smith's teachings about ordination. In order "to prevent disputes," the First Presidency members printed ritual texts based on the older, ordination-only tradition. Furthermore, they wrote that Joseph F. Smith was on record as stating that the difference between the form "adopted by the leading authorities of the Church from the beginning" and his new method was "a distinction without a difference"; the letter insisted that "either will do."[76] Despite the majority of First Presidency and Quorum of the Twelve members being "in favor of Smith's change" to the temple ordination text that year,[77] two years later the same council voted to revert the ordination ritual in the temple to the older form.[78]

Leaders had discouraged the distribution of example ritual texts for decades[79]; however, the shift to younger and less experienced missionaries required that missionary handbooks include them. The ordination texts in these volumes retained the old form of ordination for the bulk of the twentieth century.[80] Moreover, several general handbooks also added the old form of ordination to their instructions during the same period—the only ritual text to be so included.[81] Subsequent editions of *Gospel Doctrine* retained the First Presidency's clarifying statement until the 1960s.

Joseph F. Smith's views, however, retained some popularity. Over time, as several outspoken church leaders were wholly converted to his ideas,[82] the Quorum of the Twelve and First Presidency concluded that Smith's ordination pattern should be normative. When asked "how aggressive they [the Quorum of the Twelve] should be in making the change" in 1957, Church President David McKay responded that general authorities should teach the new form when visiting stakes and use it when performing ordinations themselves. The First Presidency repeated these instructions to the temple presidents during the April conference of that year.[83] Church leaders then included Smith's ordination pattern in the 1964 *Melchizedek Priesthood Handbook* and the 1968 *General Handbook of Instruction*.[84] These were the first such handbooks to systematically include

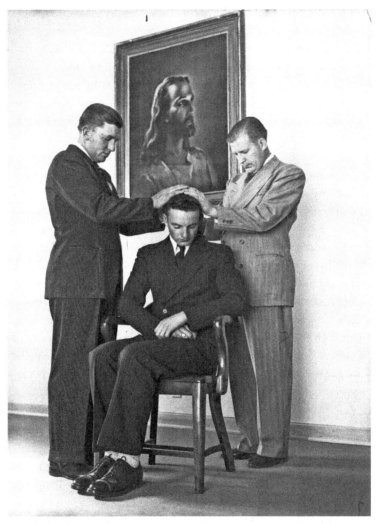

Photograph of Hyrum W. Smith, aged 17, being ordained a priest by Bishop E. Vern Breeze and Samuel L. Dial, in Hunter Ward, Salt Lake City, Utah, ca. 1950. By Jim Hansen. LOOK Magazine Photograph Collection, Library of Congress, Prints & Photographs Division, LC-L914-50-AB63, #2.

liturgical texts and to be edited by Priesthood Correlation Committee officials, and they were consequently extremely influential. This sequence of priesthood conferral and subsequent ordination to office has since become standard in the church and has been the basis of modern priesthood narratives.

The earlier concept of the cosmological priesthood of the Nauvoo temple, that existed as the material heaven on earth had essentially been independent of church ecclesiology. The decline of this cosmological framework created a space for the rise of a new understanding of priesthood. Inherent in Joseph F. Smith's argument about his ordination procedure was the idea that priesthood exists outside of the various ecclesiastical offices. An important aspect of the new priesthood narrative was the idea, increasingly taught throughout the twentieth century, that priesthood is the "power of God." This differed from earlier associations of the power of God being manifested by faith, whether that power was channeled through priesthood structures or not. The new narrative also diverged from the older idea of receiving power in the priesthood network of heaven.

In the twentieth century, with the cosmological priesthood beyond memory, church leaders came to explicitly define priesthood in terms of God's power. With the concentration of church liturgy within the priesthood ecclesiastical structures[85] and the rise of the Priesthood Correlation reforms, which emphasized priesthood keys as an organizational principle,[86] the power of God became inseparable from the church ecclesiology. As President N. Eldon Tanner expressed it: "The priesthood is the power by which all things were created and the power by which God has done those things about which Bishop Vandenberg spoke this evening[87]; but for us as individuals, it is the power of God that has been delegated to us to act in his name in the office which we hold. And it is a great privilege, a great blessing, and a great responsibility to have that priesthood bestowed upon us."[88] This definition of the priesthood as the exclusive power and authority of God, with specific reference to the creation, was codified in the 2004 manual *True to the Faith* (a youth catechism of sorts), the 2010 General Church Handbook of Instructions, and the 2016 *Doctrinal Mastery* document for all youth.[89]

Women and the Priesthood

Another important aspect of this shift in understandings of priesthood is the place and role of women. The cosmological priesthood of the Nauvoo Temple required the integration of women for the priesthood itself to exist because it was essentially familial—where there was no priestess, there was no priest. However, as the priesthood ecclesiology was intrinsically male, the expansion of that priesthood required the exclusion of women to maintain coherence. Church leaders consequently wrestled for the next hundred years trying to integrate women into that revised conception of priesthood. This tension has been particularly evident during periods of major public criticism of women's roles in the church by Mormon and formerly Mormon activists. In the late 1970s and early 1980s, activists like Sonia Johnson demonstrated against the church for its position on the Equal Rights Amendment and its structural inequalities.[90] In the early 2010s, the Ordain Women movement demonstrated against church policies regarding women.[91]

Ambiguities about women's roles in Mormonism have been complicated by the ongoing participation of women in the temple liturgy, and their historical participation in the healing liturgy. Both men and women who have passed through the temple liturgy in turn perform the "priesthood ordinances" of the temple for others of their own sex. This tension has been resolved in several manners. For example, Kristen Moulton, a female convert, wrote in a 1980 *Ensign* article: "Although women do not hold the priesthood, they are partakers of every blessing necessary for salvation. The temple endowment makes this clear. The general ordinances of the temple are all performed by authority of the priesthood, and women have access to all of them."[92] In other words, women perform rituals by priesthood authority without actually having any priesthood. One hundred and thirty-four years earlier, the women who performed rituals in the Nauvoo Temple were recognized as having a sealed position in the cosmological priesthood, and their authority to extend that station to others was implicit. With the lexical shift in regard to priesthood, that authority became somewhat mysterious to participants, and a tendency arose to conflate the cosmological priesthood functions of the temple with the ecclesiastical priesthood of the church.

Sheri Dew, a prominent former general leader of the Relief Society, wrote in 2013 about how many women wrestle with this tension:

> Although women are not ordained to the priesthood, they do have authority to officiate in priesthood ordinances in the temple. On the other hand, women, unlike men, are not required to be ordained to the Melchizedek Priesthood in order to enter the house of the Lord, though the ordinances performed there are all priesthood ordinances. Neither are women required to be ordained to the priesthood to serve as leaders in the Lord's Church. Why is this the case? We don't know the answer to these questions, either.[93]

Dew's conclusion highlights the acontextual status of both the temple liturgy and structures of authority in modern Mormon belief. The liturgy and ecclesiology of the church are largely experienced and explained without any connection to the beliefs and antecedents that gave rise to them. Whereas the temple liturgy has changed relatively little since its formalization in the nineteenth century, the cosmological priesthood that grounded it is beyond memory.

In the case of female participation in the healing liturgy, which was explicitly supported by church leaders well into the twentieth century, Dew demonstrates the difficulties of situating such a practice within the modern framework of priesthood: "What are we to make of the fact that these statements don't square with Church doctrine and practice today?" she asks. "I don't know why Joseph Smith appears to have sanctioned females blessing the sick, though I've pondered different possibilities: Were these statements recorded accurately?" She wondered, too, how "women could participate in priesthood blessings."[94] The reality that healing rituals and miraculous healings could be performed without priesthood office is outside of her perceptual framework, so her solution is to question the historicity of the phenomenon.

Academic observers of Mormonism have made similarly presentist conclusions, though often on the other side of the question. Several authors writing in *Women and Authority: Re-emerging Mormon Feminism*, published in 1992, presented path-breaking research and insightful analysis on topics such as the rise of priesthood–motherhood complementarianism in the twentieth-century church. However, authors also argued that by participating in the temple liturgy, women received a priesthood that was tantamount to the modern ecclesiastical priesthood of the church, and that the performance of healing rituals by women was evidence that they held the priesthood.[95] Like many contemporary church leaders and members, the book's editor, Maxine Hanks, described several ways in which women "receive priesthood *power* (or the power of God)."[96] The fundamental premise of these authors—that the priesthood comprises all of God's power and authority—was mirrored within the twentieth-century church. Absent an understanding of the "cosmological priesthood" and its contexts, and based on a belief that the modern liturgy concentrated within the ecclesiastical priesthood was historically normative, scholars have often distorted the past as much as clarified it.

In 2013, in response to questions regarding the church's longstanding commitment to male-only ecclesiastical priesthood, several church leaders, both male and female, addressed the participation of women in the church in terms of priesthood authority and power. That same year church leaders released a series of training videos that focused on priesthood. These videos reiterated the idea that priesthood is the power and authority of God and emphasized the concept of priesthood "keys" for church government—essentially the governing authority within the priesthood. Apostle M. Russell Ballard took the lead in these training videos and also spoke expansively on the priesthood at the April General Conference:

The power by which the heavens and earth were and are created is the priesthood . . . . Not only is the priesthood the power by which the heavens and the earth were created, but it is also the power the Savior used in His mortal ministry to perform miracles, to bless and heal the sick, to bring the dead to life, and, as our Father's Only Begotten Son, to endure the unbearable pain of Gethsemane and Calvary—thus fulfilling the laws of justice with mercy and providing an infinite Atonement and overcoming physical death through the Resurrection.[97]

The primacy of this commanding new conception of priesthood, in which all possible godly power, authority, and action is equated with priesthood, has created space for church leaders to make innovative comments regarding women in the church.

As leaders seek ways to integrate women into this new cosmology, two specific areas have appeared in tension: access to priesthood *authority* and access to priesthood *power*. Previously, church leaders taught that while men held priesthood office, the "blessings" of the priesthood were available to all.[98] That is to say, the salvific rituals and blessings of health and comfort were available to all, even though these rituals were exclusively performed by men. In the 2010s, church leaders began to teach that while priesthood offices are specifically reserved for men, church authority is necessarily priesthood authority, with women who hold ecclesiastical positions in the church wielding priesthood authority by delegation. Others have argued that any manifestation of God's power is priesthood, and that while women do not have access to priesthood authority in the church, they can be active conduits for priesthood power.

On April 5, 2013, the LDS Newsroom published a joint interview with Relief Society General President Linda Burton, Young Women General President Elaine Dalton, and General Primary President Rosemary Wixom. In a discussion of priesthood, the moderator asked, "How do you utilize the priesthood as you are leading and guiding your individual organization?" President Wixom related a story of being asked a question by an apostle who indicated that she, not he, would receive the revelation to answer it. She then stated that her "calling came from our prophet, and he was allowing me to carry that mantle, and I would be the one—with the help of my counselors and the board and, above all, inspiration from our Heavenly Father—to come to the conclusion to the answer of that question." Presidents Burton and Wixom then related an account of how they had traveled to the Pacific and, after a tour, been asked by members of the area presidency there for their impressions. Taken together, these women's responses to the moderator indicated that they believed that they "utilized the priesthood" by receiving a stewardship or assignment from priesthood officers.[99]

The observation made by Presidents Burton, Dalton, and Wixom that women can exercise priesthood authority without having a priesthood office has become more common among LDS leaders. Leveraging the heuristic of "keys" that has been emphasized as part of the Priesthood Correlation reforms, Apostle M. Russell Ballard told participants at Brigham Young University's August 2013 Education Week:

> Those who have priesthood keys—whether that be a deacon who has keys for his quorum or a bishop who has keys for his ward or a stake president who has keys for his stake or the president of the Church who holds all priesthood keys—literally make it possible for all who serve or labor faithfully under their direction to exercise priesthood authority and have access to priesthood power. All men and all women serve under the direction of those who have keys.[100]

Thus, he argued, by working under priesthood officers who hold keys, women may wield priesthood authority.

Two days earlier, Apostle Dallin Oaks had addressed church members at a stake conference, and responded to the "misleading idea" that women are not equal to men because they do not hold the priesthood. He described how women exercise priesthood authority in terms similar to those used by Ballard: "Sometimes we speak as if the authority of the priesthood is only to be exercised by men who quote unquote 'hold' the priesthood. That's not true." A woman who was about to start a full-time mission for the church, he said, "will be set apart by one holding the keys of that office. That is the stake president. He will set her apart as a full-time missionary of the church and he will give her the authority and the responsibility to preach the gospel." That authority, he said, "is the authority of the priesthood." Oaks then mentioned a Relief Society president and identified the authority with which she acted as "not the authority of the city, state or federal government, but the authority of God, the authority of the priesthood because everything that happens in the Church of Jesus Christ involves the authority of the priesthood." Oaks concluded that all "teachers, officers, male and female, missionaries, and workers in the temple, throughout the church" operate under "the authority of the priesthood." Then, speaking of his own mother, who had been widowed when he was seven years old, he proclaimed that she "was the head of our family in exercising the authority of the priesthood, which she had by virtue of [the] temple marriage of my parents. She presided over the family. She exercised the authority of the priesthood in that setting and I saw that as I was growing up."[101]

Oaks made these ideas accessible to the entire church at the April 2014 General Conference. Acknowledging that they represented an important shift in church teachings, he reviewed comments made by Apostle Joseph Fielding Smith at the October 1958 General Relief Society meeting about women wielding authority

in the church and in temples. In his 1958 address, Smith had discussed the particular authority that Mormon women have in the Relief Society and the temple;
however, he had been fastidious in his demarcation between them: "Authority
and Priesthood are two different things."[102] Historically, church leaders had
also commonly made such distinctions in reference to female ritual healing.
While Oaks quoted Smith's statements about women having authority, he did
not quote Smith's qualification about authority being distinct from priesthood.
Instead, Oaks observed: "We are not accustomed to speaking of women having
the authority of the priesthood in their Church callings, but what other authority
can it be?"[103] All authority in the church, according to Oaks, is priesthood.

One immediate consequence of Oaks's sermon was that curriculum editors
swiftly updated the Young Women (age twelve to eighteen) Sunday lesson titled
"What are the duties of priesthood holders?" and renamed it "What are my
responsibilities in the work of the priesthood?" Editors replaced sections focusing on priesthood holders and their actions with sections focused on women as
"participants" in the "work of the priesthood."[104] An essay written for the church's
youth magazine in 2016 presents this idea forcefully: "Let's say your friend just
had the worst day ever at school. You decide to send her a quick text of encouragement. Does that also fit under 'work of the priesthood'? Absolutely! And that
applies whether or not you actually hold the priesthood."[105]

Less than two months after Dallin Oaks's General Conference sermon on
priesthood, General Relief Society President Burton published a series of questions and answers on priesthood in the *Ensign*. Her responses were likely finished
and slated for publication well before Oaks delivered his address and offer an
interesting parallel development in thought about Mormon priesthood. Notably,
she claimed that "there is a difference . . . between priesthood authority and
priesthood power. Priesthood authority is conferred by ordination, but priesthood power is available to all."[106] Burton followed the safe strategy of quoting
church leaders' recent comments on the expansive relationship between priesthood and the power of God before reiterating that women are to have the power
of the priesthood.

Similarly, in her 2013 volume on women and priesthood, Sheri Dew wrote
that "the Lord has made it clear that He desires to have a righteous, pure people
who both qualify for and seek to have access to His power, which by definition
is priesthood power." Simply stated, Dew explained, "priesthood is the power of
God. It is the all-encompassing power by which He works." Such priesthood is
manifest in the temple, where "both men and women are endowed with the same
power, which by definition is priesthood power." Speaking of her status as a single
but endowed woman, she stated, "I do not have a priesthood bearer living in my
home, but I do have access to priesthood power in my home." Dew also provides

an excellent example of how many Latter-day Saints read this new priesthood approach into older texts. Quoting the Book of Mormon prophet Nephi's statement that "the power of God" was to descend on the covenant people of the Lord, she editorialized that this power is priesthood.[107] Sidestepping the issue of authority, but highlighting the incorporation of these teachings on priesthood power into regular church instruction, church leaders included these same verses, ideas, and statements in the June 2017 "visiting teaching" message for all women in the church, entitled "Priesthood Power through Keeping Covenants."[108]

Conclusion

In October 2015, the church published an essay titled "Joseph Smith's Teachings on Women, the Temple, and Priesthood" as part of a series designed to treat challenging historical material in an open and accessible way. The essay reviewed Joseph Smith's organization of the Relief Society and revelatory endorsement of women performing healing rituals. Perhaps clarifying official church teachings about priesthood, it also adopted Dallin Oaks's framework as an interpretive tool: "Today, Latter-day Saint women lead three organizations within the Church: the Relief Society, the Young Women, and the Primary. They preach and pray in congregations, fill numerous positions of leadership and service, participate in priesthood councils at the local and general levels, and serve formal proselytizing missions across the globe. In these and other ways, women exercise priesthood authority even though they are not ordained to priesthood office." The essay concludes expansively stating that "in ecclesiastical callings, temple ordinances, family relationships, and quiet, individual ministry, Latter-day Saint women and men go forward with priesthood power and authority."[109]

Such reflections point to the sweeping changes that have occurred in Mormonism with regard to conceptions of priesthood. When Osmer Flake left his family in December 1897 to travel without purse or scrip in the American South, his participation in the temple liturgy and ordination as a seventy before leaving was absolutely critical. But Flake's ordination also revealed a moment of transition. At that moment, the temple cosmology that had been elucidated in the Nauvoo Temple liturgy had faded, and church ecclesiology was on the verge of massive reforms. Four months after Flake was ordained, church leaders formally called the first full-time female evangelists to Britain.[110] Women had previously led and presided over other women and children, but preaching and praying among the general public and membership of the church had been the sole responsibility of priesthood officers. For all but the last few years of the nineteenth century, Joseph Smith's declaration that Mormons "believe that a man must be called of God by 'prophesy, and by laying on of hands' by those who are in authority to preach the gospel and administer in the ordinances thereof" had described the ordination of evangelists as seventies. With the addition of female evangelists, women were still called by prophecy and the laying on of hands, but they were not ordained to ecclesiastical priesthood offices. Like male missionaries who had previously been ordained, they were simply "set apart" to the ministry.[111] Over one hundred years later, church leaders began to categorize the authority of these sister missionaries as the priesthood.

Any discussion of the authority of male and female missionaries in the LDS Church, however, is largely a discussion of ecclesiology. Conceptions of Mormon priesthood have ranged far beyond the cloister of church office. The concept of a priesthood of heaven—what I have described as the cosmological priesthood, constituting the material network of salvation, kinship, and government of the Nauvoo Temple cosmology—is essential to understanding the fundamental role of priesthood in the ordering of Latter-day Saints in life and death. That Latter-day Saints grew to use other terms than "priesthood" when describing this ordering over time allowed for a newer understanding of priesthood rooted in the ecclesiology to take hold. The challenge for recent Mormons has been to understand the historical restrictions against the full participation of black people in the church and the integration of women into the contemporary priesthood framework. The connections that formed the basis of the cosmological priesthood—the sealing of women and men as spouses and children—have remained a constant priority of church leaders and members regardless of these shifts. The next chapter illuminates what these sealed relationships have meant and how leaders have managed their construction over time.

2

Sealings

*Verily verily I Say unto you, if <a> man marry a wife according
to my word, and they are Sealed by the Holy Spirit of promise,
according to mine appointement, and he or she shall commit any
sin or transgression of the new and everlasting covenant whatever
and all manner of blasphemies and if they commit no murder,
wherein they Shed innocent blood yet they Shall come forth in the
first resurrection and enter into their—exaltation but they Shall
be destroyed in in the flesh and Shall be delivered unto the buf-
fetins of Satan unto the day of redemption Saith the Lord God.[1]*

JOSEPH SMITH, revelation, July 12, 1843

IN 1878, MARY ATHERTON GLOVER was fifty years old, married, and the mother
of ten children. She was a member of Lancashire's working poor, and she snuck out
late one night with her family to be baptized by the Mormon elders from Utah. The
Glovers didn't want their neighbors to know of their conversion and "persecute the
older members of the family and cause them to lose their jobs." In 1880 and 1881, as
church members in the Great Basin sponsored their immigration, the family broke
apart and reunited in Johnson, Utah. When Mary's husband James died in 1883,
she married William Johnson. With William, she traveled to St. George, where she
participated in the temple liturgy for the first time. Temple officiators sealed Mary
and William for time and all eternity as husband and wife.[2]

The questions Mary and her children faced after her sealing were personally
and cosmologically critical: What of Mary's first husband, and to whom should
the adult children be sealed? James Glover was the only father the children had
known, and he had died in full faith. Mary and James had never gone to the temple, likely because they were poor—the long trip through the desert was beyond
their pecuniary reach. With William Johnson's first sealed wife, Jane, Mary wrote
to the First Presidency to inquire as to the most prudent course of action.[3] The
secretary of the First Presidency responded on behalf of President John Taylor,

Photograph of St. George Temple ca. 1880. By Charles R. Savage. Courtesy of the L. Tom Perry Special Collections.

who decided "that it will be proper for Sister Glover's living children to have their choice as to whom they will be sealed or adopted." If they decided to be sealed as children to their mother and her new husband, then they should also do all the proxy rituals possible for their biological father. "He having been a member of the Church, [he] will not have to be baptized for, but he should have his [proxy] endowments, and some one or more women that he had been acquainted with or that would be suitable for him should be sealed to him, so that he will not be alone," the president directed. Mary and James had also had several children who were no longer living. Taylor indicated that Mary could have those children sealed to her, "yet the President suggests that if she feels like letting two of the children that are dead go with their father it will be all right, but in this she can use her own pleasure and judgement."[4]

In the fall of 2008, a young man drove home on a Utah freeway late into the night. His wife received a call from the state troopers that he had been in an accident and was in the hospital. The attending physicians were helpless to save him, and he passed away. In the subsequent week, the young man's extended family gathered for the funeral. They tied the robes of the holy priesthood on his broken body and then laid it to molder among his kin.[5] Four weeks earlier, he had knelt across a temple altar and covenanted to his wife for all eternity, being sealed together for all time.

After a period of mourning, this young widow began her studies anew and met someone she wished to marry. The LDS Church prohibits living women from being sealed to multiple men, and her new fiancé, who had never previously married, wished to be married in the temple. She consequently began the process of having the First Presidency dissolve the sealing to her first husband and approve her remarriage in the temple. As in the case of widowers or divorced men who wish to be sealed to multiple women while living, the First Presidency asked all parties related to the possible action to write down their feelings, thoughts, and concerns. As part of this process, the mother of the dead man was to write about the prospective canceling of her son's sealing.[6]

In both these cases, one in 1883 and one in 2008, Mormons struggled to find their eternal families among the detritus of mortality. In the former, they struggled to fairly construct the material heaven that reflected their familial reality. In the latter, they struggled to repair the material heaven that was fractured by their reality. When Latter-day Saints enter their temples to seal the living and the dead, they build the eternal structure of the cosmos. As soon as they leave those sacred edifices, the entropic forces of reality begin to chip away at the mortar. Beyond death and remarriage, the Saints have faced singlehood and single parenthood, divorce, abuse, disbelieving partners and children, and sin in all its manifestations—endless possibilities that are incongruous with the interconnected structure of the cosmological priesthood.

In the previous chapter, we explored the cosmological priesthood and the shift in priesthood language to describe the temple liturgy. This chapter probes the fundamental characteristics of the cosmology resulting from the sealing liturgy as it evolved over time from the persevering material network of heaven to the aspirational reward of the faithful. From the time Joseph Smith revealed the practice, church leaders have anxiously regulated the details of temple sealings. Smith jealously guarded the authority to seal, and subsequent leaders regularly wrestled with the details of practice. Critical to these church leaders' efforts has been the integrity of the heavenly network. Knowing that they were creating something that endures forever, they wanted to ensure the creation was done well.

Ultimately, micromanaging the construction of heaven proved not only confusing for church leaders, but spiritually unsatisfying. From the last years of the nineteenth century through the first years of the twenty-first, church leaders directed a shift toward a more open and flexible approach to sealing, in which God would sort out the details and ambiguities of these mortal actions in the next life. And the ambiguities multiplied, especially with regard to polygamy. Polygamy was associated with sealing from its first revelation, and since that moment Latter-day Saints have wrestled with its implications both temporally and eternally. While Mormons stopped living in polygamy over a century ago, sealing practice has maintained and supported polygamy on a cosmic scale, though with increasing ambivalence in each passing decade.

Perseverance

"Sealing" as a ritual act dates to the first years of the Restoration, when elders with the High Priesthood sealed up church members and congregations into eternal life. With successive waves of Mormonism's liturgical development, sealing expanded in meaning. In the Kirtland House of the Lord, Elijah appeared to Joseph Smith and Oliver Cowdery as part of a broader theophany, and delivered to them, according to later readings, the power and authority to seal people together in relationships that persist beyond death. In Nauvoo, Smith situated this power in response to Calvinist election and Arminian backsliding.[7] But he revealed that it was impossible to be sealed up into eternal life as an individual— one's "calling and election" being "made sure" was entirely relational.[8] The relationships that these sealings created were the material network of the cosmological priesthood. The power of Elijah, Smith taught, was the power to "bind or seal" husband to wife and child to parent.[9] This understanding was manifest in the temple, where both biological children and nonbiological relations became heirs of the priesthood through sealing rituals. Those who had not been sealed in marriage and those who had not been sealed to parents were to be "single & alone" for eternity.[10] They were outside of the heavenly structure.

Joseph Smith began sealing men and women together several years before he revealed the totality of the Nauvoo Temple liturgy. And while he taught that children were to be sealed to their parents, he also refused to perform child-to-parent sealings until the temple was finished—something that did not occur until after his death. Perhaps because of this protracted introduction, church leaders commonly sealed women and men as husband and wife outside the temples along the trail west and in Mormon settlements into the twentieth century.[11] Yet sealings of children to parents and adoptions, which Brigham Young described as the highest ritual performance in the church, were strictly reserved to the temples.

The relationships formed by sealing are the basis for Joseph Smith's understanding of perseverance. Perseverance is the theological concept in Christianity that once individuals are saved, they "can neither totally nor finally fall away from the state of grace."[12] As one temple quorum member and subsequent Nauvoo Temple worker described them, these relationships were "the 'bundle of eternal life.'"[13] On August 13, 1843, Smith preached a funeral sermon describing how the sealing of couples together passed to their biological children: "When a seal is put upon the father and mother it secures their posterity so that they cannot be lost but will be saved by virtue of the covenant of their father."[14] While Smith taught that perseverance was a blessing of various discrete temple rituals, he did not intend to create discrete liturgies. Instead, he revealed a single unified liturgy. The temple rituals worked together to create the fabric of the cosmos. Mormon sealing, whether for marriage, for children, or for the fullness of the priesthood, sealed in the traditional sense of guaranteeing salvation inasmuch as it created the eternal and interconnected bonds of the cosmological priesthood. These bonds were the material heaven, and they were sure.

As mentioned in the previous chapter, during the summer of 1842, a few months after revealing the Nauvoo Temple initiation ceremony and dramatic liturgy, Joseph Smith approached his close friends and fellow church leaders Newel and Elizabeth Whitney with a shocking proposal. Despite being married to Emma Hales Smith, he wished to marry their daughter Sarah Ann. The Whitneys ultimately agreed to Smith's proposal, and he dictated a revelation promising the family's integration into the cosmological priesthood through the act. This revelation also included a text for the sealing ritual. Newel Whitney was to pronounce Joseph Smith and Sarah Ann husband and wife, through life and eternity. The ritual concluded with Whitney declaring: "Let immortality and eternal life henceforth be sealed upon your heads forever and ever."[15]

One year later, Smith's brother Hyrum requested a revelation in the hope that he could use it to convince Emma Smith, Joseph's first wife, to accept polygamy.[16] The text Joseph Smith dictated was later canonized and remains LDS scripture as Doctrine and Covenants 132. For the first decade of its existence, however, those who knew of it kept it a secret. Besides justifying polygamy, the revelation included near-antinomian[17] assertions of perseverance for those whose relationships had been sealed. In it, the voice of the Lord declared that "if <a> man marry a wife according to my word, and they are Sealed by the Holy Spirit of promise," that is by the sealing power,[18] "and he or she shall commit any sin or transgression of the new and everlasting covenant whatever and all manner of blasphemies and if they commit no murder, wherein they Shed innocent blood yet they Shall come forth in the first resurrection and enter into their—exaltation." The idea that those who were sealed as husband and wife would receive all that God had to offer as long as they did not murder in cold blood may have been reassuring, but to many it was also troubling. Evoking Paul's counsel in 1 Corinthians 5 regarding a man who had sex with his stepmother as one possible example of familial disruption, the revelation said that those sealed individuals who continued to sin "shall be destroyed in in [sic] the flesh and Shall be delivered unto the buffetin[g]s of Satan unto the day of redemption Saith the Lord God."[19] The structures created by sealings were to endure despite earth and hell.

Heber and Vilate Kimball were one of the earliest couples sealed by Joseph Smith. Just over a month before Smith dictated the 1843 revelation for his brother, Heber left on a mission to the eastern United States. The day before he left, Vilate wrote a letter to him anxiously expressing her affection and invoking their sealing: "I am yours in time and throughout all eternity. This blessing has been sealed upon us by the Holy Spirit of promise, and cannot be broken only through transgression, or committing a grosser crime than your heart or mine is capable of, that is, murder."[20] Similarly, after going to the finished Nauvoo Temple in January 1846 with his spouse, one individual wrote, "We were according to the holy order of the Priesthood Sealed together for time and all eternity and Sealed up unto eternal life and against all sin except the sin against the Holy G[h]ost."[21] As with the marriage sealings of their parents, by being sealed as children in the temple, individuals were "sealed unto eternal life" and "sealed against all sins and blasphemies," except the sin against the Holy Ghost.[22] In sermons, Smith used both cold-blooded murder and the nebulous "sin against the Holy Ghost" as constraints on complete perseverance and sometimes equated them as the "unpardonable sin."[23]

Even during Joseph Smith's life, the durability of these sealings was tested, and church leaders began to recast what perseverance meant. Cold-blooded murder was a high threshold for the loss of perseverance, and the early community of Saints was disrupted by far less. Some Mormons who had been sealed apostatized from the church, including church leaders such as Apostle and Patriarch William Smith, Apostle John Page, and stake president William Marks. On the trail west, Brigham Young organized traveling companies by gathering those who had been adopted to the Twelve, or who had committed to be adopted, and disagreements and discontent were ubiquitous. Church leaders held court over matters of sexual misconduct, theft, and abuse. The case of John D. Lee likely weighed particularly heavily on Young during the first decade in the Great Basin. In Nauvoo, Lee had worked as a scribe in the temple and with his first spouse had been sealed to Young as an adoptive child; consequently, the case was as personal to Young as it was public. Soon after arriving in Utah Territory, church leaders received testimony of Lee's abusive and lewd conduct toward his family, and he was disciplined by an ecclesiastical court. Later, Young learned that Lee had been a leading participant in the 1857 massacre at Mountain Meadows.[24] Before Mountain Meadows, Young had stated that the adoptive sealing "chain saves all men but those that shed innocent blood."[25] After the massacre, in contrast, Young publicly stated that adults sealed to him, as Lee was, would be judged according to their works, and that their salvation was entirely contingent.[26]

Nevertheless, Young remained emphatic that any children born to those sealed in marriage were connected to their parents in ways that could not be broken. For him and for other Latter-day Saints, this concern was very personal. Young had many children who did not participate in Mormon lived religion. Anxiety over children's salvation is a persistent theme in Christian history, and it is consequently not surprising that the perseverance of the sealed child-to-parent relationship has been the most enduring aspect of the cosmological priesthood. Privately, Young claimed that "himself & Br. Heber, would be able to draw their children to them again, even if they should turn away. All they had to do, was to do right themselves."[27] Publicly, he affirmed that whether those sealed have "one child or one hundred children, if they conduct themselves towards them as they should, binding them to the Lord by their faith and prayers, I care not where those children go, they are bound up to their parents by an everlasting tie, and no power of earth or hell can separate them from their parents in eternity; they will return again to the fountain from whence they sprang."[28]

Integrity of the Cosmological Priesthood

Polygamy can be viewed as the solution to a problem faced by a generation of converts to Smith's restored church who found themselves in a cosmological bind: if heaven could only be realized in the material bonds formed by sealing rituals, and if heaven was to integrate the believers in Nauvoo, then those believers needed to be sealed together in some way. Despite teaching that child-to-parent sealings would be available in the temple, Joseph Smith only sanctioned sealings between husbands and wives during his lifetime. If marriages between couples were the only sealing rituals available to be performed, generations would pass before the first generation could even possibly be connected together.

Within this cosmology of sealing, children born to parents who had been sealed were "heirs to the priesthood," or what later church leaders described as being "born under (or in) the covenant." These children were sealed to their parents by birth. No temple ritual was needed. When Smith introduced sealing rituals in Nauvoo, however, virtually all church leaders were married and had children already. All of the children were thus outside of the covenant and needed to be sealed to their parents by a ritual similar to that performed for marriage. Joseph and Emma Smith had one child born in the covenant—David Hyrum Smith—who was born four months after Joseph was killed. The rest of their children remained unsealed. If all the believers in Nauvoo had been sealed to one spouse, and had their children either been born in the covenant or sealed to them in the completed temple, and had those children married in the community and continued the pattern, eventually over generations the descendants would have been sealed in enough ways that the first generation of Saints would have been connected to each other. In other words, people in Nauvoo could have been connected to each other through normal patterns of monogamous marriage as their faithful grandchildren and great-grandchildren married each other. However, many of the first generation of Mormons were convinced that God had commanded them to be sealed to multiple people in the present—that is, God had commanded them to engage in polygamy, a practice that immediately created the material connections of heaven within the community.

Beyond polygamy, church leaders in Nauvoo also revealed another type of sealing ritual that connected adults in the cosmological network. After Joseph Smith died and the temple was completed, Brigham Young initiated a practice that long confused both Mormon insiders and outsiders: adoption. In December 1845, the Nauvoo Temple was finally ready for its intended use. The following weeks were a flurry of activity as officiators performed 1,097 marriage sealings, and 90 sealings of biological children to parents.[29] Officiators also sealed 211 adults as adopted children to sixteen couples to whom they were not biologically related.[30] This practice of sealing otherwise unrelated individuals together was a way to build the material heaven in parallel with polygamy as it similarly bridged the gaps between families. And, like polygamy, being sealed as a child to someone other than one's biological parent was not without controversy. Brigham Young reasoned, however, that it was simply expedient. On February 16, 1847, during an extended discourse on ritual adoption, he posited the hypothetical scenario of having a father who was dead and who had never heard the gospel during his life. Young asked whether it was proper to seal the deceased father "into some mans family" and then "be adopted unto my Father?" He rejected this possibility: "If we have to attend the ordinances of redemption for our dead relatives we then become their saviors," he explained. Young continued: "Were we to wait to redeem our dead relatives before we Could link the Chain of the Priesthood we would never accomplish it."[31] The first generation of Saints were to be the nucleus from which the network of heaven—the links in the chain of the priesthood—was to extend. And this nucleus was created by polygamy and adoption.

From Nauvoo to the end of the nineteenth century, the integrity of the cosmological priesthood was of paramount importance. Church leaders approached the problems of first establishing the eternal network and subsequently expanding it with the utmost caution and solemnity. The policies governing sealing performance hinged on the matter of maintaining the cosmological chain intact.

Every sealing mattered because it was an exclusive connection for an individual to heaven. From the first child-to-parent sealings—whether for biological or for adopted children—the parents, whether living or dead, had to have been members of the church in good faith. Church leaders reasoned that if being connected to the network of heaven was imperative, then one person's connection to it should not be jeopardized by basing it on a sealing to someone who might or might not accept the gospel in the next life. While sealing rituals materialized heaven and persevered, they also required the unequivocal assent of all parties to be in force.[32] Proxy sealings were consequently entirely conditional on their acceptance by the dead. By this same reasoning, church leaders refused to seal widows to their deceased husbands when those husbands had not accepted the restored gospel while living. Widowers, however, were not under the same proscription, as they were able to have multiple sealing relationships.

In an effort to extend sealings to as many deceased relatives as possible, church leaders directed the sealing of unmarried female ancestors as wives to living descendants. The rationale was straightforward: marriage and posterity in the eternities were viewed as the highest blessings, but not every individual in history had been married or had children. Wilford Woodruff described Brigham Young's solution to this problem: "He told me to have the single women of my father's and mother's households sealed to me. I asked him 'how many?' He said if there was not over nine hundred and ninety-nine to take them." Woodruff estimated that he had had approximately three hundred such women sealed to him as wives.[33] Joseph Smith may have initiated the practice during his life, but if so, it was uncommon in the Nauvoo period.[34] However, it was fairly common among those individuals who invested in genealogy and temple work during the nineteenth-century-temple era.[35] As with the case of widows and widowers above, the sealing of unmarried ancestors was also asymmetrical, limited to single women. As women could only be sealed to one man, there was simply no similar avenue possible for deceased single males to be similarly connected.

This impulse to tie up loose ends was also manifest in mortality, particularly in cases of women who were married to men who were not interested in Mormonism. One such woman in 1880 wrote the First Presidency to see if she could be sealed to a practicing Mormon man while still remaining civilly married to her nonpracticing husband. Church President John Taylor approved the request, with the stipulation that she maintain complete honesty and openness with her civil husband. She would be sealed for eternity to a practicing Mormon man while living as a wife to her legal husband for the duration of her life.[36]

Opening the Liturgy

Without question, nineteenth-century Saints wrestled with a tension between the impulse to micromanage the construction of heaven and the universalism attendant in the concept of a proxy liturgy. On April 8, 1894, President Wilford Woodruff and First Counselor George Cannon addressed the General Conference gathered at the Tabernacle and delivered the most significant resolution of that tension in the history of Mormon revelation.[37] The Manifesto of 1890 that had discontinued public plural marriage ceremonies was still fresh, but Woodruff offered an even more dramatic revision of Mormon sealing practice.

After a brief introduction by Woodruff, Cannon set the stage for the president's forthcoming announcement by revisiting the history of sealing as salvation from the time of the scriptures to Joseph Smith. He openly acknowledged that the "power which records or binds on earth, and binds in heaven . . .may seem to some to be a very bold doctrine." This power, Cannon claimed, was the power that Jesus had given Peter and that was active in the ritual of baptism, whether for the living or the dead. Woodruff, returning to the stand, then emphasized the necessity of revelation, noting that "we have not got through revelation." Brigham Young, he explained, "did not receive all the revelations that belong to this work; neither did President Taylor, nor has Wilford Woodruff." He then demanded the attention of the temple presidents, two of whom were apostles, and declared: "You have acted up to all the light and knowledge that you have had; but you have now something more to do than what you have done. We have not fully carried out those principles in fulfillment of the revelations of God to us, in sealing the hearts of the fathers to the children and the children to the fathers."

Just two years earlier, Woodruff had finally had his father ritually adopted to Joseph Smith, and he described his feelings about this step to the conference: "I was adopted to my father, and should have had my father sealed to his father, and so on back; and the duty that I want every man who presides over a temple to see performed from this day henceforth and forever, unless the Lord Almighty commands otherwise, is, let every man be adopted to his father." But even this was not enough. "We want the Latter-day Saints from this time to trace their genealogies as far as they can, and to be sealed to their fathers and mothers," he said. "Have children sealed to their parents, and run this chain through as far as you can get it . . . . This is the will of the Lord to this people." Latter-day Saints, Woodruff directed, were to be sealed to their biological ancestors, regardless of those progenitors' status as believers.

In the same speech, Woodruff introduced an additional change with regard to marriage sealings: individuals who wished to be sealed to a spouse who was no longer living and had never joined the church could now do so. With this revelation, Woodruff invoked a principle that may have catalyzed his change in perspective regarding adoptions. Reminiscent of Joseph Smith's penchant for sacramental universalism, and perhaps reflecting trends in liberal Protestantism at the turn of the century,[38] Woodruff stated plainly, "There will be very few, if any, who will not accept the Gospel." Those who were suffering in hell, Woodruff said, would "doubtless gladly embrace the Gospel, and in doing so be saved in the kingdom of God."[39] Woodruff thus broke with decades of logic that reasoned that one's ancestors could not be relied upon to function as links in the chain of divine inheritance. No longer were Mormons to be saviors in being, but saviors in doing—performing proxy rituals for the dead and sealing the lineal chain as far back as possible. In this way, the tension between micromanaging the structure of heaven and universalism was clearly resolved in favor of universalism. But this revelation required a reconceptualization of sealings themselves. Henceforth, Mormons were to perform proxy rituals according to their best efforts and trust that God would manage the outcomes.

Days before publicly announcing this revelation, Woodruff met with the First Presidency and Quorum of the Twelve to discuss it, with the leaders unanimously and enthusiastically agreeing. Perhaps because this revelation resolved what many perceived to be problems within the temple cosmology, the discussion immediately turned to post-Manifesto marriage practice and what the Quorum perceived to be the remaining significant problems. George Cannon described two issues. First, he pointed out that both widows who had been sealed to their husbands but had never had children and sealed women who were still married but biologically incapable of having children would leave their husbands without posterity in the eternities. Second, he pointed to the "surplus" of young women who were unable to find righteous husbands. Cannon gave several specific examples, including that of his son David, who "died without seed, and his brothers cannot do a work for him, in rearing children to bear his name because of the Manifesto." Cannon grieved that one of his sons could not take David's widow as a levirate plural wife to bear children for David. Because a woman could be sealed as a wife to only one man in life or death, Cannon feared that unmarried men would be unwilling to marry sealed widows, since those widows would remain with their first husbands in eternity. Without plural marriage, there simply were not enough good men to marry all the available Mormon women.[40]

The magnitude of these challenges to the cosmology of the church leaders is evident in the possible solutions entertained after Cannon outlined them. Cannon proposed the possibility of concubinage, or extramarital procreation, in which church members who could not enter into a plural marriage would make a temporal covenant to have children together and, when the woman had not previously been sealed, be sealed at the death of the first partner. "Perhaps such sentiments might shock some of my brethren," Cannon wrote in his journal, stating that he "did not mean to occupy the position of an advocate of a system of concubinage, but to throw these thoughts out for consideration." Still, several church leaders, including Woodruff, seriously considered the possibility that some form of concubinage might be possible as a resolution to the predicaments Cannon described.[41] That a practice so clearly alien to all of the participants would be even remotely considered is indicative of how strained their cosmology was at that moment.

Within the next five years, however, two primary ideas appear to have converged and successfully mitigated the problems Cannon raised for the ensuing generations. The first idea was the one revealed several days after the meeting by Woodruff: that virtually all people would eventually accept the gospel. The second idea was the assurance that God was just and fair, a theological premise captured by the Book of Mormon's teaching that unbaptized children will be saved, as well as by Joseph Smith's entire revelation of proxy liturgy. A third and later addition was a view of the Millennium as an opportunity for injustices to be made right. Brigham Young had long prophesied that the Millennium would be the time when the bulk of proxy temple work would occur, and that it would be directed by angels with knowledge of kinship relations throughout the centuries.[42] After Young died, Joseph F. Smith expended significant effort to recast some of his uncle Joseph Smith's sermons indicating that deceased children would be resurrected and live through eternity in the form of children. Instead, Joseph F. Smith reasoned that deceased children would be resurrected as children and then be raised to adulthood during the Millennium by their resurrected parents.[43] So too would all the blessings due to the faithful be given in the Millennium.

On May 8, 1899, Lorenzo Snow, Wilford Woodruff's successor as church president, addressed congregants at the St. George Tabernacle. "I understand that there are in St. George about eighty widows and about one hundred marriageable sisters, and there seems to be considerable lamentation in regard to this condition," he stated. "There is no need of this particularity." He then described a thirty-eight-year-old woman who came to his office who felt "very badly" that "opportunities for getting a husband had not been favorable." She wondered about the eternal status of her soul if she did not get married. Snow noted that similar questions were likely common among women in the church, and that "some very foolish doctrine has been presented to some of the sisters" on the topic. Snow emphatically stated:

> There is no Latter-day Saint who dies after having lived a faithful life who will lose anything because of having failed to do certain things when opportunities were not furnished him or her. In other words, if a young man or a young woman has no opportunity of getting married, and they live faithful lives up to the time of their death, they will have all the blessings, exaltation and glory that any man or woman will have who had this opportunity and improved it. That is sure and positive.

Snow then described his famous sister and former general Relief Society president Eliza R. Snow as a faithful example of someone who was unable to have children in this life. He concluded that "The Lord is merciful and kind, and He is not unjust. There is no injustice in Him; yet we could scarcely look upon it as being just when a woman or a man dies without having had the opportunity of marrying if it could but be remedied in the other life."[44] From that point forward, Latter-day Saint leaders taught that God's justice would prevail, and that He would direct the appropriate temple rituals for the faithful during the Millennium. Though exceptional cases are documented as late as 1950, no longer were unmarried dead female relatives to be sealed to male descendants.[45]

Though the place of single Mormons in the church has been particularly fraught,[46] throughout the twentieth century church leaders repeated and reaffirmed the idea that the faithful will receive all the blessings of an eternal family in the next life, regardless of the opportunities in this life.[47] However, perhaps because of church demographics during this period, women received the bulk of church leaders' consolation. Twentieth-century church leaders' discourse about single members was typified by the speeches of Church President Ezra Taft Benson in 1988. That year he delivered sermons addressed "To the Single Adult Sisters of the Church"[48] in the General Women's Meeting, and "To the Single Adult Brethren of the Church"[49] in the Priesthood Session of the General Conference. These sermons were reprinted in pamphlet form along with Benson's sermons to mothers and fathers, respectively, and were widely distributed. In his sermon to unmarried women, Benson recognized the reality that not all women will have "an opportunity for marriage and motherhood in mortality." However, if such women are faithful, Benson taught, they "can be assured of all blessings from a kind and loving Heavenly Father—and I emphasize *all blessings*. I assure you that if you have to wait even until the next life to be blessed with a choice companion, God will surely compensate you." While Benson may have technically thought the same was true for single men in the church, he continued a long tradition of not publicly recognizing it. In a dominant culture of masculinity, men had the burden of actively finding a wife and starting a family, whereas women were to passively wait to be courted. Benson quoted the previous president of the church's description of advising a thirty-five-year-old returned missionary who had not yet married: "I shall feel sorry for this young man when the day comes that he faces the Great Judge at the throne and when the Lord asks this boy: 'Where is your wife?' All of his excuses which he gave to his fellows on earth will seem very light and senseless when answers the Judge." According to Benson and other church leaders, "I did not find the right girl" would be an insufficient excuse before the bar of the Almighty.

Women, Men, and Modern Plural Sealings

After Wilford Woodruff's 1894 revelation on sealings transformed the possibilities for proxy ritual performance, Mormons embarked on a flurry of activity, spurred by a new impulse to find their deceased ancestors and connect themselves together. Within months of the revelation, the Utah Genealogical Society had formed to act as the facilitator of the modern Mormon zeal for family history

Plate 23.—The Sealing Room for the Dead, ca. 1911. This is the room where officiators performed proxy sealings of couples and children to parents, published in James Talmage, *House of the Lord* (Salt Lake City: Church of Jesus Christ of Latter-day Saints, 1912), 286. Photograph by Ralph G. Savage, PH 600, LDS Church History Library, Salt Lake City.

work.[50] Even with only nine months remaining in the year when Woodruff announced his revelation, proxy child-to-parent sealings in 1894 increased 675 percent over the previous year.[51] Genealogy boomed, and Latter-day Saints began to create "family group sheets"—documents that contained genealogical data for entire nuclear families. Mormons took these sheets to the temple, where they performed the proxy rituals in order for all members of the family, sealing the relationships formed on earth over the temple altars. However, how church leaders directed sealing of women differed dramatically from how they directed them for men.

Following Woodruff's issuance of the 1890 Manifesto pronouncing an end to new plural marriages, church leaders began a protracted journey away from polygamy. It took the better part of two decades and multiple subsequent manifestos before the church systematically shut down all new polygamous unions, and by the end of the process, several members of the Quorum of the Twelve had been sanctioned and ultimately removed from church leadership because of their reluctance to support the new position. Monogamy became the Mormon ideal, and the practice of polygamy an excommunicable offense. However, into the second half of the twentieth century, many church leaders viewed the cessation of polygamy as only a temporary accommodation—a compromise for this world that would be corrected in the future.[52]

While the church during this period did not countenance lived polygamy, as late as 1966 church leaders approved of new polygamous sealings between living and deceased individuals who had not been married to each other in life.[53] These cases, however, were rare. More commonly, church policy allowed men to be sealed to multiple women if the marriages were civilly recognized and temporally sequential. For example, widowers and male divorcees were able to be sealed to subsequent spouses in the temple, a practice that continues to be permitted under church policy today. While lived monogamy is strictly enforced upon penalty of excommunication, the church's sealing practice suggests that polygamy may be operative in heaven. Church leaders have been consistently circumspect in discussing this aspect of sealing policy, as distancing the church from polygamy has been a goal of paramount importance. However, with time church leaders seem to have grown a genuine theological ambiguity regarding sequential sealings, perhaps evolving towards a position in which sealings grant the blessings of heaven but the actual relationships involved are mutable. For example, when a prominent Mormon widower began dating a woman seriously in the late 1970s, the couple took the question of how multiple sealings to one man played out in the eternities to Church President Spencer Kimball. Kimball said that "he did not know exactly how these relationships will be worked out, but he did know that through faithfulness all will be well and we will have much joy." After the couple expressed some hesitancy about the prospect of causing offense to the deceased first wife, "President Kimball's demeanor seemed to change. From being somewhat hesitant in his earlier answers, he now became sure and spoke with firmness. He looked right at [the woman] and with a tear forming in his eye, he said, 'I do know this: you have nothing to worry about. Not only will she accept you, she will put her arms around you and thank you for raising her children.'"[54]

In 2006, filmmaker Helen Whitney interviewed Apostle Dallin Oaks for a PBS documentary and asked specifically whether "polygamy is part of the afterlife." Oaks began his response by noting that this was an area "where the prophet has not chosen to make doctrinal statements." Nevertheless, he acknowledged that "a lot of people, myself included, are in multiple-marriage situations." Furthermore, he elucidated,

> for people who live in the belief, as I do, that marriage relations can be for eternity, then you must say, "What will life be in the next life, when you're married to more than one wife for eternity?" I have to say I don't know. But I know that I've made those covenants, and I believe if I am true to the covenants that the blessing that's anticipated here will be realized in the next life. How? Why, I don't know.[55]

In spite of this ambiguity, the church's maintenance of the policy that women cannot be sealed to sequential husbands is at least suggestive that the polygamous cosmology of the past is continuing to direct the sealing policies of the present. Moreover, many Mormons today view these policies as clearly endorsing eternal polygamy and struggle spiritually and emotionally to reconcile this cosmology with their beliefs in romantic monogamy.[56] It is also possible that this ambiguity is the result of church leaders viewing the cessation of polygamy as not temporary, but cosmologically necessary. Regardless, such a position allows individuals in sealed relationships the freedom to invest those relationships with the complete weight of eternal and romantic monogomy, while not having to negate the founding generations of Mormons' marriages.

In contrast to men, living widows and female divorcees must have their first sealing canceled by the First Presidency before they can be sealed to a subsequent spouse. Today, however, there is one case in which women can be sealed as wife to multiple men: when they are all dead. It is perhaps surprising that such a dramatic shift in policy was a consequence not of women petitioning church leaders for change or of a particular sealing being reviewed by church leaders but instead as a result of the Genealogical Society adopting computer technology. In the decade after World War II, the First Presidency struggled to deal with cases of war widows who wanted to remarry.[57] In some rare cases, the First Presidency even authorized the sealing of living widows to a second man, without canceling the first sealing.[58] But even more urgent for church leaders' consideration in the latter half of the twentieth century was the problem that member participation in the proxy temple liturgy was increasing to a point at which there was a real risk of not having sufficient names of the deceased at the temple to support them. Church leaders consequently invested in computer technology as a solution to the dearth of names. Increasingly, names for proxy temple work became the output of ana-lytical algorithms, not the manual family history work of individual members. Whereas members had traditionally brought data for entire families to the tem-ple, this automated process resulted in individual names that were extracted from genealogical records. And it was not immediately evident to church leaders how to perform sealings for individuals.[59]

After wrestling with the problem, the First Presidency approved a new policy in 1969. As historians James Allen, Jessie Embry, and Kahlile Mehr, in their his-tory of the Genealogical Society, summarized: "Children could be sealed to their parents even if they were not yet tied together in family groups and even if the names of the parents were not yet known. If a child were sealed to parents (that is, if the word parents, rather than specific names, was used in the temple ceremony), there would be no doubt that the child would, in fact, be sealed to his or her correct parents."[60] Moreover, because names and marriages were often extracted from parish records, it was extremely difficult to distinguish between first or sub-sequent marriages, so the First Presidency approved the performance of sealings for all marriages so extracted.[61] These changes were not without controversy, and subsequent church presidents reconsidered them.[62]

In light of these changes in practice, in 1969, Apostle and Genealogical Society President Howard Hunter approached the First Presidency to suggest that members be allowed to consciously seal deceased female relatives to all the husbands they had had during their lives. If women were only sealed to their first husbands, he argued, descendants of subsequent marriages had no "positive line to follow" in their gene-alogy work. He further indicated that the leaders of the Genealogical Society had concurred that such a change "would be better." Unlike cases in which men had multiple viable sealings, however, "this would still give the woman the right to make her selection in the hereafter."[63] President McKay approved the change.

When church leaders included this new policy in the next edition of the General Handbook, published in 1976, they were careful to note that despite the possibility of deceased women being sealed to more than one man, there was no such thing as polyandry in heaven. While the status of men's multiple sealings remained ambiguous, that of women's multiple sealings was clear: "A deceased woman having had more than one civil marriage, but having been sealed to one of her husbands during life, cannot be sealed to any other husband by proxy because she exercised her election to be so sealed during lifetime." A woman who died without having been sealed could be sealed to all the men she had been married to in her life, but this would leave "to the woman and to the Lord the decision as to which one, if any, of the sealings will become effective."[64]

This policy was reiterated in subsequent editions of the General Handbook. Then, on December 8, 1988, the First Presidency wrote a circular letter to local and regional church authorities that included instructions that deceased women could be sealed to all of their mortal husbands regardless of whether they had been sealed during their lives or not.[65] After this letter, the General Handbooks began including the same instructions.[66] The most recent Handbook notes that both deceased men and deceased women may be sealed to all spouses to whom they were legally married during their lives. However, while a deceased male may have spouses sealed to him if they are living or dead, a deceased female may only be sealed to multiple men when all her husbands are deceased.[67]

Attenuation of Perseverance and the Justice of God

The idea that Mormons could receive sealing blessings in the next life if they were faithful in this one—in contrast to Joseph Smith's earlier vision of the next life being made real today—was a shift in the conception of heaven that moved Latter-day Saints further toward that of traditional Protestantism. Instead of a heaven made in the temple, heaven would one day be received as a reward. This further attenuated the sacerdotal perseverance of the Nauvoo Temple liturgy, though these earlier beliefs did persist in Mormon thought, primarily in relation to children.[68] Apostle Orson Whitney spoke at the April 1929 General Conference, and delivered a statement that continues to be widely quoted by church leaders to the present:

> The Prophet Joseph Smith declared—and he never taught more comforting doctrine—that the eternal sealings of faithful parents and the divine promises made to them for valiant service in the Cause of Truth, would save not only themselves, but likewise their posterity. Though some of the sheep may wander, the eye of the Shepherd is upon them, and sooner or later they will feel the tentacles of Divine Providence reaching out after them and drawing them back to the fold. Either in this life or the life to come, they will return. They will have to pay their debt to justice; they will suffer for their sins; and may tread a thorny path; but if it leads them at last, like the penitent Prodigal, to a loving and forgiving father's heart and home, the painful experience will not have been in vain.[69]

Apostle Joseph Fielding Smith reiterated this idea in the 1948 *Church News*. After quoting Brigham Young's statements on the matter, Smith affirmed that "those born under the covenant, through all eternity are the children of their parents. Nothing except the unpardonable sin, or sin unto death, can break this tie. If children do not sin as John says, 'unto death,' the parents may still feel after them and eventually bring them back again."[70]

When Bruce McConkie edited this text for inclusion in the widely distributed *Doctrines of Salvation*, a collection of Joseph Fielding Smith's writings, in 1955, he followed it with a Joseph Fielding Smith letter that is currently unavailable in holograph form. According to McConkie's volume, Smith wrote that "all children born under the covenant belong to their parents in eternity, but that does not mean that they, because of that birthright, will inherit celestial glory. The faith and faithfulness of fathers and mothers will not save disobedient children."[71] Smith's vision of the persistence of the familial relationship thus appears somewhat different than that posited by the material structure of heaven. This seemingly subtle revision represents a major change to a century of Mormon thinking. After the declension of the cosmological priesthood as the context for the temple, Latter-day Saints mapped out their eternal relationships onto the tripartite heavenly rewards of founder Joseph Smith's "Vision," expressed in Doctrine and Covenants 76.

The question of the eternal fate of wayward children continued to vex the Saints. In 1946, a ward in Rockland, Idaho, held a fireside chat with several members of the stake leadership and other visitors. One of these visitors taught that "all children born under the Covenant, and by virtue of the sealing power of the priesthood would be saved in the Celestial Kingdom." One of the attendees was confused by this statement and wrote to Apostle John Widtsoe for clarification: "This [teaching] seems contrary to reason but he claimed the Prophet Joseph Smith for authority and I allowed the matter to drop without involving too much discussion."[72] Widtsoe responded: "When children are born under the covenant, they are entitled to all the blessings that are inherent in the kingdom of God, providing, of course, they live proper lives . . . . However, these blessings may be forfeited in part or completely by improper living. It would not be reasonable to expect that because a person is born under the covenant, he can sin to his heart's desire and still retain the blessings of the kingdom."[73] The specter of antinomianism was simply too terrible. Orthopraxy, or correct behavior, became a dominant theme throughout the twentieth century. Joseph Smith's teachings were, however, difficult to shake. Church leaders continued to regularly quote Orson Whitney's sermon about the "tentacles of providence" to comfort parents into the twenty-first century.[74]

In 2014, Apostle David Bednar wrote in the *Ensign* an article designed to dispel "doctrinal misunderstandings" derived from readings of nineteenth-century church leaders regarding the perseverance of sealed relationships to children. "The statements by Joseph Smith and Orson F. Whitney are construed by some members of the Church to mean that wayward children unconditionally receive the blessings of salvation because of and through the faithfulness of parents," Bednar stated, before marshaling extensive scriptural evidence to argue that God will judge individuals on their own merits. "The 'tentacles of Divine Providence' described by Elder Whitney," Bednar wrote, "may be considered a type of spiritual power, a heavenly pull or tug that entices a wandering child to return to the fold eventually. Such an influence cannot override the moral agency of a child but nonetheless can invite and beckon. Ultimately, a child must exercise his or her moral agency and respond in faith, repent with full purpose of heart, and act in accordance with the teachings of Christ."[75]

Since Joseph Smith's revelation of the temple rituals, it has not just been children who have failed to meet the ideal. Parents too have strayed from the fold, or divorced and sought cancellations of their sealings. Children from such marriages have naturally wondered about the status of their sealings to their parents. Joseph Fielding Smith explained in a letter published in 1955 that if sealed parents do not keep their covenants, "the children may be taken away from both of them and given to somebody else, and that would be by virtue of being born under the covenant." A child who has been born "under the covenant" is not to be sealed to other parents during his or her life, Smith explained, "but by virtue of that birthright," the sealing "can be transferred" in the eternities.[76] In this view, God can rearrange sealed relationships to make sure the faithful are connected together.

With the changes in sealing practice initiated in 1969 in response to computer extraction of names for temple work, church leaders allowed deceased individuals to be sealed to unknown parents with the understanding that God would make all relationships right. It was perhaps within this context that in 1975 a General Authority assistant to the Quorum of the Twelve wrote in the *Ensign* about children "in the next life when there has been a cancellation of sealing of the parents." He noted that such a cancellation "does not cancel the sealing of the children to the parents, since they were born in the covenant," though it would cancel the parents' sealings to each other. This meant that in the eternities, "the decision as to with whom they [the children] will go will be determined by the Lord."[77] Church leaders began to refer to sealing blessings of children as the promise of "eternal parentage," even if it was unclear who would fill the role of parents.[78] The standard letter written during the late 1970s and 1980s to inform individuals that a marriage sealing had been canceled stated: "Please note that a cancellation of sealing of a wife to her husband does not affect children born in the covenant or previously sealed. Such children are entitled to birthright blessings, and if they remain worthy, are assured the right and privilege of eternal parentage regardless of what happens to their natural parents or the parents to whom they were sealed."[79] Perhaps recognizing the potential disconcertion resulting from such ambiguity, church leaders wrote in the 2010 Handbook that "members who have concerns about the eternal nature of such relationships can find peace in the knowledge that Heavenly Father is loving and just. He will ensure that eternal family relationships will be fair and right for all who keep their covenants."[80] The current letter sent upon the cancellation of marriage sealings states that "for each of us, the realization of eternal blessings is conditioned upon personal worthiness and individual agency. Such blessings, including our eternal family relationships, will be determined by our wise and loving Father after we have completed our mortal probation."[81]

Excommunication and Perseverance

One of the clearest examples of church leaders' shifting views on sealing perseverance relates to the liturgical policy surrounding excommunication. Rebaptism was common among Mormons during the nineteenth century, being employed as a means to renew covenants generally or as part of church discipline. A Saint might be rebaptized when arriving in Utah as an emigrant, before participating in the temple liturgy, before joining a communitarian "United Order," or as part of a healing ritual. Likely because rebaptism was so widespread and requisite for all excommunicants (though not just excommunicants) to regain fellowship within the church, Mormons have viewed excommunication as nullifying the baptismal "ordinance." Consequently, when church leaders shed rebaptism in most circumstances in the 1890s, they nevertheless kept it in the case of excommunication. The Church of Jesus Christ of Latter-day Saints may be the only Christian church in operation today that cancels the baptisms of its excommunicants.

Sealings, however, are not nullified by excommunication. When a man is excommunicated, the sealing to his wife is not canceled.[82] Only the specific and recorded nullification by the First Presidency can break sealings, either for spouses or for children. Even if the couple legally divorces and the man remains outside of the church, a woman who wishes to be sealed in a new marriage must obtain a formal cancellation of the previous sealing from the First Presidency. The status of an individual who has been sealed in marriage but excommunicated by the church is analogous to that of a child "born in the covenant" who has left the church.

In the twentieth century, however, church policy changes eroded this notion of the irrevocability of temple sealings. While the First Presidency had previously decided that the children of an excommunicant were still born in the covenant, in 1965 President David McKay decided that children born to a parent who had been excommunicated were not, although an "illegitimate" child born to a woman who had been sealed but merely had undergone a civil divorce was indeed born in the covenant.[83] In 1968, the Priesthood Correlation Committee updated the General Handbook to note that children born after an excommunication and before a restoration of blessings were not considered born in the covenant and needed to be sealed in the temple to their parents.[84] The 1983 Handbook introduced language stating that while the sealing of an excommunicant still existed, it was considered to be temporarily "suspended."[85] Then, in 1998, church leaders changed the language of suspension to revocation, though the sealing was maintained for faithful spouses and children.[86] Today, a divorced women still need to receive a sealing cancellation before being sealed in a new marriage, even if her ex-husband has been excommunicated.

The policy in place today is somewhat softer, though not as forgiving as the customs of the nineteenth century. The 2010 Handbook describes the sealings of excommunicants as being "revoked"; however, "the sealing blessings of the innocent spouse and of children born in the covenant are not affected."[87] After church leaders are convinced of the true penitence of an excommunicant who has been rebaptized into the church, they then administer a "restoration of blessings" ritual. This simple blessing by the laying on of hands was established to resolve ambiguity about the status of temple rituals that were not canceled by excommunication and to formalize the belief that such rituals are active and in force for the penitent.

Conclusion

Henry Eyring of the First Presidency posted a Facebook update on August 7, 2016, that captures the normative position of current church leaders with regard to sealings. In this post he describes how once, after having some anxiety that "the choices of others might make it impossible for our family to be together forever," an otherwise unidentified "prophet of God" told him that if "you just live worthy of the celestial kingdom," then "family arrangements will be more wonderful than you can imagine." This blessing, Eyring wrote, was for "all of those whose personal experience or whose marriage and children—or absence thereof—cast a shadow over their hopes."[88] Regardless of how the details of these relationships may be resolved, one can hope for a fullness of joy.

Perhaps more than any other aspect of Mormon liturgy, the sealing of family relationships over temple altars orders the Mormon cosmos. It is precisely because Mormons view the grand structures of the eternities as intersecting with and amplifying the quotidian experiences of individuals interacting with those closest to them that they have such power in the lives of Latter-day Saints. There is no question that Mormons find absolute comfort and strength in the eternal relationships formalized in these rituals, even in the face of less-than-ideal family conditions. The prospect of eternal marriage and eternal relationships has been a consistent and successful emphasis in modern proselytizing efforts.[89] There is also no question that many believers are confused by the tension between the church's laser focus on sealing ideals and the messy reality of mortality. As one practicing Mormon woman described, "The sealing ordinance is both extremely important ('Never settle for less than being married/sealed in the temple!') and not important at all ('You are still sealed to your abuser? Don't worry about—God will sort it out in the hereafter!')."[90] Another woman who was recently sealed as the second sequential wife of a divorced man wrote, "I know several women in similar situations—still sealed against their will [e.g., after a civil divorce], or forced to choose between being polygamously sealed, or not at all. There is really nowhere to discuss this sort of thing in church."[91]

The tension described by these Mormons derives from ambiguities church leaders have consciously introduced into the church cosmology. When Joseph Smith began ritually sealing families together, he revealed that the bonds formed by sealing were sure. They comprised the material heaven, and where the bonds didn't exist, there was only lonely disconnection—a terrorizing prospect to Smith. As the temple liturgy, including the attendant sealing rituals, became available to more than the small group surrounding Smith during his life, the complexities of managing ritual performance also expanded. Smith's successors viewed the connections to the material network of heaven to be crucial, so much so that only those who accepted and lived the restored gospel during their lives could be relied upon to connect individuals. To that end, adoption and polygyny were normative.

With Wilford Woodruff's 1894 revelation opening the sealing liturgy for the dead, and with the First Presidency's further approval of ambiguous sealings in 1969, church leaders shifted from micromanaging the construction of a material heaven to distributing the promises of a future eternal relationship contingent on individual agency and God's justice. Certainly this development has prevented and resolved countless conundrums faced by Mormons as they work through the maze of family relations to bring their ancestors' names to the temple. However, individuals like Mary Glover, described in the opening vignette of this chapter, still must navigate sealing policies that are clearly informed by and descended from male-centered polygyny. Still, many church members find comfort in the promises of leaders like Henry Eyring who teach that despite the unknowns and complexities, a heaven replete with kin is within reach.

3

Baby Blessing

She has form'd the dear connexion
That has won her father's name;
And thro' which the resurrection
And the priesthood's power she'll claim.[1]

ELIZA R. SNOW, poem memorializing the death of a two-year- old child, 1847

ON THE EVENING of October 16, 1857, Brigham Young was conversing with some of his friends and fellow church leaders when the topic turned to stillborn babies. Young noted that in some cases in which babies were carried into their third trimester but then ceased to develop or died before they could be delivered, church members had blessed and named them. "But," Young noted, "I dont do it for I think that such a spirit has not a fair Chance." He continued: "I think that such a spirit will have a Chance of occupying another Tabernacle and develop itself." Wilford Woodruff, who recorded Young's remarks in his journal, editorialized that while Young's remarks represented a new teaching, "it looks Consistant."[2] Mormonism's concept of a premortal life where all spirits exist and await mortality is indeed consistent with Young's idea that such spirits might get fair access to a viable body.[3] However, the practice of blessing and naming a stillborn child, on which at least some people insisted, is also consistent with Mormon cosmology, though in different ways.

Typical Mormon baby blessings offer numerous promises of life's bounty, but the stillborn child has no mortal life to live. Moreover, it is not clear why a naming ritual would be at all necessary for such a child. This chapter demonstrates why a parent in the early Utah era would have sought to have any child blessed, whether living or dead. Blessing babies is one of the earliest documented rituals of the church and has been part of its formal liturgy since a small group gathered in upstate New York to incorporate the Restoration. As with all rituals, the meaning of baby blessing has changed with the people who have participated in it. In the nineteenth century, baby blessing was an important demarcation of Mormonism's communal salvation. In the twentieth century, the practice became an important element of Mormon manhood. These features of baby blessing help to reveal key aspects of the familial and priesthood cosmology of church members as it has developed over time.

Naming Christian Children

With the rise of general infant baptism in the first centuries of the Common Era, baptism became a de facto naming ritual during which parents presented their infants to the church to be baptized and eventually to have their names recorded.[4] Children then grew up as candidates for church membership, preparing for initiation into a formal relationship with the church through confirmation. The baptism and naming of infants continued through the Reformation but became more controversial during the colonization of America. The place of children in the colonial Christian church was a contested space.[5] Among the first Puritans, membership in the tax-supported church was contingent upon an individual's appropriate confession of sin's conviction and subsequent regeneration. Although infant children of church members were baptized, they did not have access to the sacrament of the Lord's Supper and eventually needed to make the same profession of faith that their parents had made in order to be admitted to the church. These children (and subsequent grandchildren) did not manifest high rates of evidence for church membership and, as only full members could have their children baptized, successive generations had increasing proportions of unbaptized individuals. This attenuated the influence of the church both temporally and spiritually, leading to the emergence of the "halfway covenant" as a solution to help extend the church and, many hoped, persuade more people toward a confession of faith. The halfway covenant was a rule that allowed the children of those individuals who had themselves been baptized but had not as yet been accepted as full members to be baptized. These grandchildren of full members did not have access to the communion table, but they did at least have some connection to the church.[6]

The halfway covenant was extremely controversial, but it was also popular among lay members. It was this popularity that led Jonathan Edwards to lose his long-time ministerial appointment in Northampton, Massachusetts. Edwards rejected the halfway covenant, believing, as summarized by George Marsden, that "the hypocritical betrayers of Christ . . . did not deserve to have their children baptized."[7] With disestablishment and the rise of popular evangelicalism after the Revolutionary War, church membership both increased and came to be regulated by diverse borders. Methodists formally named their babies as part of the baptismal ritual,[8] but Baptists, who rejected child baptism, accounted for a large proportion of the newly churched population. While some Baptist parents surreptitiously had their children baptized by non-Baptist ministers,[9] generally parents raised their children to expect a conversion experience, at which point they would be baptized. Despite a lack of traditional Christian initiation, the Separate Baptists, localized in Virginia in the late eighteenth and early nineteenth centuries, engaged in a practice that some called "dry christening." In this ritual, parents brought their children "to the minister, who either takes it in his arms, or puts his hands upon it, and thanks God for his mercy, and invokes a blessing on the child; at which time the child is named."[10] This practice preserved the naming of children within the church while maintaining a healthy distance from the rite of baptism. The Separate Baptists were, however, generally anomalous in their performance of this ritual and appear to have abandoned it early in the nineteenth century.[11] No comparable ritual was common among other credobaptists until many decades later.[12]

Mormon Baby Blessing: Early Cosmology

The blessing of children was part of the first formal liturgy Joseph Smith revealed to his nascent church, and it appears, with the exception of the Separate Baptists, to be anomalous on the landscape of antebellum American religious practice. In the days immediately after the organization of the Church of Christ in 1830, Joseph Smith prepared the Articles and Covenants, which functioned as the law of the church. Included in this instructional document was the commandment that "every member of this church of Christ having children, are to bring them unto the elders before the church who are to lay hands on them in the name of the Lord, and bless them in the name of Christ."[13] Oliver Cowdery's anteced-ent "Articles of the Church of Christ," which apparently governed believers in 1829 and early 1830, did not include any mention of baby blessings.[14] Though it is highly unlikely that Smith was aware of Separate Baptist practice, it is possible that in including baby blessings in church liturgy he was reacting to pressures similar to those the Baptists faced, namely, the drive to include children in church communion.

At the time the short exhortation on baby blessings included in the "Articles and Covenants" was written, the highest office in the church was that of elder. Moreover, the document included no mention of when or how the blessing was to be delivered, beyond the necessity of it being performed before the body of the church. This lack of specific detail resulted in diverse manifestations of ritual per-formance. As was common in Mormon liturgy, instructions such as precisely how and when to bless children were dictated by oral instruction and by proximate example. Two of the earliest aspects of the ritual to develop were the practice of giving blessings to children eight days after birth and the framing of the ceremony as a naming ritual.

One of the earliest documented baby blessings of which I am aware is Joseph Smith, Sr.'s blessing of Hyrum Smith's child on "the 8th Day," September 30, 1832.[15] Though there is no extant explanation of this practice, it is likely that a specific eighth-day blessing was evocative of the Abrahamic practice of circumcision,[16] which Smith's Bible revision indicated was to show "forever that children are not accountable before [God] till eight years old."[17] The eighth-day blessing was immediately normative, though not universal, and remained a feature of Mormon liturgy into the twentieth century. Reminiscent of the Puritan view of baptism as sealing the lineal Abrahamic covenant on their children,[18] Mormons evoked the same covenant as they presented their children to the church.

The earliest evidence for the naming of children as part of the ritual is tied to both sacred record keeping and communal salvation. On January 1, 1834, Oliver Cowdery responded to a letter from John Whitmer in Zion, the settlement in frontier Missouri that Mormons hoped would be the New Jerusalem. Whitmer had posed Cowdery several questions, and his response is one of the few early texts that deals with liturgical matters. Long before Joseph Smith's revelation that proxy baptism required a formal record to be effectual, Cowdery wrote:

> When a child is brought forward to be blessed by the Elders, it is then necessary to take their nam[e] upon the church Record. Put down the name of the man, his place of birth, and when, &c. and also of his family. If he . . . apostatis [apostatizes] write, opposite his name that he has. If he begets children after that and they do not come into the church their names are not known with their brethren in the book of remembrance.[19]

The directive to register the names of blessed children in the "book of remembrance" was a profound invocation of a letter that Joseph Smith had written on November 27, 1832, in which he slipped in and out of the voice of the Lord. Before Cowdery responded to Whitmer, he and Smith discussed this letter, which had been printed in the church periodical.[20] Highlighting the cosmological function of church records and the role of John Whitmer as the "Lord's clerk," Smith had written that "all they who are not found writen in the book of remmemberance shall find none inheritence [in the land of Zion] in that day but they shall be cut assunder and their portion shall be appointed them among unbelievers."[21] Smith's commandment regarding the "book of remembrance" was itself a recapitulation of events described in his Bible expansion, published after his death as the Book of Moses.[22] In this text, Adam created the archetypal "book of rememberance," which was written "according to the pattern given by the finger of God."[23] Smith intended the modern church record to be the delimiter of citizenship in the city-state of Zion, itself an explicit mark of communal salvation.[24] Much as

Smith's later "Book of the Law of the Lord" reified the Deuteronomists' "Book of the Law of God,"[25] the "book of remembrance" was to be a concrete, material testament that the Saints moved within a sacred and cosmic trajectory.[26] The Saints were to find their children as well as other covenant believers in the city of God, where they would also find peace from the cataclysms of the eschaton. Zion was "a land of promise . . . flowing with milk & Honey, upon which there is no curse"; it was a place that the Lord gave as an inheritance "while the Earth shall stand" and to "Posses it again in eternity no more to pass away."[27] As Mark Ashurst-McGee has written, in Zion, "salvation itself was a social affair."[28] And when church elders blessed a child, that child's name was to be written in the sacred record that guaranteed his or her inheritance of an eternal place within that society. Unfortunately, no book of remembrance from this early period is extant, being most certainly among the records from that period that are lost.[29]

The failure to realize a territorial Zion refocused the impulses of church members and leaders alike. In 1839, John Corrill summarized contemporary church practice regarding infants: "The members of the Church are required to bring their children under eight years old [the set age for believer's baptism], into meeting, and have the elders lay hands on and bless in the name of the Lord. This they say was according to the custom of the ancients, also of the Saviour, who commanded little children to be brought to him for that purpose."[30] In the absence of formal records of baby blessings, it appears that this ritual was performed both among family, as with the practice of bestowing eighth-day blessings, and also regularly during meetings of the church.

The hope to record the name at the moment of blessing likely indicates that the blessing of children also functioned at times as a naming ritual in ways similar to baptismal "christening" within Christianity more broadly. However, due to a lack of documentation from this period in the 1830s, explicit evidence for the naming of babies as part of their blessings is not extant. In one potential example of naming, Joseph Smith, Sr., blessed his grandchild "& named [her] Susan[n]ah [Baily Smith]" during a November 3, 1835 patriarchal blessing meeting that coincided with the child's eighth day.[31] However, naming did not always accompany infant blessing, as evidenced by the fact that large numbers of children were regularly blessed at both general and regional church conferences.[32] For example, at the 1838 April conference of the church, ninety-five children were blessed as part of the regular proceedings,[33] and certainly not all of these children were neonates. Any formal naming aspect of the blessing would consequently have been highly contextual.

While the two practices of eighth-day blessings and baby blessings at church may have been in tension, there is some indication that at least in the case of evangelizing elders, ritual performance was exclusive to regular church meetings. For example, on September 8, 1833, Orson Pratt held Sunday services in Bath,

Vermont, during which the missionaries "laid hands upon the little children and blessed them in the name of the Lord."[34] In January 1836, Wilford Woodruff, while proselytizing in Arkansas, blessed nineteen children "in the name of the Lord" in three of seven daily meetings.[35] In England during the summer of 1837, Joseph Fielding wrote of organizing a meeting at which the missionaries "had Sacrement, blessed about 12 Children the first that had been blessed publicly there the Saints were much pleased with the Ordinance."[36] No further records were kept for these rituals, and again, the children were not likely newborns; consequently, the emphasis appears to have been on blessing the children, not naming them. Without any record of what words were spoken in the blessings, it is difficult to recapture any cosmological implications members may have associated with the ritual, though one evangelist in England noted after a Christmas meeting that the many children who were blessed there "reminded us of the Account of Christ blessing the Children [in the] Book of Mormon."[37] Baptisms similarly lack documentation while clearly wielding cosmological heft.[38]

The earliest extant baby blessing texts date to the period of the Nauvoo Temple, perhaps because of that temple liturgy's emphasis on record keeping.[39] With this liturgy's basis in the radically expanded cosmology, where priesthood, salvation, kinship, and government were synonymous, the early vision of the city-state of Zion gave way to a material heaven on earth, constructed at the temple altar. As detailed in chapter 1, this cosmological priesthood incorporated and required the ideas of eternal inheritance and sacred community. The language of those who experienced the new temple liturgy became saturated with references to this cosmology, and the surviving examples of baby blessings capture this language in explicit detail.

Whereas in the fall of 1835 Joseph Smith had blessed a number of children with "the blessings of the new and everlasting covenant,"[40] in Nauvoo he expanded the phrase to comprise the sealed relationships of the cosmological priesthood.[41] Wilford and Phoebe Woodruff left for Great Britain before the temple was complete but had been endowed and sealed as husband and wife in Nauvoo. When their son Joseph was born in 1845, Phoebe held him in her arms while Wilford performed the eighth-day blessing. In this ritual, he took oil that had been consecrated by the twelve apostles and anointed the child, declaring him an heir to "the priesthood"—"the first fruits of the Priesthood unto thy parents since there endowment." The boy was also declared an heir to the "blessings of Abraham Isaac and Jacob" and to the "blessings of the new & Everlasting Covenant," and Woodruff affirmed that he would take his "station in the celestial kingdom in the linage of thy Fathers in the family organization of the celestial world."[42] That same year, before the temple was finished in Nauvoo, the temple quorum gathered to bless several "children of promise"—children born after their parents had been sealed—in conjunction with a prayer circle. Apostle Willard Richards blessed Heber and Vilate Kimball's six-month-old son, declaring that "the holy Preast hood rested on him from his Mothers womb."[43] Taken together, these blessings are strong evidence that the cosmological priesthood was the dominant framework for ordering the Latter-day Saints during this period.

In this vein, like other temple participants, John and Leonora Taylor took their children to the operative temple where they washed and anointed them, claiming them as children in a recasting of the baby blessing ritual performed in anticipation of their temple sealings.[44] Similar to the washing and anointing for health ritual that church leaders developed during this same period, and to the temple initiation from which it drew, this blessing required John and Leonora to anoint the various parts of their children's bodies "according to the ordinance which he [the Lord] has established in his church" and, "preparatory to further ordinances," declaring a "father's blessing."[45] The children were then sealed to John and Mary Ann Taylor, materializing their eternal relationship. Two years after he performed these rites, John Taylor bestowed an eighth-day blessing upon his infant son Richard, again "accord[ing] to the ordinances which God has appoint in his Church." However, this child, unlike his siblings, who had been blessed at the temple, was born after his parents were sealed in marriage and was consequently what church leaders called at that time a "natural heir."[46] Taylor's blessing on Richard invoked "the bless[ings] of Abraham & Isaac & Jacob & the bless[ings] of the New & Ever[lasting] Cov[enant]." Reiterating the perseverance bestowed by the cosmological priesthood, Taylor continued: "As thou art a child of the New & Ever[lasting] Cov[enant] I seal thee up unto Eternal Life that though mayest come forth with the sanctified in the First Res[urrection]."[47]

Similarly, when Brigham Young held his son Moroni in his arms for Heber C. Kimball to bestow an eighth-day blessing in Winter Quarters, Kimball blessed the baby "with the blessings of Eternal lives, and with the blessings of Abraham & Isaac & Jacob, & of your father." Emphasizing the lineal nature of these blessings, Kimball affirmed that "thy seed shall be blessed with the Holy Priesthood, & he [Moroni] shall be become partaker of the Priesthood of thy father."[48] Whereas the baby blessings in the 1830s acted as a sort of alternative to infant baptism in incorporating children into the salvific community of the church, for participants in the Nauvoo Temple liturgy, the baby blessing became an annunciation of the child's sealed position in the cosmological priesthood of heaven and earth.

At Church or at Home

On February 9, 1847, Solomon, the son of Apostle Heber Kimball and Vilate Kimball, was eight days old. Brigham Young and Bishop Newel Whitney came to the Kimball home in Winter Quarters and laid their hands on him to bless him.[49] While there, they blessed two of Heber's children from two other wives— a nineteen-month-old daughter of Sarah Perry Peake Kimball and an eleven-month-old son of Sarah Whitney Smith Kimball.[50] With the hasty exodus from Nauvoo and the subsequent ad hoc living arrangements, it had been difficult to maintain regular church practice. The prospect of blessing children from polygamous relationships anywhere near the disapproving gaze of outsiders had surely been discomfiting, but in Winter Quarters the Saints felt free to live their religion and claim their families more publicly.

The next month, Newel Whitney convened a bishops' meeting during which he specifically asked about the church's policy on baby blessing. At the time of the meeting, many men were preparing to leave with the vanguard company to the Great Basin, a departure that would split their families across the continent. Two aspects of the meeting in particular characterized the tension that would define baby blessing practice for the balance of the century. First, the meeting was a "Bishop's meeting," emphasizing the new and evolving pastoral function of bishops in the church and their role as presiding elders over congregational wards. Second, much of the discussion centered on the role of fathers in blessing their own children. As the bishops discussed the proper order of recording blessings and their content, and whether fathers should bless their own children, one bishop remembered that Hyrum Smith had taught that fathers should bless their own babies. Brigham Young reiterated "that any father who held the Priesthood was A Patriarch to his own family & when He blessed his children it was a patriarchal Blessing." The idea that church Patriarchs were to bless those without parents in the church was the foundation of their labor, even though the possibility of a blessing from a dedicated oracle was too attractive for most individuals to resist, regardless of the extent of familial conversion.[51]

Young's discourse during this period was saturated by the cosmological priesthood, a key concept of which was the passage of the priesthood of heaven from parents to children. In many ways the extant baby blessing texts show a convergence between this ritual and patriarchal blessings. However, he said during the bishop's meeting, "when an elder Lays his hands on a child to bless him [it is] not a Patriarchal Blessing. the Blessing has hold on him till the years of accountability." Willard Richards encouraged the bishops to bring blessing texts and descriptions of blessings to the recorder's office, in line with Joseph Smith's revelation that a record must be kept. However, the practicality of the church maintaining records of family acts and not just those performed by the priesthood ecclesiology was daunting. As Young explained, "If a man wrote the Blessing of his Children & Could get the Historian to write it it was well enough but the Historian could not write all the Children Blessings in the Church."[52]

The practice of bishops blessing children did not take hold until the Saints reached the Great Basin. In the first decades in Utah, bishops or other church leaders frequently blessed children, either when eight days old or as part of church services. In 1850 Brigham Young hosted a bishop's blessing meeting at his home where Bishop Newel Whitney assisted him in blessing nine of his children, among others. On this occasion Young reiterated that "those faithful in the Priesthood" had the right of "bestowing blessings upon their offspring."[53] However, the experiences of church leaders like Brigham Young are not particularly representative of most church members. Few church members could host a ward meeting in their homes or had the influence to organize a bishops' meeting. Instead, local bishops and other leaders took the initiative in blessing the children of the Saints, often at fast meetings.[54]

The Palmyra–Spanish Fork area of Utah County provides an excellent example of this practice. Steven Markham, the presiding elder of the Palmyra settlement, blessed children as an "acting bishop," and the official record includes texts of these blessings.[55] The Palmyra record includes forty-six blessing texts from 1853 to 1856 and includes details about the children blessed, their birth dates and birthplaces, and their parents. Fifty-nine percent of the blessings in the record were performed at church meetings, with approximately forty percent of those meetings also coinciding with the eighth-day blessing of one of the children. Following a similar format to that followed in the blessing of the Kimball children in Winter Quarters, Markham typically performed the eighth-day blessing, to which church members brought other children, often siblings who were years older, to be blessed at the same time. These other children had frequently been born in the transitional settlements in the east. Blessing meetings were generally held on Sundays. Approximately half of the blessings that did not occur at meetings were eighth-day blessings.[56]

In many respects, Markham's blessings are typical of patriarchal blessings in an era when the cosmological priesthood was prominent. Markham called the children by name and pronounced blessings expressing hopes for their futures. In all but five cases he declared an Abrahamic lineage for the children, generally specifying the tribe of Ephraim, and the associated inheritance of the kingdom and priesthood. For example, on one boy Markham pronounced that he delivered a "Bishop's blessing because that is the order that is instituted in the last days at Eight days old that thou may be a Lawful heir in the Kingdom of God and have the priesthood."[57] Children received promises of future gifts that would have been commonly recognized among the community of Saints. Markham declared that girls as well as boys would have power over the devil, have the ability to cast out evil spirits and heal the sick by the laying on of hands, and come forth on the morning of the first resurrection. This pattern continued for decades. For example, Markham blessed Alvaretta Butler, whose father became a bishop of Spanish Fork, the settlement created after the abandonment of Fayette. Butler continued the practice,[58] as did the two subsequent bishops after him.[59]

The Cedar City Stake began blessing babies in earnest in 1856, perhaps in response to the Mormon Reformation, a period of intense retrenchment.[60] In November and December of that year, church leaders blessed numerous children—often siblings of various ages—in mass blessing meetings. During meetings on December 8 and 9, the Cedar City bishopric blessed seventy-seven children. Over the following years, the bishopric generally blessed newborns at regular meetings.[61]

George D. Watt, the primary shorthand transcriptionist in Brigham Young's office, also freelanced in blessing recordation, advertising in the 1853 *Deseret News* that "when any of the Wards call a meeting for the blessing of children, it may be found for their benefit to have G. D. W. present on such occasions."[62] On September 1 of that year, Watt recorded dozens of blessings at a Sixteenth Ward fast meeting, a number of which were for Brigham Young's children.[63] Similarly, when Young hosted an Eighteenth Ward fast and baby blessing meeting in the Lion House in Salt Lake City in 1859, Watt recorded forty-five blessings,[64] including those of Young's children.[65]

Despite these records, baby blessing texts are rare. Of the surely tens of thousands of baby blessings performed in the first century of the LDS Church, relatively few blessing texts are found in the primary repositories of Mormon-related documents. That scarcity may be explained by the decentralization of the duty of blessing babies, in contrast to patriarchal blessings, which occurred under the authority of a patriarch, who ministered to large regions of Saints and worked with dedicated transcriptionists. As Brigham Young explained in Winter Quarters, the recording of baby blessings was logistically challenging and not required by the church.[66] These challenges were compounded by the fact that while bishops and other church leaders blessed many children in the church, men holding Melchizedek Priesthood office also blessed their own children, generally on the eighth day after birth, at home.[67]

In 1849 and 1851, an elder in England published a catechism that began with several questions about baby blessing. After asking the name of the reader, the catechism asked: "Who gave you that name?" The response was: "My father." The next question, "When did he give you that name?" was answered: "When he gave me up to be blessed by the elders of the church."[68] In the first decades of the church, and especially in areas where evangelizing elders worked, male converts generally were not ordained to Melchizedek Priesthood office.[69] Most fathers in these areas simply could not bless their own children. However, in areas where the temple liturgy was available and participation in it required ordination to

Melchizedek Priesthood office, men increasingly held the proper ecclesiastical office to bless their own children. As seen previously, even couples who had participated in the temple liturgy often had bishops and other church leaders bless their babies. However, a significant number of families gathered to have the father or another relative who did not hold leadership office bless their own babies. In both cases mothers often labored to make white layettes, often from imported materials.[70]

These two practices—blessing by fathers and blessing by church leaders—existed in tension with one another. In 1873, the Salt Lake School of the Prophets—a regular meeting of church leaders—met and read the section of the Articles and Covenants about baby blessing, and debated whether children should be blessed at home by family members or at church by priesthood leaders. One participant noted that "every Father is a Patriarch to his own family." Orson Pratt, however, remarked that he "did not question the right of a Father being a Patriarch over his own house, neither in blessing their own children, but that does not exonerate us from observing the order of the church."[71] The order of the

Photograph of Sarah Martha Newman Twitchell holding baby in long dress, circa 1900s. By Wilford W. Emery. LDS Church History Library, Salt Lake City.

church was that babies were to be brought to church meetings for leaders to bless them. Quorum of the Twelve President John Taylor came to a similar conclusion in 1878. Speaking for the governing body of the church, Taylor wrote in a general circular, "If we are not misinformed it has been taught that there was no need of parents bringing their infants before the Church to be blessed by the Elders, but it were better for the father to attend to this rite at home, for if he did not he lost a very great privilege as well as a right to, and power over his children that he might otherwise retain." While Taylor indicated that he did not "object to the father taking his babe on the eighth day and giving it a father's blessing," he also indicated that the practice should not "interfere with our obedience to that law of the Lord." Quoting the Articles and Covenants of the church, he reiterated that having the church elders bless the child in public was not a mere custom but "a direct command of Jehovah."[72] In making such a statement, Taylor was reluctantly advocating for babies to be blessed twice. The pattern of double blessings introduced by Taylor had been practiced by a few Mormons as early as the 1860s,[73] but after Taylor's instruction it became a common, though not exclusive, practice. As one non-Mormon observer of Utah described in 1894: "According to the Mormon customs, when the child is eight days old its father ought to bless and name it. Then on a fast day,—they come on the first Thursday of every month,—the baby is blessed and named by the Elders, with laying on of hands."[74]

Coincident with Taylor's epistle on baby blessings at church was a new focus on maintaining records, both in the stakes and in the missions. Baby blessings began to be reported in the general statistics of the church, as well as in reports of evangelization.[75] The statistical report delivered at the April 1886 General Conference noted that there were 24,758 families in the church, and that over the previous year, 2,739 babies had been born and 2,673 blessed.[76] That same year, however, John Taylor privately noted that not all church statistics were accurate. After reaffirming the double blessing policy and recognizing the reality of ongoing federal polygamy prosecutions, Taylor counseled that for the public blessing, children "should be taken to the proper meeting and be blessed and a record be kept." However, Taylor noted, there may be cases "in these days of persecutions where it may not be wise to bless children in public, as it might betray their parents. In such instances the parents should keep a record."[77]

The keeping of a record was a paramount concern. While again acknowledging that fathers had the right to bless their babies at eight days of age, George Cannon wrote that "there is, however, an order in the Church that children should be blessed in the ward, under the direction of the bishop. One reason for this is that there may be a proper record kept of the birth of the child, its parentage, the name that is given to it, etc., so that its name may be numbered among the names of the Saints of God."[78] This emphasis culminated in 1900 with the introduction of new procedures for recording church rituals.[79] In many respects, this emphasis on record keeping was a recapitulation of the earliest Mormon practice of recording babies' names in the Zionic book of remembrance. These babies were to be recorded members of the church.

Early blessing texts generally opened by addressing the baby directly and stating his or her name. Consistent with the emphasis on recording the name of the child being blessed, blessings after the 1880s included specific language explicitly pronouncing the naming function of the blessing. For example, a baby blessing in a ritual text used by a missionary in 1897 opens by calling the child "Little One" and then proceeds to "give you the name of —— by which you shall be known to the children of men."[80] Similarly, Matilda Ruesch remembered "practicing a little innocent sacrilege" when she was a schoolgirl in the 1890s during recess: standing with a group of girls, she held a doll and said, "We bless this little baby; we give it the name of Ruth (or Edith, etc.)."[81] When Church President Lorenzo Snow blessed Lydia and Rudger Clawson's baby in 1899, he addressed the entire blessing to the Lord, asking him "to smile upon us in compassion and look upon this little child, whose name is now to be given. It is Lorenzo Snow Clawson, and may this name be recorded in the Lamb's book of life and there remain from eternity to eternity."[82]

Concurrent with the shift toward formal naming conventions and record keeping was a shift away from incorporating elements of the cosmological priesthood and patriarchal blessings into baby blessings—a declension that was mirrored in virtually all aspects of church liturgy and teaching. In 1899 George Cannon wrote that including in blessings language bestowing "keys and powers and blessings of the new and everlasting covenant" or "the blessings of Abraham, Isaac and Jacob" was both "entirely unsuitable and improper" and "all wrong." Cannon noted that "there is, or should be, no necessary distinction between the blessing conferred upon children whose parents do not belong to the Church and those whose parents do."[83]

Some of the liturgical shifts that occurred at the turn of the twentieth century were due to the changing demographics of the church. By that time, the first and many of the second generation of Latter-day Saints had passed away. As liturgical history was generally transmitted orally and by proximate example, it is not surprising that questions arose about proper ritual form. Those who had had immediate contact with Joseph Smith or witnessed the revelation of church liturgy were no longer present to attest to the validity of tradition. With regard to baby blessings, church leaders during this time fielded questions about the invocation of authority during a blessing,[84] whether to bless or how to choose the name of a baby when the parents were not married,[85] which names to state in the blessing,[86] and whether to hold the baby or lay hands on its head.[87]

Fatherhood and the Rise of the "Patriarchal Order" of the Nuclear Family

It is clear that the church's emphasis on record keeping and the bestowal of blessings at church meetings led to a higher institutional value being placed on such blessings over that associated with the eighth-day or other naming and blessing done by a father outside of church meetings.[88] As early as 1897, some leaders instructed bishops to not reserve baby blessings entirely to themselves.[89] When Joseph F. Smith became president of the church in 1901, however, he approached the subject of baby blessings with the memory of only performing one blessing, typically on the eighth day, as was common before John Taylor's proclamation.[90] Smith, who was concerned about ritual repetition more generally, in 1903 noted that it was common for parents to bring their children to be blessed to fast meetings, where the bishopric would typically allow the father, if he was an elder, to participate in the blessing circle. However, Smith also noted that "many Elders desire to perform this ordinance within the circle of their own families on or about the eighth day of the child's life. This also is proper, for the father, if he be worthy of his Priesthood, has certain rights and authority within his family, comparable to those of the Bishop with relation to the ward." He then encouraged all worthy men to bless their children at home, as such a practice would magnify their role as fathers. In answer to the original question, "If an Elder performs the ordinance of naming and blessing his own child at home, is it necessary that the ordinance be repeated in the ward meeting?" he responded, "We answer, No; the father's blessing is authoritative, proper, and sufficient."[91]

Francis M. Lyman, an apostle managing the British Mission, read Smith's censure regarding double blessings and felt compelled to make clarifying comments two months later. Echoing statements he had made in a stake conference years earlier,[92] he wrote that "it is a rare exception that a father blesses his children at home and does not take them before the Church," and that as the ritual was not like the healing of the sick or the bestowal of general blessings by the laying on of hands, baby blessings "should be with the consent of the presiding officer in the ward or branch." "When there is some special reason for it, the infant may be blessed in the home by the father, but he must obtain the consent and assistance of the branch president, who will make a record at the time of the sacred ordinance," Lyman concluded. "Otherwise the revelation [the Articles and Covenants] should be followed."[93] Such institutional support for the performance of blessings at church resulted in President Smith's direction against double blessings to gain little traction, if any.[94] Moreover, the consistent preference for the Articles and Covenants text over received tradition led church leaders to discount the use of the terms "father's blessing" and "bishop's blessing" in relation to the ritual.[95]

The first General Handbook of Instructions to discuss baby blessings was issued in 1913. It decreed that people should have their babies blessed in their own wards, but that when the babies were taken to other wards, the bishops there were authorized to bless them as well.[96] The 1928 and 1934 General Handbooks of Instructions made provisions for both the performance of baby blessings at church under the direction of the bishop and the performance of blessings at home under the direction of the parents.[97] A lesson plan in the 1933 *Instructor* commented that eighth-day blessings by fathers were still common.[98] However, the 1940 General Handbook removed the provision for a home blessing under the parent's direction, noting that any home blessings were to be performed at the direction of the bishop and then only "under exceptional circumstances."[99]

On this issue, as on many others, Joseph F. Smith occupied an important position at the dawn of the twentieth century. He was the last church leader to have lived in Nauvoo and was essentially a living receptacle of liturgical history. While he introduced dramatic innovation in the case of ordination, as we saw in the opening chapter, he also worked to retain aspects of nineteenth-century cosmology. This was especially the case with regard to the familial features of the cosmological priesthood. Although the cosmological priesthood existed outside of the 1835 canon on which Smith relied for his recasting of priesthood ordination, fatherhood as well as motherhood were still the apex of the temple liturgy. The result was that in authoring the shift in focus to an expanded ecclesiastical priesthood, Joseph F. Smith maintained a claim that a father "has certain rights and authority within his family," but framed them ecclesiastically as being "comparable to those of the Bishop with relation to the ward." This statement reflected Mormon leaders' changed understanding of the concept of "patriarchal order." In nineteenth-century Utah, the "patriarchal order" of marriage and kingdom had been a euphemism for plural marriage.[100] In 1902, Smith asserted the vital importance of understanding and teaching the "patriarchal order" of the family, as well as of the kingdom and government of God, but he redefined the term for the post-Manifesto era. According to the "patriarchal order," Smith taught that "in the home the presiding authority is always vested in the father, and in all home affairs and family matters there is no other authority paramount." To illustrate his point, he pointed to the ritual anointing and blessing of the sick:

> It sometimes happens that the elders are called in to administer to the members of a family. Among these elders there may be presidents of stakes, apostles, or even members of the first presidency of the Church. It is not proper under these circumstances for the father to stand back and expect the elders to direct the administration of this important ordinance. The father is there. It is his right and it is his duty to preside. He should

select the one who is to administer the oil, and the one who is to be mouth in prayer, and he should not feel that because there are present presiding authorities in the Church that he is therefore divested of his rights to direct the administration of that blessing of the gospel in his home. (If the father be absent, the mother should request the presiding authority present to take charge). The father presides at the table, at prayer, and gives general directions relating to his family life whoever may be present.[101]

While Smith's suggestion that fathers had complete and proper authority to perform their children's eighth-day blessing as the sole blessing of the church gained no traction, the impulse behind his position—that the priesthood-bearing father was the rightful administrator of blessings to his children—most certainly did. Some church leaders continued to refer to "patriarchal orders" or "patriarchal priesthoods" in discussions of the office of patriarchs,[102] but increasingly they taught that the patriarchal order was the organizational principle of the nuclear family in the church.[103] By the end of World War II, fatherhood had become discursively synonymous with priesthood—but in a way entirely different than it had been in the cosmological priesthood of the temple. It became identical with the ecclesiastical priesthood of the church and rendered cosmological American social trends.[104]

Rituals demarcating important life events, salvific or otherwise, were naturally also family events, and the father increasingly became the officiator of these performances. In relation to baby blessings, this role is vividly illustrated in a 1955 article published in the *Improvement Era* by William Palmer, a professor and historian of southern Utah. In this article Palmer relayed an anecdote about a vagabond he had met who grew up as an orphan and never knew his own last name. Palmer described this lacuna in painful terms and then offered a contrast in the standard of the church:

> When a child is blessed in church, the elder officiating says words to this effect: "We present this child before this congregation to give him a name and a father's blessing. We give him the name John (not John Jones) by which he shall be known among men, etc." . . . When John's father took him to Church for blessing that act said to the congregation and to the whole world, "I acknowledge this child as mine. He is heir to my name with all that it stands for, and he is heir to my possession." Such acknowledgment gives to little John the best start he could possibly have in the world. It is a father's greatest blessing upon his child.[105]

According to Palmer, the primary function of the baby blessing was for a father to document his claim on his children.

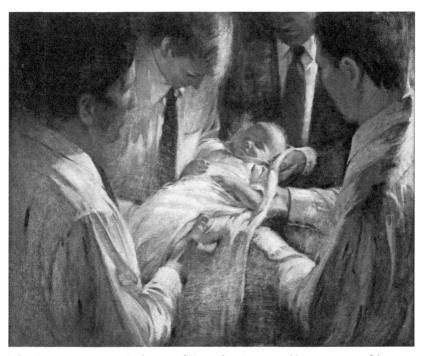

"Bless Them in His Name," oil on panel. By Walter Rane. Used by permission of the artist.

Other church publications in the second half of the twentieth century high-lighted other aspects of the father's role in blessing his children. In 1963 the *Instructor* published an article on baby blessings by Paul Cracroft, a local church leader who lived in Salt Lake City, that was to be incorporated into Sunday School lessons. Cracroft's article opened with a description of the biblical Jacob blessing his sons. While Cracroft acknowledged that "few men are Jacobs," he argued that "many of the men in the Church today share Jacob's birthright of Priesthood. They have the privilege of naming their sons and daughters and of blessing them often. Naming and blessing little children gives them a proper moral and spiritual start in life, and serves to dedicate them to the Lord." Cracroft acknowledged that the blessing of babies was far more than a simple naming ritual and noted that a father should "tighten up his 'spiritual gear' and prepare for a soul-searching trip" in preparation for the blessing. The father, that is, should prepare to wrestle with the Lord as Jacob did in his quest to find inspiration for the blessing. Then the father "can exercise his Priesthood" by blessing his child "with the power to make the proper decisions at the proper times: to seek baptism, to welcome advance-ment in the Priesthood, to prepare for missionary service, to protect his or her virtue at all cost, to choose eternal marriage over civil, to serve the Church loyally but not blindly, and to put on the name of Christ in every action."[106] Though the blessings viewed by the community as appropriate had shifted over the preceding century, the baby blessing was still viewed as a moment to impart the promise of a fulfilled Mormon life. Reiterating the importance of priesthood to this process, a similar article written for use in Sunday School a few years later noted, "The power of the priesthood gives authenticity to the ordinance of blessing babies in a manner similar to the blessings given to little children by Jesus."[107] Fathers had become the vicars of Christ.

Inclusion and Exclusion

As the ritual of baby blessing has become a principle exercise of Mormon father-hood, questions have arisen about which persons should be included in the blessing circle and whether children from family situations that the church sees as less than ideal should be excluded from the blessing. For example, some have wondered about babies whose fathers did not hold a Melchizedek Priesthood office. In a meeting on February 1, 1940, the Quorum of the Twelve ruled "that a father may hold his child when it is being blessed, regardless of the office he holds in the priesthood," a policy that was codified in the handbook for church leaders and reiterated in the *Church News*.[108] In February 1957, the Presiding Bishopric informed church leaders that while those who did not hold a priest-hood office were not to participate in the blessing circles, fathers holding an Aaronic Priesthood office could stand in the circles and hold their babies during the blessings,[109] a policy President David McKay affirmed.[110] The month after these instructions were delivered, however, the Presiding Bishopric took a more strict approach, instructing that "only those who bear the Melchizedek Priesthood should be invited to stand in the circle or to participate in any way in the performance of these ordinances."[111] However, two years later, the Presiding Bishopric wrote again to indicate that the First Presidency had ruled that, while it was not to be encouraged, a father, "whether a member of the Church or not, [who] requests the privilege to hold his child during the blessing . . . may be per-mitted to do so."[112] The 1964 leaders' handbook maintained this more permissive policy but reiterated that the practice "should not be encouraged,"[113] and in 1975, the *Ensign* published an item stating that any father "at his request, may hold his child when a name and blessing are given."[114] In 1976, the First Presidency issued a statement that "certainly we should give new and additional emphasis to the role of the father in giving blessings to children in the family." The state-ment further stipulated that fathers could declare lineage as part of this blessing, as they would in patriarchal blessings.[115] The provision for nonmember fathers remained in church handbooks until 1989, when the language changed to state that "only those who hold the Melchizedek Priesthood should participate in the ordinance,"[116] and that leaders were "encouraged to inform their members of this policy."[117]

Despite the limitations on non–priesthood holders' participation in the baby blessing ritual, church leaders remained committed to the participation of fathers in the liturgy. In 2010, the new General Handbook instated a policy that anyone performing confirmations, Melchizedek Priesthood ordinations, or ecclesiastical setting-apart rituals must hold a current temple recommend—a small card indicating that an individual has met the requirements of belief and practice to participate in the temple liturgy.[118] However, fathers who did not qualify for a temple recommend but also didn't have "unresolved serious sins" were nevertheless permitted to bless their babies, baptize their children, ordain their sons to Aaronic Priesthood offices, and stand in the circle for other ordinations or setting-apart rituals.[119] Speaking at General Conference that same year, Apostle Boyd Packer spoke on the integral role of the priesthood-bearing father in the family and humorously referred to the performance of priesthood rituals by less-than-prepared fathers as a "battlefield commission."[120] Helping men perform their sacerdotal fatherhood was more important than maintaining worthiness standards.

The ritual of baby blessing raised questions about not only whether certain men could participate in such blessings if they lacked Melchizedek (or any) Priesthood office but also whether women could as well. Since the 1990s, church leaders have not referred to families in terms of a patriarchal order, and since the publication of the Proclamation on the Family in 1995,[121] they have instead focused on husbands and wives being "equal partners."[122] In 2005 Apostle Dallin Oaks spoke at a General Conference about the relationship between priesthood authority and the family. Speaking of his experiences after his father died when he was only seven years old, he confessed that he had been puzzled by his mother's authority in the home because he had been taught that "the priesthood presided in the family." "When my father died, my mother presided over our family," he concluded. "She had no priesthood office, but as the surviving parent in her marriage she had become the governing officer in her family."[123] It is thus no surprise, in an era when the roles of fathers and mothers are viewed as collaborative and when mothers can preside at home,[124] that Mormon women are interested in participating more directly in liturgical matters involving their families.

In the case of baby blessings, some Mormon mothers have requested that they be allowed to hold their baby during the blessing ritual. The results of these requests have been mixed. In one case in 2012, a family asked its bishop to allow the mother to hold the baby. The bishop did not immediately respond but instead visited the temple to consider the problem and pray about it before discussing the issue with the counselors in his bishopric and subsequently the members of the ward council. After discussing the matter with the family again, the bishop took the matter to the stake president, who also prayed on it and ultimately took the question to the regional leadership. After several more conversations between the family, the bishop, and the stake president, the stake president left the decision to the bishop, who then indicated to the family that he trusted them and their motives, and that they could do as they chose. At the appointed time, the mother held the baby for the blessing during the regular church meeting.

In another case in 2015, however, a family asked the bishop to allow the mother to hold the baby for the blessing at home or at church. The bishop asked the stake president, who indicated that it was in no way possible for a mother to be a member of the blessing circle. The bishop then communicated this decision to the family, who clarified that they were not interested in the mother joining the blessing circle but rather simply wanted her to hold the child while the priesthood officers formed the circle. The bishop raised this clarification with the stake president, who directed the bishop to decline the request, citing the current General Handbook. The father then blessed the baby at church without the mother holding it.[125]

Ecclesiastically, the mother who holds a child as part of the blessing is not technically different than the non-priesthood-holding father who was allowed to do the same for much of the twentieth century. There is historical precedent for such an act: Phoebe Woodruff, for example, held her baby while her husband Wilford blessed him in England, as discussed early in this chapter. However, the inclusion of a mother in the blessing circle, even if she is not numbered among those blessing the child, is challenging to those sensitized to the political incursions of women advocating for female ordination. Moreover, non-priesthood-holding males were and otherwise "unworthy" men still are allowed to participate in the ritual in a performative sense that reifies the sacerdotal character of fatherhood. Some leaders clearly want to limit any sacerdotal valence to motherhood.

Current church leaders are demonstrably concerned with the cosmological character of the entire family as well as the sacerdotal character of the father. In November 2015, several months after the United States Supreme Court ruled that same-sex marriage is legal in every state, members of the First Presidency and Quorum of the Twelve Apostles updated the digital version of the General Handbook for church leaders to define participation in a same-sex marriage as apostasy. This definition required that a church disciplinary council be held for members in same-sex marriages and barred the children of same-sex couples from the ordinances of church membership, including baby blessings.[126]

The children of polygamist schismatics have long been excluded from participating in the liturgies of the church. This policy was developed in response to efforts by some polygamists who recognized the authority of the church hiding their practices and beliefs in order to join LDS congregations and ultimately be allowed in the temples. Church leaders who wanted to distance the church from polygamy and protect the sanctity of its temples thus established high fences to prevent such incursions into the church. While there is no evidence that gay couples have sought clandestine access to temple altars, church leaders have institutionally categorized gay marriage alongside unauthorized polygamy. It is likely that they fear the normalization of gay marriage among Mormons and view a similarly high fence as necessary to prevent such a development.

Church leaders subsequently sought to clarify the new policy on families with gay parents, casting it in terms of preventing excessive cognitive dissonance in the children of same-sex couples.[127] They have also limited the prohibition against blessings to those children who are in the primary custody of gay parents.[128] The message of church leaders, however, remains clear: same-sex relationships are outside of Mormon cosmology and are not to be normalized. Blessing a child of gay parents would result in that child being a member of the church, and church leaders view such close proximity between the church and a gay family to be a threat to Mormonism's cosmological integrity.[129]

Conclusion

Today, Mormons are familiar with the idea that their rituals are salvific—that those rituals do in fact change the fabric of the universe. Baptism creates the covenant relationship with Christ that allows sins to be forgiven and demonstrates an individual's entrance into the church. Confirmation bestows the permanent gift of the Holy Ghost and ratifies church membership. The sacrament of the Lord's Supper is now the renewal of the baptismal covenant. Ordination bestows authority to ratify ritual performances in heaven and earth and to direct the church. These rituals were all included in Joseph Smith's first revelation to the church after its organization—the Articles and Covenants. But there are other liturgies as well, some of which have less obvious cosmological functions. The blessing of children is one of those performances, a ritual that is not considered by the church to be essential for salvation. Revealed in the "Articles and Covenants" along with the core salvific liturgies of the church, its function, like those of the other rituals, has changed with time. Moreover, like these other rituals, the blessing of children has directed the lived experience of church members in important ways.

Nineteenth-century church members frequently performed the first baby blessings on the eighth day after birth, but they also performed them in regular meetings. The blessings' documentation in the records of Zion as evidence for inheritance is the first example of communal salvation in the church, an idea that would be expanded and reified at the altar of Nauvoo's temple. After Joseph Smith introduced the temple liturgy, baby blessing became an annunciation of the child's place in the material heaven on earth. This context was easily forgotten as those who had encountered the Nauvoo liturgy firsthand became a small minority, and the ritual came to be imbued with different meaning by those who witnessed it. In the twentieth century, baby blessings became an important demonstration of a reconceptualized sacerdotal fatherhood. Whereas the cosmological priesthood of Nauvoo had created an eternal relationship between father and mother as king and queen in a material, interconnected network, the priesthood-wielding father in the twentieth century was to extend his role of provider and teacher into the eternities. Even those men not generally considered worthy and authorized to participate in priesthood functions could perform their fatherhood by participating in the blessings. The heteronormative cosmology of the church, however, has consistently bound this performance to a conception of fatherhood well suited to the twentieth century but increasingly challenged in the twenty-first.

4

Healing, Authority, and Ordinances

*Signs such as healing the sick, casting out devils should follow
all that believe whether male or female.*[1]
JOSEPH SMITH to the Female Relief Society of Nauvoo, 1842

*Only Melchizedek Priesthood holders may administer to the
sick or afflicted.*[2]
LDS Church Handbook of Instruction, 2010

IN THE SPRING of 1889, Louisa Fanny Newman was twenty-three years old. Almost two years earlier she had married Cyrus Gold as a plural wife, and she was now pregnant with her first child. In order to prevent federal prosecutors from indicting her husband for unlawful cohabitation, she hid in northern Utah County in what Mormons at the time called "the underground." As part of this diffuse group of fugitives, she was unable to associate with friends or family in Salt Lake City, but she wanted a blessing in the hope that she would safely deliver her child. On May 21, General Relief Society President Zina D. H. Young, who was attending meetings in Alpine and Lehi as part of a leadership tour of the region, took time to lay on hands, anoint, and bless dozens of women, some suffering from "fits" or "paralysis," and others who were sick or "very poorly." Louisa was among several pregnant women who desired to be blessed for their "confinements." Young carefully washed, anointed, and sealed blessings upon Louisa and her unborn child.[3] Perhaps the best-documented healer in the history of Mormonism, male or female, Young performed hundreds of rituals a year, but Louisa needed only one.

Mormonism's healing liturgy is historically diverse, in terms of both rituals and the authorized administrators of those rituals. As such, healing is an incredibly rich area to probe Mormon conceptions of life, death, and the order of the universe. But analyzing the healing liturgy is also challenging, as it has evolved so much that historic practice is entirely foreign to modern believers. Not only are women currently forbidden from performing formal healing rituals in the church, but many of the rituals that Zina D. H. Young and other Mormon men and women performed lie far beyond the horizon of current church members' memories. This vivid contrast between Mormonisms provides one of the best opportunities to analyze the concept of authority that is so fundamental to the Latter-day Saint narrative.

Today, Latter-day Saints frame the basis of Joseph Smith's Restoration in terms of authority. The materials that serve to train Mormon missionaries and provide them with proselytizing content narrate a history of humanity that has been punctuated by periods of collective rejection of God and his church. "When widespread apostasy occurs," the principle guide explains, "God withdraws His

Zina D. H. Young, Relief Society General President and one of the most documented administrators in the Latter-day Saint healing liturgy. Photograph courtesy of the Utah State Historical Society.

priesthood authority to teach and administer the ordinances of the gospel."[4] As discussed in chapter 1, priesthood language and cosmology have shifted throughout Mormon history, particularly in relation to the temple, women, and authority. Not all ritual acts in Mormonism have required officiation by a priesthood officer, especially in the faith's early decades. However, in the twentieth century, church leaders concentrated liturgy within the priesthood ecclesiology and established the formal "ordinances" of the church—the salvific and other rituals that are only considered efficacious when performed with priesthood authority. This chapter reviews the history of the Latter-day Saint healing liturgy and outlines an analytical framework that historicizes Mormon liturgical authority and the features that distinguish it from other authority in the church.

The Development of the Mormon Healing Liturgy

When Joseph Smith held the engraved plates that grounded angels, miracles, and an open heaven in history, Christianity had generally given up on formal healing liturgies. Catholic anointing had become a deathbed ritual during the Carolingian Renaissance.[5] Since the schism of the Reformation, numerous groups had wrestled with the Bible's clear affirmation of healing and anointing rituals, but they generally did not withstand the constant press of cessationism. Before 1830, healing rituals were ephemeral on the American landscape, though threads connected believers from such disparate small groups as the Welsh Baptists, the Separate Baptists, and the Rogerenes. The most temporally proximate to Joseph Smith were the German Baptist Brethren, a group also called "Tunkers," who anointed the sick three times on the head and had congregations in Ohio in the 1830s.[6] Mormonism was thus one of the earliest American Christian denominations to establish a common and lasting healing liturgy. Early Mormons situated their healing practice explicitly in response to Christian cessationism.[7] Thus, in many ways, Mormonism is a prime antecedent to both the Divine Healing Movement and Pentecostalism.[8] Like early Methodists, Mormons prayed for healing and saw God's hand in an auspicious recovery. However, unlike the Methodists, Mormons rapidly ritualized healing, producing a healing liturgy that channeled the power of God.

On October 25, 1831, William McLellin attended a conference in Orange, Ohio, where he first met Joseph Smith and several other church leaders. The following day he travelled the approximately twenty miles back to Kirtland. He recorded the details of that journey in his diary:

> I stepped off of a large log and strained my ankle very badly—thence I rode; and just as I was abo[u]t to start to bed I asked brother Joseph what

he thought about my ancle's being healed. He immediately turned to me and asked me if I believed in my heart that God through his instrumentality would heal it. I answered that I believed he would. He laid his hands on it and it was healed although It was swelled much and had pained me severely.[9]

In this short vignette, McLellin described several acts that challenged the fundamental premises of American Christianity, at least as taught by authoritative religious leaders at the time.[10] From the moment Joseph Smith revealed the Book of Mormon, with its warning about the lack of healing miracles in the modern world, he consistently sought to endow his people with the power of God and to reveal rituals that would channel God's power to heal.[11]

Like the apostles described in the New Testament, in the first years of the restored Church of Christ, elders either commanded the sick to be made whole or prayed over the sick and laid their hands on them,[12] reflecting divine instruction that exhorted the Saints to administer healing rituals.[13] However, these early healings were not viewed as the exclusive exercise of priesthood authority but instead as general spiritual gifts available to all Saints. Instead of invoking priesthood as the authority for healing, the Saints healed "in the name of Jesus Christ," and this gift was shared by all members—both male and female.[14] When Joseph Smith, Sr., started pronouncing patriarchal blessings on believers, he bestowed the gift of healing on both men and women and specifically authorized women to perform healing rituals.[15] The gift to heal was a matter of receiving God's power, even if the healing rituals employed by Latter-day Saints were essentially liturgical.

Joseph Smith introduced consecrated oil to the Latter-day Saints as part of the Kirtland Temple liturgy in 1836. The ritual, which recapitulated the Israelite consecration of priests and was meant as a preparation for the promised endowment of power, comprised a washing, an anointing of the head, and a sealing of the anointing by laying hands on the head and bestowing blessings. Drawing on New Testament support for anointing the sick (Mark 6:13; James 5:14–15), Latter-day Saints took not only the consecrated oil from the temple but also the ritual forms of the temple—anointing and sealing—for use in healing rituals performed outside the temple walls. Anointing immediately became the dominant form of healing ritual, with anointings on various afflicted parts of the body as well as the head. For example, a few months after William McLellin, then an apostle, participated in the Kirtland Temple rituals, he, along with others, "anointed, prayed for and laid our hands upon A. Culbertson's sore leg."[16] Likely influenced by a preference for botanical remedies, the drinking of consecrated oil for healing also became common and was often used in conjunction with other healing rituals.[17]

The relationship between the newly introduced temple and its associated liturgy and healing was a profound one. Today, the only "sealing" rituals performed outside of Mormon temples are the sealings of anointings for the sick. For the first eighty years of the church, however, healing and temples were far more interconnected, with Joseph Smith and other church leaders intensifying the association in Nauvoo. Smith envisioned the temple as a sacred place for healing. Not only did the temple rites and healing rites both include anointing, but from the first formal day of baptisms in the Nauvoo Temple font, people were baptized for their health, a practice that soon became common outside the temple.[18] In addition, the expanded initiation rituals of the Nauvoo Temple liturgy—washing, anointing, and sealing, as well as the prayer circle, a form of group prayer limited to temple initiates—were also adapted for healing purposes.[19] Thus, almost every aspect of the temple ceremonies had a healing analogue. And, as with the Nauvoo Temple liturgy, women served as regular administrators of the healing liturgy. Women performed the same rituals as men: they anointed, they sealed anointings, and they blessed. The only exception to gender parity in the healing liturgy was baptism for health, which only priesthood officers administered. Women remained regular and recognized healers into the twentieth century.

Ecclesiastical, Liturgical, and Priestly Authorities

After the April 19, 1842, meeting of the Female Relief Society of Nauvoo, a woman "was administered to for the restoration of health, by [Relief Society Presidency] Councillors Cleveland & Whitney." Joseph Smith attended the subsequent meeting on April 28. According to the minutes of that meeting, Smith arose and drew attention to 1 Corinthians 12, Paul's discussion of spiritual gifts and the proper order within the body of Christ. After discussing potential jealousies between members with different church offices, Smith "said the reason of these remarks being made, was, that some little thing was circulating in the Society, that some persons were not going right in laying hands on the sick." What then followed was an explicit endorsement of female ritual healing, one that concluded with Smith stating that his "instruction respecting the propriety of females administering to the sick by the laying on of hands—said it was according to revelation &c. said he never was plac'd in similar circumstances, and never had given the same instruction."[20]

In discussing the performance of healing rituals by women, Smith emphasized two major points. The first was that women in the church had the authority to perform the rituals. In defense of this claim he pointed to the commission that the resurrected Jesus gave to the ancient apostles: "Go ye into all the world." "No matter who believeth," Smith declared, "these signs, such as healing the sick, casting out devils &c. should follow all that believe whether male or female." He also appealed to the ordering of the church outlined in Paul's letter to Corinth. Then:

> He ask'd the Society if they could not see by this sweeping stroke, that wherein they are ordaind, it is the privilege of those set apart to administer in that authority which is confer'd on them—and if the sisters should have faith to heal the sick, let all hold their tongues, and let every thing roll on. He said, if God has appointed him, and chosen him as an instrument to lead the church, why not let him lead it through? Why stand in the way, when he is appointed to do a thing?

Some have argued that Smith's statement referred to women being "ordained" to heal the sick. No contemporaneous evidence exists for such a reading, though later evidence suggests that Smith did bless women in their roles as healers. Instead, Smith was showing that those who took umbrage with members of the Relief Society Presidency for healing—women who had demonstrably been ordained to their offices—were actually taking umbrage with the order of the church as revealed by Smith. Later in his discourse he reiterated that "those ordain'd to lead the Society, are authoriz'd to appoint to different offices as the circumstances shall require."[21]

Smith then shifted topics to the temple liturgy, which he revealed a week after this meeting. He told the women that "the keys of the kingdom are about to be given to them, that they may be able to detect every thing false—as well as to the Elders." Three days later Smith preached a Sunday sermon on these "keys of the kingdom" near the temple construction site in which he declared that "the keys are certain signs & words by which false spirits & personages may be detected from true.—which cannot be revealed to the Elders till the Temple is completed." Similarly, he said, "There are signs in heaven earth & hell. the elders must know them all to be endued with power."[22] Smith thus taught that both women and men were to receive the keys of the kingdom as part of the temple liturgy.

Smith's April 28 Relief Society speech addressed three areas of Mormon authority. First, he affirmed the propriety of women participating in the healing liturgy. Second, he discussed the ordination of women to offices in the church and the resulting ecclesiastical order. Last, he introduced the participation of both women and men in the temple liturgy, through which they were to receive the keys of the kingdom. Priesthood had been associated with all three of these areas of church practice, and Smith's secretary captured the resulting complexity in a short entry for Smith's journal describing the discourse: "Gave a lecture on the pries[t]hood shewing how the Sisters would come in possession of the priviliges & blesings & gifts of the priesthood—& that the signs should follow them. such as healing the sick casting out devils &c. & that they might attain unto these blessings."[23] The minutes of the meeting confirm that before delivering his address, he indicated that the reason he was at the meeting was "to make observations respecting the Priesthood, and give instructions for the benefit of the Society." Smith had earlier claimed that "the Society should move according to the ancient Priesthood."[24] Participants in Relief Society meetings similarly reiterated that the Society was the "order of God connected with the priest hood" and that "the Order of th[e] Priesthood is not complete without it."[25] Unlike his systematization of priesthood revelations in Kirtland, as described in chapter 1, Joseph Smith never systematized the new concepts of priesthood he introduced in Nauvoo. In the time since these statements, historians, church leaders, and interested observers have all struggled to understand the relationships between priesthood and the three areas Smith addressed.

In a previously published study, I employed a taxonomy to divide Mormon authority into three areas: (1) ecclesiastical authority, derived from church office; (2) liturgical authority, derived from membership in the church to participate in general rituals of worship; and (3) priestly authority, derived from participation in the Nauvoo Temple liturgy or cosmological priesthood, described in chapter 1. I argue that over time church leaders and members have used the term "priesthood" in reference to various aspects of these authorities.[26] Joseph Smith affirmed that women received ecclesiastical authority when ordained to an office in the Relief Society, that women in the church held liturgical authority to perform healing rituals, and that women were to receive priestly authority in the temple.

While church offices in the first years of the church were coterminous with the priesthood offices organized up to 1835, in Nauvoo, church ecclesiology expanded beyond the early revelation texts. While Smith's contemporaries remembered the organization of the Society being patterned after the priesthood or acting as an appendage of the priesthood, no one appears to have claimed that it fit into the priesthood organization formalized in Kirtland. However, participants frequently referred to the cosmological network materialized through the Nauvoo Temple liturgy as the priesthood. While one of Joseph Smith's published revelations did exhort church elders—a priesthood office—to lay on hands and bless the sick, this authority was not seen as exclusive to elders. Smith and his contemporaries classified the authority to participate in the healing liturgy in a similar manner as the authority to publicly pray, exhort, and translate glossolalia in church meetings. Aside from the controversy that elicited Smith's comments, the authority to participate in the healing liturgy remained uncontroversially vested in women for the balance of the nineteenth century. Several people did question, however, what authority that was.

By What Authority?

The cosmological priesthood was foundational to the Nauvoo Temple liturgy. However, as the decades passed and waves of immigrants settled in Utah Territory, not all Latter-day Saints had the context to situate language associating priesthood with the temple, a connection common in the statements of church leaders. For example, in a public sermon in 1879, John Taylor asked, "Do they [women] hold the priesthood? Yes, in connection with their husbands and they are one with their husbands."[27] When Orson Pratt edited an account of Joseph Smith's teachings for inclusion in the 1879 Doctrine and Covenants, he added an editorial clarification that the "Order of the Priesthood" required for the highest eternal blessings was "the new and everlasting covenant of marriage."[28] Some church members naturally associated these statements with the ecclesiastical priesthood of the church and not the cosmological priesthood of the temple, a misreading that has persisted to the present. Some church members then extended this conflation between priesthoods to the healing liturgy.

One illustrative example of this conflation appears in an 1885 debate between two British converts, Charles W. Stayner and Joseph Pollard, that was taken before the Salt Lake High Council. Stayner had been born in England in 1840 and emigrated to Utah in 1855. He had served a mission in Britain and in the 1880s lived in Salt Lake City serving as a home missionary, an office that preached to local congregations and exhorted the Saints to righteous behaviors. On October 4, 1885, Stayner visited the Fifteenth Ward and delivered a sermon encouraging the congregants to be sealed in the temple and not married civilly. To support this exhortation, Stayner stated that "a young Sister who was married by the sealing power became a partaker of the priesthood which her husband held but could not if she married him by any other means." Moreover, he declared that "if she had a child after this marriage, and it should become sick and afflicted, she could, in the absence of her husband and the absence of the Elders, herself lay hands upon her child by virtue of the priesthood she held in connection with her husband."

After Stayner finished, the bishop of the ward, Joseph Pollard, took the stand to disagree with Stayner, and ultimately, they decided to take the matter to the stake high council to adjudicate. "I never heard this doctrine before," Pollard declared. "I have been in the Church a great many years, and I have tried to inform my [sic] concerning the principles of the Gospel but that is something entirely new to me." Pollard had also been born in England, in 1819, converted to Mormonism in 1849, and travelled to Utah two years after Stayner.

The confusion between the two men over the ecclesiastical priesthood of the church and the cosmological priesthood of the temple was natural. The high council's deliberations at this time had been focused intently on whether women could receive ecclesiastical priesthood authority, an idea they had unanimously agreed was neither supportable nor desirable. Presiding officer Joseph E. Taylor stated that a "man ordained to the Melchisedek Priesthood has the right to command in the name of Jesus and by the authority of the Holy Priesthood; and to him also belong the sealing power, and this too because of the priesthood which he holds. This power never was conferred upon woman either singly or in connection with her husband."[29] The "sealing power" mentioned here was the authority to formalize family relationships at the temple altars. However, men and women had regularly sealed anointings since consecrated oil was introduced in Kirtland. While Taylor conceded that women could "petition" and "ask the Father in the name of Jesus to let the blessings sealed upon the oil prove efficacious to the healing of her child," one of the other high councilors said that he had seen Zina D. H. Young anoint in the regular way, which would have included sealing, and that Brigham Young had said, "Amen" to her work.[30] The men discussed women blessings their own children in their homes, but the brief mention of Young was the only hint of broader female healing practice in the minutes. A prolific public healer, Young performed hundreds of rituals a year of the sort that opened this chapter and in public meetings also encouraged all Mormon women to participate in these rituals.[31] Taken together, the contrast between this isolated high council meeting and the practices prevalent within the Mormon community highlights the heterogeneity in Mormon belief resulting from the absence of textual systematizations of authority.

Stayner's interpretation of statements associating priesthood and temple sealings was surprising to Bishop Pollard and rejected by the high council. However, without the Nauvoo-era context of the temple liturgy, it was certainly a reasonable reading and was likely representative of the beliefs held by thousands of Mormons who converted, emigrated, or were born after the Nauvoo era. In fact, over the next twenty years, this view became sufficiently popular that Church President Joseph F. Smith decided to write an article against it in the general church periodical.[32]

Perhaps in response to questions similar to those raised in the Salt Lake High Council meeting, one year before it took place, Eliza R. Snow, then the General Relief Society president, introduced a dramatic shift in Latter-day Saint teachings about liturgical authority. In 1884 she taught that a prerequisite of female administration of the healing liturgy was participation in the one place that women unambiguously sealed anointings with proper authority: the temple liturgy. However, unlike Stayner, Snow did not connect this authority to any priesthood resulting from temple sealings. She published a letter "to the branches of the Relief Society" in which she answered the question: "Is it necessary for the sisters to be set apart to officiate in the sacred ordinances of washing and anointing, and laying on of hands in administering to the sick?" Snow reaffirmed church practice since the Kirtland era that, "It certainly is not." Authority to perform healing rituals was not ecclesiastical in nature, she concluded. But she continued:

> Any and all sisters who honor their holy endowments, not only have the right, but should feel it a duty, whenever called upon to administer to our sisters in these ordinances, which God has graciously committed to His daughters as well as to His sons; and we testify that when administered and received in faith and humility they are accompanied with all mighty power.
>
> Inasmuch as God our Father has revealed these sacred ordinances and committed them to His Saints, it is not only our privilege but our imperative duty to apply them for the relief of human suffering. We think we may safely say thousands can testify that God has sanctioned the administration of these ordinances by our sisters with the manifestations of His healing influence.[33]

Male and female church leaders understood Snow to be teaching that women needed to participate in the initiation and endowment ceremonies of the temple before performing healing rituals. Instead of conflating ecclesiastical authority with liturgical authority, Snow's argument conflated the priestly authority of the temple and the liturgical authority to heal. Moreover, unlike Stayner's misreading of the term "priesthood" as used in relation to the temple, Snow was well aware of the cosmological priesthood context of the temple. Instead, her conflation of the two concepts of authority appears to have been deliberate. While intentional, it was also short-lived. The First Presidency met with Snow shortly after the letter was published and "*corrected* her."[34] After she died in 1887—three years after writing the letter—church leaders reverted the policy and affirmed that all women in the church, including the unendowed, could participate in the healing liturgy. However, because church members viewed Snow as such a reliable purveyor of Joseph Smith's teachings, confusion over the policy persisted for several decades.

Ecclesiastical Priesthood Authority and Healing

In the temple, now as in the past, Melchizedek Priesthood officers perform sealings at the temple altars, binding husbands to wives and parents to children. The performance of these sealings has always been strictly reserved to offices of the Melchizedek Priesthood. However, as Eliza R. Snow presciently suggested in her attempt to associate healing authority with the priestly authority of the temple, women sealed anointings as part of the temple liturgy from the time Joseph Smith revealed it. Anointing with oil for health and subsequent sealings of anointing were forms derived from the earliest temple rituals. In the Utah temples in the late nineteenth century, women were explicitly set apart and authorized to perform temple rituals. The question among many was whether women needed a similar discrete conferral of authority to heal in or outside of the temple. Both male and female church leaders repeatedly stated that this was not the case, but the fact that men could receive an ordination and that the office of elder was biblically associated with healing created confusion. Some, like Joseph E. Taylor, the counselor in the Salt Lake Stake Presidency who presided at the high council meeting discussed earlier, concluded that the ritual of sealing anointings outside the temple should be connected to Melchizedek Priesthood office.

At a meeting of home missionaries in 1883, Taylor answered questions in relation to healing and addressed the hypothetical situation in which an ordained teacher (an office in the Aaronic Priesthood) was asked to administer healing rituals for the sick when other Melchizedek Priesthood officers were present. Taylor explained that he "would not ask him to lay on hands with me, because the power to seal blessings had not been conferred upon him; but if an emergency existed, a Teacher has the right, if the spirit should so incline him," to "take the oil that had been blessed by the authority of the Melchisedek Priesthood" and anoint. However, that teacher would have "no right to command by the authority of his Priesthood; neither has he the authority to rebuke in the name of Jesus; neither to seal in the name of Jesus; this belongs exclusively to the Melchisedec Priesthood." Taylor concluded that "it is safer for the Priest, Teacher and Deacon to confine themselves to prayer alone and never even anoint the sick" unless the Holy Spirit expressly dictates the action.[35] If Taylor believed that a man holding an Aaronic Priesthood office was not authorized to seal an anointing, he would have also almost certainly rejected the idea of women doing so, since they held no ecclesiastical priesthood authority. Taylor was clearly an outlier in his beliefs, as evidenced by the widespread support of church leaders for female ritual healing. However, with each passing decade, beliefs such as Taylor's became more normative.

Nearly ten years after Taylor made these claims, the *Juvenile Instructor*—a magazine intended for the youth of the church—ran a story of a healing performed by a boy who had been ordained as a deacon in the Aaronic Priesthood. The boy's sister had been sick for years, in spite of regular prayers, fasting, and a trip to the Salt Lake Temple, where she was baptized for her health. One day the boy asked his father, the author of the account, "Pa, has a Deacon authority to rebuke disease?" His father responded, "Yes, if he is administering to the sick." The boy then walked into the sick girl's room and took her by the right hand, commanding her to arise and be made whole in the name of Jesus Christ, which she did.[36]

After reading this article, a superintendent of a local Sunday School wrote to the magazine, questioning the correctness of the father's response. The magazine then ran two successive editorials addressing the question, which were likely written by George Cannon, a member of the First Presidency and the publication's editor. In the first editorial, the writer noted that all church members, including women, frequently healed, and that mothers in particular blessed their children with great effect. "This, we suppose, no one of experience in the Church will question," he concluded. On the question of the deacon's authority to heal, he noted that as long as the deacon did not invoke "the authority of the holy Priesthood (the Melchisedek Priesthood)," he was authorized to rebuke disease "in the name of Jesus" with perfect propriety.[37]

After reading this article, another individual wrote to the magazine stating that "he does not understand the difference between rebuking in Jesus' name and in the authority of the Priesthood." In the second editorial, the writer responded that "there is a great efficacy in the use of the name of Jesus, and every faithful member of the Church, in times of distress, sickness and peril can appeal to it for help and deliverance." However, he cautioned readers that "we must not be understood as saying that a member of the Church, whether man or woman, has the right to rebuke disease in the sense and with the same authority that those do who bear the Holy Priesthood."[38] While asserting that all church members had access to the power of God when participating in the healing liturgy of the church, the editor clearly believed in the distinction accorded by priesthood ordination.

Joseph F. Smith was one of the leaders that most regularly supported female participation in the healing liturgy. He joined in healing blessings with women and received blessings from at least one of his wives.[39] Moreover, he explicitly taught that women "can seal their blessings in the name of the Lord Jesus."[40] But at the turn of the twentieth century, many church members and leaders experienced a sort of crisis in authority in response to the rise of non-Mormon Christian healing ritual performance. This, coupled with other shifts in the post-Manifesto organization of the church, and perhaps in response to the persistence of Eliza R. Snow's teachings, resulted in Joseph F. Smith changing his mind and recommending in 1900 to Church President Lorenzo Snow that the healing liturgy be bifurcated, with only men being allowed to seal anointings.[41]

That year, members of the Relief Society in Mexico wrote to the First Presidency indicating that because they were far from the temple and consequently the examples of female healers who worked there, they wanted clarification on the proper methods to perform healing rituals. In its response, the First Presidency maintained the right of women to continue administering healing rituals but stated that women were to "confirm" anointings, not "seal" them.

Priesthood officers during this time often confirmed anointings as well, and many women were confused by the change, as it was both explicit and exclusionary. Some of the confusion was the result of the policy being announced in a *Deseret News* editorial, an outlet that lacked the imprimatur of the First Presidency. A former editor of the *Woman's Exponent* wrote incredulously to the editor of the newspaper to confront him with the then-common understanding that Eliza R. Snow had been instructed "from the Prophet Joseph Smith" to always seal the anointings.[42] At one meeting of the General Young Ladies Mutual Improvement Association, Helen Woodruff, wife of the young Apostle Owen Woodruff, testified that "Aunt Zina & Aunt Bathsheba," both general Relief Society presidents, had sealed a healing anointing on her and that "she took them as very good authority."[43] These women had in the past been viewed as the ultimate authorities on female healing ritual performance.

Eliza R. Snow was, however, dead; her successor, Zina D. H. Young, had also just passed away. Joseph F. Smith was then one of the most experienced church leaders with regards to female healing, and his support of the practice did not waver. Despite his alteration of the ritual women were permitted to perform, he was the most prolific church president on the topic. He explicitly and repeatedly sustained the right of women in the church to administer healing rituals, both by performatively participating in such rituals with his wives and by writing letters from the office of the First Presidency. Demonstrating this support in 1914, the First Presidency wrote a general circular letter to all church leaders in support of female healing on the same day that Joseph F. Smith spoke to the General Relief Society Conference and reinforced the same assertion.[44] However, granting ecclesiastical priesthood holders exclusive access to areas of healing ritual performance undoubtedly created a hierarchy within the healing liturgy, making Melchizedek Priesthood office ascendant.

Priesthood Ordinances

Despite continued teachings by both male and female church leaders that the traditional and more accessible healing liturgy was still normative in the church, the early twentieth century witnessed an increased emphasis on Melchizedek Priesthood authority in the performance of healing rituals. The official manuals for the Aaronic Priesthood from 1904 to the 1950s stated that even twelve-year-old deacons could anoint the sick by virtue of the priesthood authority they held.[45] However, this practice was sufficiently uncommon that I have been unable to find documentation for any actual ritual performance, and church leaders during this time taught to the contrary. Apostles James Talmage and David McKay wrote in 1921 and 1935, respectively, that Aaronic priesthood officers should not administer healing rituals,[46] and later in 1960 general church leaders instructed publicly that Aaronic Priesthood officers (and specifically those serving in the capacity of home teachers) were "unable to anoint or seal the anointing."[47] Female participation in the healing liturgy, on the other hand, remained well documented for decades, and the Relief Society handbook made provision for women performing healing rituals until 1968.[48] Ultimately, church liturgy was formalized within the priesthood ecclesiology during the twentieth century, and church leaders isolated performance of the healing ritual—or healing "ordinance"—to men holding a Melchizedek Priesthood office.

Key to understanding the centralization of liturgical authority within Mormon priesthood ecclesiology is recognizing how Mormons have viewed their ordinances and the work those ordinances perform in ordering the cosmos. Before the Reformation, the liturgy of Western Christianity centered on the sacraments of the church. Sacraments were necessary within Catholic theology, as means of transmitting the grace of God to humanity. These sacraments were salvific: they performed a divine function not entirely predicated on the faith of the recipient. Reformers rejected not only most of these rituals as extrabiblical, but also the theology that supported them. Many, especially Baptists, preferred the term "ordinance" when referring to baptism and the Lord's Supper. This term was employed in a manner similar to that used today when referring to rules and regulations established by governing bodies. Thus, municipal ordinances are the laws established by city governments. According to reformers, the ordinances of the church were rituals and activities established, or ordained, by Jesus. They were Jesus's laws. And whereas sacraments were efficacious mediums for divine action, ordinances were simply righteous acts necessary (or potentially unnecessary) because of divine command. For example, John Wesley wrote that members of Methodist Societies were "constantly to attend on all the Ordinances of God," namely, church attendance, the Lord's Supper, Bible reading, daily and family prayer, and Friday fasting.[49]

While Presbyterians and others frequently came to call the Lord's Supper "the sacrament," antebellum anti-Catholicism was so ubiquitous that other uses of the term "sacraments" carried the whiff of popery. Joseph Smith and other Mormons adopted this convention. Smith described baptism as *an* ordinance, but the Lord's Supper as *the* sacrament—this despite Mormonism's early and clear sacramentalism.[50] Moreover, Smith's revelations, sermons, and letters employed the term "ordinance" in the broader sense used by the early reformers—that is, in the context of commandments and laws.[51] Thus Smith could write with perfect consistency in what became the church's canonized "Articles of Faith" that "through the atonement of Christ all mankind may be saved by obedience to the laws and ordinances of the Gospel" and that "these ordinances are 1st, Faith in the Lord

Jesus Christ; 2d, Repentance; 3d, Baptism by immersion for the remission of sins; 4th, Laying on of hands for the gift of the Holy Ghost."[52] According to Smith, faith and repentance were ordinances of the gospel. The antecedent "laws and ordinances" is a legal doublet—a standard phrase used in a legal context that pairs two near-synonyms.[53] Common legal doublets are "aid and abet," "free and clear," and "null and void." A few months after releasing this statement, Smith published the Nauvoo City charter, which repeatedly employed the "laws and ordinances" doublet when referring to the laws of the city.[54]

Smith's successors grew to employ the term "ordinance" in a manner similar to the way some Roman Catholics employ the term "sacraments." Mormons grew to see ordinances as a category of venerable rituals set apart to be performed by priesthood officers. By the end of the nineteenth century, Smith's categorization of faith and repentance as ordinances had become sufficiently incomprehensible to Mormon leaders that despite its then-canonized status, they rewrote the section of the "Articles of Faith" dealing with them. Discussing the matter, the Quorum of the Twelve and First Presidency "decided to change the fourth article of Faith to read 'We believe that the first principles and ordinances of the Gospel are,' etc. This is to overcome the error which occurs where it says in the third article 'We believe that mankind may be saved by obedience to the laws and ordinances of the Gospel', and fourth 'We believe that these ordinances are,' etc., when faith and repentance are not ordinances but principles."[55] Or, in other words, faith and repentance were not rituals performed by priesthood officers.

In 1889 Zina D. H. Young stood up at the first General Relief Society Conference of the church and declared that "it is the privilege of all Sisters living as they should to administer the ordinances to their Sisters in sickness & the little ones in faith & humility even being careful to give God the Glory."[56] Church members and leaders had commonly referred to women's participation in the healing rituals as performing the healing "ordinances," but acting Church President Wilford Woodruff had stated one year earlier that this ritual "is not, strictly speaking, an ordinance, unless it is done under the direction of the priesthood."[57] The disparity between Young's and Woodruff's views on whether female healing rituals were ordinances reflects the degree to which the church liturgy as a whole was at that time not formalized, having still-shifting lexical values for terms like "ordinances." Clearly, if an ordinance was defined as a ritual performed by the authority of a priesthood officer, then rituals performed by lay women were not ordinances, but this usage did not become universal until decades later.[58]

A century after Young's and Woodruff's respective comments, the Mormon healing liturgy was wholly composed of a Melchizedek Priesthood officer anointing, sealing, and blessing the sick by laying hands on the head, with the General Handbook stating that "only Melchizedek Priesthood holders may administer to the sick or afflicted."[59] The idea that Mormon women could, and at one time did, perform healing "ordinances" is so incongruous to contemporary Mormon conceptions of authority as to be nearly transgressive. The connection between historical beliefs and practices and those of the present has been entirely obfuscated in Mormon lived religion. According to modern definitions, if a woman is to perform an ordinance outside the temple, she must also hold a priesthood office.

Priesthood Correlation

The centering of the healing liturgy within the priesthood ecclesiology was a part of the broader shifts in redefining ordinances and centralizing church administration that took place during the priesthood reform movement of the early twentieth century and the priesthood correlation movement in the latter half of the twentieth century.[60] Both movements worked to alleviate heterogeneity in belief and practice, and a controlling feature of this systematization was the steady expansion of the role of priesthood ecclesiastical structures. Throughout the twentieth century priesthood ecclesiology generally subsumed church liturgy. For example, baptisms have traditionally included official witnesses. Up through much of the twentieth century, these witnesses could be any church member, male or female, ordained or not.[61] However, in 1976 church leaders ruled that all baptisms must be witnessed by two people "who hold the Melchizedek Priesthood."[62] Requiring a priesthood officer for this ritual act was one of many similar changes initiated as part of the priesthood reform and priesthood correlation movements in the church.

Church liturgy was diffuse throughout the nineteenth century, with new rituals developed and old rituals repurposed. As seen earlier in this chapter, heterogeneity in belief and practice was normative. In nineteenth-century Mormonism, loyalty was often valued more than doctrinal orthodoxy or participation in regular worship services. At the turn of the century, however, church leaders surveyed the state of believers and became deeply concerned that the younger generation of Saints lacked the commitment that their pioneer progenitors had demonstrated in immigrating, colonizing the Great Basin, and then building their temples and tabernacles. The advent of the twentieth century coincided with a turn toward progressivism in the church, emphasizing efficiency, systematization, and performance.

Progressives believed that by implementing the proper system, people and their work could be elevated. Poverty, illness, and immorality could be eliminated. Prohibition was just one policy initiative designed to better humanity. A key tool in this revolution was "scientific management," which promised that measurement and systems control would lead to dramatic reforms in industrial engineering, social work, and clinical medicine. Progressives believed that education and efficient government could transform America's poor and degenerate inhabitants into productive, virtuous members of society. Within the Relief Society, the progressive impulse resulted in a series of centralized reforms. The General Relief Society established a new periodical that included lesson plans incorporating advice on hygiene, gardening, and many other practical life skills, as well as instruction on literature and music that aimed to elevate the cultural refinement of church members. Relief Society leaders worked with government programs to bring health care and social services to members of the church and their broader communities.[63]

For the governing quorums of the church, the strengthening of priesthood quorums and their members was paramount, and toward that end they instated focused programs to measure and improve participation in church activities. They also worked to reconceive and systematize several of Mormonism's key rituals. Understanding the concurrent changes that took place in three ritual areas—the sacrament of the Lord's Supper, grave and home dedication, and prayers in church meetings—is essential to understanding the dynamics of liturgical authority at play in healing during the same period.

The Sacrament of the Lord's Supper

As part of the priesthood reform movement, the sacrament of the Lord's Supper was recast as a renewal of the baptismal covenants, replacing rebaptism in the church, and was restructured around priesthood offices.[64] Before his death in 1877, Brigham Young had moved to extend Aaronic Priesthood offices to boys. As part of the progressive reforms of the turn of the century, the offices of deacon, teacher, and priest became stepping stones for boys to progress to Melchizedek Priesthood offices as adults. Boys were to be ordained as deacons at age twelve, and at regular intervals be ordained teachers, and then priests. One of the main questions church leaders faced was what actual duties these young priesthood officers were to have.

Aaronic Priesthood quorums had generally not been used in the church in nineteenth-century Utah, and the Lord's Supper was administered by ward leaders. The Articles and Covenants of the church had dictated that church elders and priests had authority to bless the "flesh and blood of Christ" but stated that "neither the teacher nor the deacon has authority to baptize nor administer the sacrament."[65] Women often prepared the bread and water (or wine) and cared for the linens, cups, and trays associated with blessing and passing them.[66] The priesthood reforms formalized priests as the regular officers to break the bread and bless the sacrament, teachers (and sometimes deacons)[67] as the officers to prepare the emblems to be blessed and manage the vessels and linens, and deacons as the officers to pass the sacrament to the congregation.

Some members and leaders questioned whether such assignments were proper in light of the Articles and Covenants' prohibition against teachers and deacons "administering the sacrament." Church leaders responded by indicating that passing the bread and water was not "administering" and consequently was not technically a priesthood function, noting that women regularly passed the trays down the benches during the service.[68] Rather, they argued, young priesthood officers needed a regular duty to perform. Their canonical duties—"to warn, exhort, expound and teach and invite all to come to Christ"—were certainly still in effect but were also impractical to systematize among young boys. Participation in the weekly ritual of the Lord's Supper was something meaningful and regular for the boys to do.

While the Presiding Bishopric had to remind local leaders not to have women prepare the sacrament table as late as 1957,[69] over time church members and leaders began to refer to the entire process of preparing, blessing, and passing the emblems of the Lord's Supper as "administering the sacrament"[70] and to view these duties as exclusive priesthood functions. As young boys were prepared for

Photograph of the administration of the Lord's Supper in Hunter Ward, Salt Lake City, Utah, ca. 1950. By Jim Hansen. LOOK Magazine Photograph Collection, Library of Congress, Prints & Photographs Division, LC-L914-50-AB63, #3.

their ordinations, they were increasingly instructed that their primary priesthood duties included the passing, preparing, and blessing of the Lord's Supper.

The priesthood order of the Lord's Supper was further expanded in 1946, when the First Presidency ruled that the presiding officer at any meeting was to be the first person to eat and drink the emblems; "thus, whenever the sacrament is administered, members of the Aaronic Priesthood officiating will have a lesson in Church government."[71] Despite the First Presidency ruling, change was neither immediate nor universal. In 1956, the Presiding Bishopric lamented that "passing the sacrament to the highest authority sitting on the stand is being overlooked in too many wards." The Presiding Bishopric reiterated that "No one is to receive the sacrament until after the highest authority has been served—no one!"[72] Four years later this practice was codified in the General Handbook.[73]

Grave Dedication and Home Dedication

The dedication of graves and homes emerged in the nineteenth century as folk rituals, likely evolving from the early church practice of dedicating objects, lands, and public buildings through formal ritual.[74] Latter-day Saints began dedicating homes by 1860, and dedicating graves the following decade. Like all aspects of Latter-day Saint liturgy in the nineteenth century, the practice of grave dedications was neither formalized nor codified. It was not until the early to mid-twentieth century that liturgical texts became normative. The first general missionary handbook, printed in 1937, was the first church document to include specific instruction on how to perform a grave dedication. It stated that "though one holding the Priesthood is generally chosen, any suitable person may dedicate a grave. This may be done either with or without the authority of the Priesthood."[75]

The 1940 General Church Handbook of Instructions similarly stated that anyone could offer the dedication, "whether he be a bearer of the priesthood or not." It stated that priesthood members were often asked; but in contrast to the missionary instructions, hinting at the still incomplete process of liturgical formalization, "it is not advised, however, that one so ministering should use words to the effect that he is officiating by virtue of any power or authority pertaining to the Holy Priesthood, nor that by any such authority or power he dedicates the grave. He is acting as the leader in prayer in behalf of relatives and friends there assembled."[76] Concurrently, then, two different handbooks offered conflicting advice about whether a grave could be dedicated by calling upon the authority of the priesthood or simply as a more general prayer.

The missionary handbook was reprinted in 1940 and 1944 without change. In 1946, however, a revised edition was released with different instructions: "A grave should be dedicated by one holding the Priesthood .... If no one holding the Priesthood is available for the dedication of a grave at the time of burial, any person may offer a graveside prayer, and if the kindred so desire the grave may be thereafter dedicated by one holding the Priesthood."[77] In the church question-and-answer section of the 1948 *Deseret News*, a correspondent asked whether someone ordained to the priesthood should dedicate graves. The editor responded: "In the new handbook issued by the General Melchizedek Priesthood Committee of the Church, with the approval of the First Presidency, instruction is given that graves are to be dedicated by the authority of the Holy Melchizedek Priesthood and in the name of the Savior. Inasmuch as this is the instruction, naturally one holding the authority of the Melchizedek Priesthood should perform the ordinance. Dedication of graves is considered one of the ordinances of the Church."[78] In less than eighty years, Mormons had developed a grave dedication ritual, available to be performed by any member of the church, which leaders had then transformed into a formal priesthood ordinance of the church.

Though grave dedication emerged after home dedication among Latter-day Saints, it became an "ordinance of the church" first. While a common practice among Mormons, home dedication was absent from church handbooks for virtually all of the twentieth century. It was not until 1983 that the General Handbook included any instruction on the ritual.[79] In 1998 the section on home dedication was updated to read: "Church members may dedicate their homes as sacred edifices where the Holy Spirit can reside and where family members can worship, find safety from the world, grow spiritually, and prepare for eternal family relationships . . . . To dedicate a home, a family might gather and offer a prayer that includes the elements mentioned above and other words as the Spirit directs."[80]

Similar to the beginnings of grave dedication, home dedication was not initially a ritual confined to the priesthood ecclesiology. Often men who held the priesthood performed the ritual, and in fact, many Latter-day Saints believed that the ritual performance required priesthood office,[81] but any church member was authorized to dedicate the home. In 2010 the General Handbook was updated with the addition of the following text: "A Melchizedek Priesthood holder may dedicate a home by the power of the priesthood. If there is not a Melchizedek Priesthood holder in the home, a family might invite a close relative, a home teacher, or another Melchizedek Priesthood holder to dedicate the home. Or a family might gather and offer a prayer."[82] It is clear from this text that dedication by the "power of the priesthood" is implicitly superior to a prayer by a non–priesthood holder. Moreover, following the developmental pattern of the grave dedication ordinance, the recommendation of such an exercise of priesthood authority may very well be the introduction and formalization of a new official ordinance of the church.

Prayer at Church

Church meetings in nineteenth-century Utah were generally structured around the sermons and ritual performances of priesthood officers. Both male and female members attended stake and then ward services but generally did not participate in the programs. They did not preach or pray in church meetings. Some church members patterned their home worship on this precedent. George Cannon addressed this issue in the 1899 General Conference, stating that "there are men who think that unless they pray the Lord does not hear the prayer, and they are in the habit of doing all the praying in their families." He then encouraged men to have the women in their households pray and reiterated: "Brethren, do not get the idea that the Lord will not hear your wives and daughters." Despite this injunction, the disparities between home worship and church remained.[83]

Women had been teaching and preaching in the all-female context of the Relief Society for decades, but it was the introduction of regular female missionaries in 1898 that brought female preaching to the entire church on a continual basis.[84] With this change, some women became set apart as ministers of the gospel. The first documented examples of women regularly participating in sacrament meeting services were female missionaries either leaving for, ministering in, or returning from missionary service.[85] In 1935, in response to a question by the European Mission president about whether priesthood officers were required to deliver the opening and closing prayers in sacrament meetings, the First Presidency responded that any church member could properly pray in any meeting if asked by the presiding authority to do so. "It is preferable, however," the First Presidency wrote, "to have the Priesthood officiate in prayer at a regular sacrament meeting." They also wrote that should the presiding officer choose a "boy or girl" to open other church meetings, "he is not violating any rule of the Church."[86]

In 1956 the First Presidency wrote to the Presiding Bishopric that "our sisters may participate in offering prayers in the meetings of the auxiliary organizations when desired, but we feel that the brethren holding the Priesthood should offer the prayers in sacrament meetings." The Presiding Bishopric then wrote to all local church leaders to "commend these instructions to all bishoprics and branch presidencies and suggest their careful observance."[87] The instruction that only "brethren holding the Melchizedek or Aaronic Priesthood" were to pray in sacrament meetings was reiterated in the Correlation Committee's *Priesthood Bulletin* in 1967,[88] in the first General Handbook for church leaders produced by that same committee in 1968,[89] and in *Ensign* magazine for the entire church in 1975.[90] It appears that church leaders viewed the sacrament meeting as a priesthood meeting that required a priesthood officer to pronounce the invocation and benediction.

During the summer and fall of 1978, American media began to portray the LDS Church as silencing women because of the church's fight against the Equal Rights Amendment, and in response to activist Sonia Johnson's testimony in support of the amendment before a Senate subcommittee. On September 29, 1978, Church President Spencer Kimball stood up in front of a gathering of regional church leaders. Before beginning his address, he made several announcements. As the first announcement, Kimball declared that "the First Presidency and Council of the Twelve have determined that there is no scriptural prohibition against sisters offering prayers in sacrament meetings." He stated that women were authorized to pray in all church meetings, including sacrament meetings and stake conferences and during visiting teaching, a change noted in church and Utah news outlets.[91]

This policy remained in place until the early 1990s, when, before his death, Church President Ezra Taft Benson apparently made a comment that led several members of the Quorum of the Twelve to believe that only male priesthood officers should offer the opening prayer in sacrament meetings. These apostles then orally instructed local and regional leaders that women were not to offer invocations for sacrament meetings.[92] This policy was never codified in the church handbooks, but regional leaders encouraged local leaders to maintain the exclusion, both orally and by written letter, resulting in uneven application of the policy, at least in the United States. In 2010, the General Handbook was edited to include the instruction that "men and women may offer both opening and closing prayers in Church meetings."[93]

Despite the authorization for women to pray in all meetings, prayers at the semiannual general conferences of the church had always been exclusively performed by male priesthood leaders. With limited speaking slots and scores of possible church leaders not able to participate, meeting organizers likely chose general or regional authorities of the church honorifically. In doing so, they consistently overlooked the female General Relief Society, Young Women, and Primary officers. In 2011, Cynthia Bailey Lee, a Mormon author and university professor, challenged this long-standing tradition. After writing a short article on a Mormon blog about the necessity for change,[94] she contacted public affairs representatives of the church to suggest that women be included in offering prayers. Several other authors also wrote in support of the change.[95] Two years later, on April 6, 2013, Jean A. Stevens, first counselor in the Primary General Presidency, offered the first General Conference prayer by a woman in the church's history.

The Healing Ordinance

As seen from the previous examples, the general trajectory of Mormon liturgy in the twentieth century was a reorganization within the priesthood ecclesiology.

In each case, an aspect of liturgical authority that had been available to women within the church was recast as ecclesiastical priesthood authority exclusive to men. In the case of the sacrament of the Lord's Supper, priesthood duties incidental to the actual blessing of the emblems were created and then strictly implemented, resulting in a formalized and expanded ordinance. In the case of grave dedication, church leaders took a ritual tradition of church members and created a new priesthood ordinance, a path they now appear to be following with home dedication. In the case of prayers at church meetings, church leaders began to conceptualize the ritual as requiring priesthood office. However, the vocal invocation of priesthood authority during invocations or benedictions was never employed, nor was there any scriptural antecedent for such a practice. Church leaders consequently engaged in a protracted process lasting several decades of turning away from the idea of priesthood requirements for prayers in sacrament meetings. Ultimately, church leaders affirmed the liturgical authority of both lay women and lay men to pray in those meetings.

Healing in the church interacted with all of the same dynamics, particularly the creation of formal priesthood patterns and the conflict between written instructions, memory, and oral communication. Over time, healing became an exclusive priesthood ordinance, with perhaps the largest difference between healing rituals and these other examples being the widespread and historical participation of women in the liturgy. It is quite possible that at the turn of the twentieth century, more healing rituals were performed by women in Utah than by priesthood officers.

In our lengthy study of female ritual healing in Mormonism, Kristine Wright and I argue that two significant factors contributed to the decline in female participation in the healing liturgy during the twentieth century. First, church leaders removed the healers, many of whom were women, from the temple. The temple healers administered performatively; they were institutional examples of proper ritual performance, and they anchored liturgical authority among all Mormon women. Second, while priesthood healing rituals were formalized and codified throughout the twentieth century, female healing continued to be transmitted as all Mormon liturgy had been during the nineteenth century: orally and by example.[96]

One illustration of this second key factor in the decline of female participation in the healing liturgy and the ascension of the priesthood officers is the rise of written texts codifying ritual healing practice. The first liturgical texts published by the church were created to help newly available young men and women learn their responsibilities as missionaries. The missionary handbook used from the 1930s to the 1950s included a chapter on ordinances, which declared that "those who hold the Priesthood in the Church of Jesus Christ of Latter-day

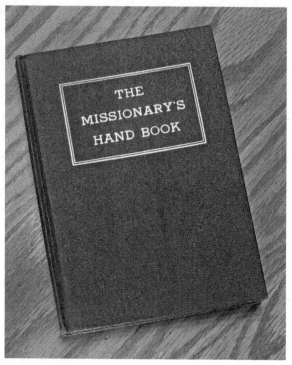

The 1936 *Missionary Hand Book*. The first handbook prepared for all missionaries contained standard texts for church rituals including ordination. Photograph courtesy of Jonathan Stapley.

Saints are divinely commissioned with the authority to perform holy ordinances that are necessary for the happiness and eternal welfare of our Father's children." The chapter included instructions and example texts for each ordinance of the church. When young men were away from home as missionaries or as members of the military, they turned to these handbooks.

Church President Thomas Monson frequently recounted the story of performing his first healing blessing to demonstrate the utility of the handbooks. In the Navy during World War II, one of young Monson's friends and fellow sailors became very sick and asked for a blessing. Monson had never performed such a ritual before, and he consequently dug out the *Missionary's Hand Book* a member of his bishopric had given him before he left home. He turned to the chapter on ordinances, which instructs "those holding the Melchizedek Priesthood"[97] precisely how to anoint and bless the sick, and he blessed his friend.[98] Absent the liturgical instructions given to him, young Monson may or may not have performed the blessing, but with the book in hand, he was able to confidently invoke his priesthood authority and heal his friend—a foundational miracle in the future church president's life. Women had no similar written resources to maintain their ritual performance.

The definitions and patterns provided in the *Missionary's Hand Book* were reiterated in church magazines, lesson manuals, General Conference sermons, and circular instructions. It is consequently understandable that church members turned to ordained elders in times of sickness and anxiety for blessings of health and comfort. With passing generations and expansive conversion during the latter half of the twentieth century, only an isolated few individuals had any firsthand experience with traditional healing rituals performed by women, which became an anachronism. The liturgical authority to heal became isolated within the priesthood ecclesiology, and priesthood officers also became the sole authorized performers of all ordinances outside the temples. In 1992, Apostle Dallin Oaks visited the Seattle area for a stake conference. His leadership address stated that "Mel[chizedek] priesthood ordinance authority comes only from a general authority to the stake president. From the ordinance back to the prophet is at most 3 steps." Furthermore, he declared, "Every priesthood ordinance performed is because the keys are delegated by the prophet of God (except the blessing of the sick)," which is available to all Melchizedek Priesthood officers.[99] Women performing healing rituals was beyond memory. However, in conjunction with a rise in historical awareness, as discussed in chapter 1, beginning in 2013 both church leaders and members began to publicly grapple with what the widespread historical participation of women in the healing liturgy means for the church's structures of authority.

Conclusion

In 1906 the Panguitch Stake comprised ten settlements spread out across south-central Utah. Each ward had a Relief Society, and Hannah A. Crosby was the stake Relief Society president. Nearly thirty years earlier she had traveled to Beaver, Utah, where Patriarch Daniel Tyler had laid hands on her head to deliver a blessing. Tyler blessed Crosby with promises typical of such moments—invocations of the cosmological priesthood, family, and Zion. Among these gifts, Tyler also declared, "Thou shalt have the gift of healing in thy family and among thy sisters."[100] Patriarchs had since the earliest years of the church blessed women with the gift of healing and administering healing rituals. Such blessings continued into the twentieth century.[101] Whether compelled by the memory of this blessing, her own constant illness, the death of her mother-in-law (also named Hannah Crosby), or a combination of these and other experiences, Crosby created a vital record of healing activity. Under her leadership in 1906, several of the local Relief Societies took their minute books and, turning to the last pages of the volumes, inscribed example texts for the washing, anointing, and sealing of blessings for pregnant women.[102] Such texts are rare—a Relief Society in Oakley, Idaho transcribed example blessings for health and pregnancy in the same decade, and the General Relief Society Offices transcribed a similar text in 1923.[103] The texts are all very similar, but the Panguitch Stake blessings are nearly identical, suggesting a written example. A mimeograph blessing text in the General Relief Society's blessing collection includes notations that indicate it originated from the Panguitch Stake and may be a copy of the ur-text.[104] Unlike the published ritual texts produced for use by missionaries and then later by all priesthood officers, these manuscripts were isolated geographically and temporally, and they swiftly passed from memory. On the page immediately after their ritual text, the Relief Society of Tropic, a small town of approximately sixty-six homes,[105] listed women who had received blessings, presumably before the record was completed in 1912—fourteen women in total. Relief Society women created similar registers over the subsequent years, but the displacement of their liturgical authority and ordinances to the priesthood ecclesiology rendered such documentary acts anomalous well before the end of the twentieth century.

Throughout the nineteenth century, the Mormon healing liturgy comprised a diverse set of rituals that could be performed by faithful men and women in the church. Priesthood office was not a requirement to perform them. However, with the complex and changing understandings of priesthood throughout Mormon history, many church members who lacked historical understandings of the church's terms and practice questioned the authority by which women could heal. At the dawn of the twentieth century, women very well may have been the most common administrators of healing rituals in the church, but by the end of that century they were forbidden from performing them. This stark shift was the result of progressive priesthood reforms that systematized ritual performance, not just of healing but of all Latter-day Saint ritual, through a new understanding of ordinances and worship as part of priesthood ecclesiology. While the healing ritual practice and beliefs regarding ordinances are pointedly germane to understanding Mormon conceptions of authority, not every interaction with the open heaven is mediated by the formal rituals of the church. Christians in all ages have yearned for the power of God in their lives, and Mormonism has interacted with the resulting folk culture in ways that further demonstrate the rise of priesthood ecclesiastical authority. The next chapter analyzes some of these sometimes surprising practices in Mormonism and contextualizes them within the broader Atlantic tradition.

5

Cunning-Folk Traditions
and Mormon Authority

*... a white stone is given to each of those who come into ~~this~~ the
celestial kingdom ...*[1]

JOSEPH SMITH, 1843

ONE OBSCURE TRADITION among nineteenth-century Mormons in Utah
was that the "woman of Endor" in the Book of Samuel was not a witch. Hyrum
and Joseph Smith, several claimed, had said that she was actually Samuel's wife,
a woman of God, and a prophetess.[2] On January 1, 1883, Charles Smith, a British
emigrant to Nauvoo, spoke at a child's funeral in St. George, Utah. His sermon
included an intriguing version of the tradition: "[He] Said that Hyrum Smith
declared that [the] new translation of the Bible shows that the witch of Endor
that Saul went to for counsel was not a witch but was a woman holding the Holy
Priesthood."[3] Smith's Bible revision manuscripts had stayed with Emma Smith
after his death and eventually passed to the Reorganized Church. Whether
drawn from actual memory of Nauvoo teachings or with enhancement by the
Reorganized Church's 1867 publication,[4] Charles Smith's inclusion of the revised
Bible in his narrative was a legitimate corroboration:

> And the woman said unto him, Behold, thou knowest what Saul hath
> done, how he hath cut off those that have familiar spirits, and the wizards,
> out of the land: wherefore then layest thou a snare for my life, to cause
> me to die *also who hath not a familiar spirit*? And Saul sware to her by the
> Lord, saying, As the Lord liveth, there shall no punishment happen to
> thee for this thing. Then said the woman, *the words of* whom shall I bring
> up unto thee? And he said, Bring me up *the words of* Samuel. And when
> the woman saw *the words of* Samuel, she cried with a loud voice: and the
> woman spake to Saul, saying, Why hast thou deceived me? for thou art
> Saul. And the king said unto her, Be not afraid: for what sawest thou? And
> the woman said unto Saul, I saw *the words of Samuel* ~~gods~~ ascending out of
> the earth. *And she said, I saw Samuel also.*[5]

In his own vernacular, Joseph Smith had translated the witch of Endor into a seer, who saw, as he had seen, words of the dead "cry from the dust"[6]—a seer remembered by at least a few of his coreligionists for decades as a priestess and a queen.

Though cunning-folk and charmers are generally unknown today, for hundreds of years they existed within Christian societies in Europe at the nexus where the threat of misfortune and malevolence met hope.[7] Extreme unction had replaced anointing the sick by the end of the Carolingian Renaissance. The Reformers sealed the heavens. Enlightenment-era skeptics stripped the clergy of astrology and divination. Despite these religious shifts, when faced with illness or loss, Christian people still sought out those who could help them. Cunning-folk, also called wise-men or wise-women, found what was lost, healed the sick, foretold the future, influenced the course of love, and, perhaps most importantly, battled witches in a time when the church had lost interest in them. Cunning-folk were semiprofessional and operated textually, relying on the deprecated sciences and cosmologies of centuries past. In contrast, charmers, also called blessers, generally viewed themselves as having a divine and holy gift to heal, operated verbally through oral tradition, and refused payment. Both cunning-folk and charmers were active in England throughout the nineteenth century.

When Joseph Smith established the Church of Christ in 1830, American villages lacked explicit cunning-men and -women, though aspects of their tradition—finding what was lost, healing, foretelling the future, and more—remained ambiguously on the fringes of society. Devils, not witches, were the Mormons' supernatural threat,[8] and, as Owen Davies has argued, "stripped of their unbewitching activities, cunning-folk were no more or less than herbalists, astrologers, and fortune tellers."[9] In this chapter I argue that Joseph Smith and other early church leaders explicitly and selectively translated aspects of this culture into the liturgy and cosmology of the LDS Church. This process was not universal, however. Smith received several revelations that condemned "sorcery." He and other church leaders also created alternatives to cunning-folk practice that were more explicitly rooted in the patterns of the Bible. Key to this process of translation and creation were the piercing of cessationism's shroud and the establishment of an institutional structure that integrated folk practitioners into the church by channeling their impulses into orthopraxic forms. In an important sense, Joseph Smith did not translate the rituals, fixtures, and charms of the cunning-folk into Mormonism; he translated cunning-folk themselves, much like the seeress of Endor, into Mormons.

Scholars have extensively examined Joseph Smith's use of seer stones, particularly in conjunction with treasure seeking and finding lost items.[10] Members of Smith's family and several other early converts also participated in the same or similar activities. Though Smith's use of the seer stones as a medium for acquiring revelatory texts declined precipitously in the first years of the church, they remained important objects, ultimately translated into the Hebrew urim and thummim, with cosmological significance.[11] With Smith's revelation of liturgical analogues to many of the other activities of the cunning-folk and charmers, he and subsequent church leaders also allowed for and sometimes even cultivated space where practitioners of cunning-folk arts could continue while remaining part of the church. The success of this integration hinged on how these activities were managed, and under what authority. By the end of the nineteenth century priesthood ecclesiology had pushed cunning-folk practitioners outside the boundaries of orthopraxy, except in the case of healing, an area in which alternative healers are still common to the present.

Accommodating an Open Heaven

On October 21, 1846, three traveling elders arrived in Preston, England. All three had lived in Nauvoo, Illinois, though one of them—George D. Watt—was coming home. Watt, the first baptized Mormon in England, was from Preston, and the elders stopped to visit his mother, Mary Brown. After discussing the rise of the church in England, Brown "told of some things a certain woman in the place had said of him [George Watt] and prophecied on his head, and which had come to pass mainly." Their curiosity piqued, the elders asked to meet her. Brown left, returning soon with Margaret Anderton. Oliver Huntington, one of the elders, wrote:

> A curious looking and acting woman she was. Coarse in word and deed. Not so coarse neither but Plain and easy. Very plain, quick and lively, with good nature . . . . [We] thought to try her, and watch her words and the run of her conversation, to see if we could not find a contradiction, but none could we find. Nothing in her did we discover contrary to the order of truth and righteousness, yet she like like [*sic*] others who have had true gifts might look unwisely, and sometimes tell that which they do not know, through over anxiety of themselves or others. She tells what she does by the Planets, from the persons looks and moles, just by looking at them as they stand or sit. She would look at a man and tell him all about himself; and such an eye I never saw. She would do just as the Prophet Joseph used to; look a person from head to toe. Her eye commencing at the face, go down and then up.

Anderton's methods were typical of cunning-folk, and she proceeded to look the two American elders over and expound on their futures, including detailed accounts of their troubles, marital relationships, maladies, and eventual deaths. She prescribed an herbal remedy that would heal an impending illness. After finishing, she delivered a verbal charm for the elders to use on their return trip home, which Huntington inscribed in shorthand into his journal: "hĕlōm, sēlōm, sĕlōm, sāvītā." She also offered the interpretation of the words: "Mighty, Holy, High God, take us safe home to our dwellings. & further, Let no man on our pathway put us away from our own dwellings. May the Lord bless us on our way home." The two American elders then left for their place of lodging, but Watt remained with Anderton at his mother's house. Anderton, being well acquainted with him, "showed him a glass; like an egg, in which she saw, and told him many things" concerning his and Huntington's wives.[12]

This encounter between three evangelizing elders and a cunning-woman in the birthplace of British Mormonism reveals several themes that can readily act as categories in the analysis of cunning-folk and Mormonism throughout the nineteenth century: institutional control, transatlantic exchange, astrology, gender, seerism, and healing.

Anderton does not appear to have been Mormon,[13] but as a cunning-woman her sympathetic reception from Mormon church officials was extraordinary in comparison to the way cunning-folk were treated by clerics in general. Huntington compared her to Joseph Smith, and his primary criticism—that Anderton was earnestly speaking beyond her gifts—framed her activities within a Mormon cosmology and was similar to a judgment later leveled by British Mission leaders against missionaries.[14] These elders were familiar with esoteric language invoking God.[15] They had witnessed the prophetic pronouncements of both men and women. The first years of Mormonism in America brought an open heaven and the concurrent struggle to regulate spiritual manifestation in the church. The result was the demarcation of spheres: the church was to be governed by priesthood bureaucracy, but individual Mormons could access the power of God in deference to that authority.[16] The town of Preston had a history of visionary Mormon women and men who, like Anderton, had prophesied about marital relations but also disrupted institutional authority.[17] Wilford Woodruff, then the presiding apostle in England, summarized the solution to this

Shorthand verbal charm in Oliver Boardman Huntington's diary, Book 3, October 21, 1846, L. Tom Perry Special Collection, Provo, Utah.

tension in the Manchester General Conference a few months before Anderton's pronouncements: "Seek to be fed through the head and not through the feet." While the feet were necessary for the body, the head was to lead. Elucidating further, Woodruff clarified who the head was to be:

> Because some woman had got a peep stone, and was picturing some great wonders, or may-be a priest had healed one that was sick here, and another there—let not the elders run after these things—such things were not given for the government of the church; it is to your presiding elders, and to your councils, that you are to look for direction and guidance. Healings and tongues are good; interpretations are good; so are visions, dreams, and prophecies; but everything in its own place.[18]

Likely informed by the conflict over democratic seership and revelation that troubled the first years of Mormonism, Woodruff's accommodation allowed him to announce that cunning-folk posed no threat to the church and their gifts could easily be viewed through the lens of the Restoration. He also was clear that church authority rested in the ecclesiastical bureaucracy of the church, and as such, his judgment was a harbinger for the eventual and complete ascendancy of ecclesiology over folk practice.

Transatlantic Traditions and Texts

Within a few years of Joseph Smith's murder there were more Mormons in England than in the United States.[19] Ninety-four percent of these converts were from the British northwest—a region with a long history of crypto-Catholicism, anticessationism, and religious enthusiasm.[20] Large numbers of English Saints emigrated to America every year, first to Illinois and then to the Great Basin.[21] Consequently, an important consideration when analyzing Mormon interactions with cunning-folk traditions is the high degree of transatlantic exchange that was occurring. British converts interacted with cunning-folk culture in differing ways than their American coreligionists. As the cunning-folk tradition in England was more coherent and structured than its American counterpart, there appears to be a distinct difference in the manner in which American and British converts to Mormonism engaged in cunning-folk practice. Some American converts used seer stones or healed using charms. However, whereas American Mormons appear to have learned to divine or heal through folk channels of instruction—that is, via oral and proximate example—British converts tended to draw from texts that supported cunning-folk more broadly in England. These texts appear to have been a locus of conflict for LDS leaders.

In 1841, Alfred Cordon, the ecclesiastical leader of Staffordshire, a county located just southeast of Preston, held a council with Apostles Wilford Woodruff and George Smith to consider the case of Mormon William Mountford, who had been brought in "for using Magic" and employing "several Glasses or Chrystals, as he called them: they are about the size of a Goose's egg made flat at each end." Cordon recorded that Mountford "also had a long list of prayers wrote down which he used. The prayers was unto certain Spirits which he said was in the Air."[22] Wandle Mace who lived in Nauvoo, summarizing the situation from two sources, later recorded details about Mountford and other church members associated with him, noting that they "practiced Magic, or Astrology. They had Books which had been handed down for many generations." Mace recorded details of the precise rituals these members performed, including invoking the name of a particular spirit to show a desired vision, commonly of family or future spouses.[23] The procedure Mountford apparently used follows those described in two occult classics: Reginald Scot's *Discovery of Witchcraft* and Francis Barrett's *The Magus*.[24] The members of the council, who were certainly familiar with Joseph Smith's revelations condemning "sorcerers,"[25] unanimously agreed that "no such Magic work be allowed in the Church."[26] Mountford apparently gave the stones and the grimoires to the council. George Smith "destroyed the books, but put the stones in the bottom of his trunk and brought them to Nauvoo. He gave them to Joseph the prophet who pronounced them to be a Urim and Thummim as good as ever was upon the earth but he said, 'they have been consecrated to devils.'"[27] The primary difference between Woodruff's condemnation of such stones in this case and later tolerance of peep stone use appears to have been based in whether use of the stone was a natural gift or a function of an occult textual tradition.

The use of esoteric texts by Mormons is most evident among British astrologers. Astrology in Mormonism was localized to Utah and can be traced almost exclusively from the conversions of John Sanderson in England and Thomas Job in Wales. Little is known about Sanderson's early involvement in the church, though he was apparently ordained an elder and voted the Rodley Branch president on December 19, 1847.[28] Sanderson immigrated to the Great Basin soon thereafter and became part of the 1851 Iron Mission that settled Parowan, in southern Utah. He taught astrology in Parowan[29] and then, within a few years, moved back north and started an astrological school in the Salt Lake area.[30] Thomas Job was a mathematics teacher who had studied grimoires as a boy and engaged in a concerted study of astrology as he grew older. His descendants remembered that he had engaged in some forms of divination and conjuration,[31] but his primary focus was the heavens. He converted to Mormonism in 1851 and immigrated to the United States in 1854. Job remembered that Sanderson's books had been stolen and that Sanderson consequently taught from memory. Upon his arrival, Job began supplying Sanderson's school with lessons from his own library.[32] The astrology school also acquired a rare copy of Barrett's important *The Magus.*[33]

John Steele, a Scots-Irish convert who emigrated to Nauvoo and was part of the Mormon Battalion, was perhaps the most successful Mormon astrologer. While Job and Sanderson both eventually became disaffected with the Utah church,[34] Steele not only remained a practicing member but took on church leadership roles, eventually becoming ordained as a patriarch. It is likely that his association with Sanderson in settling Parowan piqued Steele's interest in astrology. He began studying the subject in earnest in the decade after moving to Toquerville, Utah, procuring astrological works and subscribing to relevant periodicals. His collection ultimately became "the largest such private collection yet discovered for pioneer Utah."[35] Steele was primarily a botanic physician, but he was a consistent practitioner of astrology, and, as his papers show, he also engaged in the traditional healing techniques of the cunning-folk and astrologers. Included among his papers are instructions for curing people and animals, finding what has been lost or stolen, and creating protective amulets. Examples include an idiosyncratic version of a charm against witchcraft and hybrid amulets based on "signs" from Scot's *Discovery* coupled with Barrett's Tetragrammaton pentacle.[36]

Perhaps the most insightful texts into Steele's chimeric astrological Mormonism are his instructions for the preparation, consecration, and discharge of "a glass." These instructions, while following similar patterns to those found in Scot's and Barrett's works, are unique in their invocation of biblical imagery and use of Mormon vernacular. Instead of adhering to the typical form of a spirit conjuration, the instructions are structured as a prayer to God "in the name of Jesus Christ" asking for "ministering angels of light" of God's "heavenly host" to mediate the desired vision.[37] This translation of the traditional incantation into a Mormon vernacular is similar to the way in which English charm variants compare to their French equivalents, in that the English charms generally lack any reference to the cult of the saints. The Reformation modified but did not extinguish the charms.[38] Steele similarly translated his conjuration into a vernacular more consistent with his Mormonism.

Steele's enthusiasm for astrology is essentially unique among Utah Mormons, particularly since his practice continued into the twentieth century. More commonly, church members and leaders were ambivalent, if not hostile, toward astrology. In 1852, James Martineau, an American convert, began studying with Sanderson in Parowan. A few months later he decided "to give up that study, also of magic, thinking it too sharp tools for me to work with." However, two years later he visited Brigham Young in Salt Lake, who gave "his approval to practice Astrology, so long as I should do good, and do no hurt." Still, feeling unsure, he spoke with Young again a year later. This time Young discouraged him from this pursuit, indicating that it was "a dangerous thing to meddle with." Martineau then resolved to give up astrology and instead study engineering, a choice Young heartily endorsed.[39]

Church leaders in Utah exhibited a spectrum of belief with regard to astrology. Apostle Orson Pratt viewed it as an absurdity[40]; Brigham Young appears to have accepted it privately for a time and then rejected it[41]; others regarded it as perverted science tainted by the devil.[42] Some church members, like Joseph Smith's former secretary, the British William Clayton, sought advice from Sanderson and Job on matters of health and business into the early 1860s.[43] Similarly, British convert James Fisher consulted an astrologer to locate a woman to marry in 1857.[44] William Barton, one of Sanderson's students, however, demonstrated the practical application of Woodruff's accommodation of cunning-folk practice. When Barton's wife fell mortally ill in 1861, Barton "Cast a Astroligicle figure for Malinda in the midle of March and found that nothing but the Priesthood could save her."[45]

Ultimately, church pressure against astrology intensified. Wilford Woodruff recorded the consensus of the Salt Lake School of the Prophets in 1868 that "it

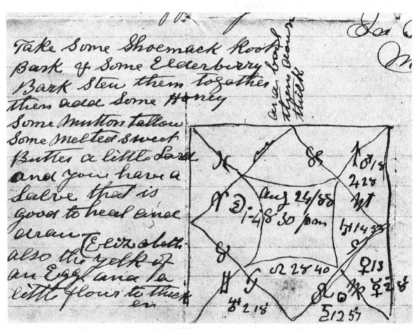

Astrological chart and remedy created by John Steele for his grandchild's illness, included in Mohonri Moriancumer Steele, letter to John Steele, August 20, 1888. From the John Steele papers, L. Tom Perry Special Collections, Provo, Utah.

was decided that Asstrology was in oposition to the work of God. Hence Saints Should not be ingaged in it."[46] Two days later the *Deseret News* ran an editorial titled "Astrology and Its Evils" that labeled astrology "the bondage of superstition."[47] From this point forward, astrology was institutionally anathema. Three decades later, prominent Mormon geologist and theologian James Talmage wrote a humorous and rational analysis of astrology in the monthly youth magazine of the church, signaling the position of the church on the matter for the subsequent century as one informed by both science and faith.[48]

Seers, Seeresses, and Seer Stones

When Wilford Woodruff elucidated Mormonism's accommodationist stance on glossolalia, healers, and seer stones at the Manchester Conference in 1845, he had seen for himself Joseph Smith's seer stone—both a catalyst for and a reification of the Book of Mormon.[49] But whereas the astrology and cunning-folk traditions predominant among the British converts were highly textual, the dominant mode of Mormon seership was more analogous to the other miraculous gifts Woodruff described: healing and glossolalia. The gift of sight was not absent from colonial and antebellum Christianity. Evangelicals of all sorts had prophetic dreams, visions, and premonitions[50]—the itinerant evangelist Lorenzo Dow even told fortunes[51]—but the Mormon accommodation of seer stones was exceptional. Latter-day Saints eventually came to call people with the innate gift to see visions in seer stones "natural seers."[52]

In nineteenth-century Utah, seers, like those who healed or spoke in tongues, were as likely to be female as they were to be male. Joseph Smith had found his seer stones by vision and later, riffing on the white stone in the Book of Revelation, taught that everyone would eventually receive a personal "urim and thummim," the white stone upon which a new name would be written.[53] This idea was generally esoteric, yet some Mormons appear to have integrated the promise into common belief.[54] When discussing Smith's seer stones with church leaders in 1855, Brigham Young recalled that "Joseph said there is a Stone for every person on the Earth."[55] Priddy Meeks, an American convert and botanic physician in Parowan, Utah, wrote that in 1857, "seer stones, or peepstones, as they are more commonly called, was very plenty about Parowan," demonstrating how popular they were. "I rather being a gifted person in knowing a peepstone when seeing one altho I had never found one yet that I could see in," Meeks continued. "A seerstone appears to me to be the connecting link between the visible and invisible worlds." Meeks had taken in a boy who was purportedly "born a natural seer" and who could identify the persons to whom the stone naturally belonged.[56]

Joseph Fish, who also lived in Parowan during this time, called it "the Peep stone craze." Fish wrote that like the young Joseph Smith, the boy who lived with Meeks put a stone

> in a black hat and looking in there he could see things. He would tell where a person's cattle were on the range . . . . Several [people] were on the watch to find a stone that they could see things in. It was claimed that every individual could see things if he could get the right kind of stone, and that there was a stone for each person if it could be found. Many had somewhat of a belief in this, but as it was proved that the seer could not always see right, those who had some faith in it lost their belief and the thing died down.[57]

Parowan in the late 1850s may have been an unusual center of seer stone activity; however, the use of seer stones among Mormons during the nineteenth century was not completely isolated either regionally or temporally. When the young Joseph F. Smith left Utah to proselytize in Hawaii in 1854, his sister and another friend wrote to him about how his cousin Mary Jane Thompson in Salt Lake City had been watching him through a seer stone.[58] In 1860 Brigham Young's nephew described a church member looking into a seer stone in the presence of a corpse in Draper, Utah, and seeing the manner of the person's death.[59] In Logan in 1884, Susan Martineau "looked in a crystal for the first time, and could see clearly in it—saw many things of much interest."[60] One anonymous critic summarized seer stone usage in the 1885 *Deseret News* as follows:

> They are found in the hands of men, women, and children . . . [who] are besieged by all classes to learn something in regard to their individual affairs; such as the whereabouts of lost animals or stolen goods, [or] the character of a man or woman with whom the enquirer is anticipating marriage. In some instances where persons are suspected of evil designs the "peep stone" has been used to verify the suspicion; the sex, as also the future of an unborn child has been enquired after. In this Western country they have been often used to determine the location of a good paying mine, etc.[61]

A few Mormon proprietors of seer stones were sufficiently gifted that their peers and coreligionists recognized them as seers or seeresses. When Henry Martineau passed through Fillmore, Utah, in the fall of 1858, he "went to see Mrs. Janvrin Dame a seeress, who derived her gift from an ordination by her father." Martineau commented that "she is thought to be almost infallible by the people of Fillmore."

This woman was either Lucinda or Lovina Dame, sisters whose Mormon father had died in Illinois in 1844. Martineau's record shows her pronouncements to have been similar to those that Margaret Anderton had delivered to the three American evangelists in 1845 in Preston, albeit with the addition of specifically Mormon details similar to the language of patriarchal blessings. Dame gave details about multiple wives, children, and mission service. She stated that Martineau was "on a broad foundation and will never desert this Cause." Martineau wrote that he recorded the details of her words "out of curiosity, to see if it will be fulfilled," but noted that "some things she told me of the past were very true, which makes me think some of the future may be."[62]

Brigham Young clearly believed in seer stones as revelatory objects. A girl living in his household once found one in which she "could see persons and animals and things in it at will, and could tell the whereabouts of lost property." Young "advised that the stone be carefully kept, and that the girl be not allowed to use it until she should become a woman of discretion" so the object would not become "the means of her own destruction."[63] However, Young himself claimed that he lacked the ability to use seer stones and on one occasion when discussing them confessed: "I don't no that I have ever had a desire to have one."[64] He was not, he repeated self-deprecatingly, a "natural seer."[65] This did not mean he did not claim to receive revelations. To the 1873 Salt Lake School of the Prophets, Young "said there were many revelations given to him that he did not receive from the Prophet Joseph. He did not receive them through the Urim and Thummim as Joseph did but when he did receive them he knew of their truth as much as it was possible for ~~them~~ him to do of any truth."[66] With Young as church president, the chief hierarch and chief revelator of the church not only did not use seer stones, but could not use them. In this way Young created an important rift in the liturgical landscape. Joseph Smith had firmly established that a seer could not receive communications from God for the church unless that seer held his position at its head.[67] Young established that the institutional position of church president did not require a seer's ability; the position alone was the formal and superior alternative to seer stone use. This rift only expanded as the priesthood hierarchy naturally became the formal channel for revelation. Seer stones were gradually maligned and relegated to the realm of folk practice alone.

The best example of this reinforcement of institutional authority is the case of Sophia Romeril Russell. A British convert from the Isle of Jersey, Russell crossed the plains as a child. At some point she acquired a seer stone that may have originally been dug out of a hill in Nauvoo.[68] By the 1880s church members widely recognized her as a seeress. In December 1890, Russell visited Fillmore, Utah, where she helped some of "the brethren" locate a mine.[69] While there she gave prophecies for several individuals. Christian Anderson, the Millard Stake high priest quorum president, who had been released from prison on his federal cohabitation sentence just weeks before, visited with her twice. "She told me," Anderson wrote, that "she could see in her stone that there was no more penitentiary for me, that I should have 3 or 4 more wives." Russell further declared, he noted, "that the future was bright for me; that the Lord loved me and that I should be blest financially and that I should gain much power and influence among my brethren." Russell prophesied about Anderson's financial well-being, the faithfulness of his posterity, and a future mission to Europe, during which "200 should be added to the church through my ministry, and they should nearly all remain faithful."[70]

Josiah E. Hickman, a young student who eventually became a prominent Utah educator, also visited with Russell during her visit to Fillmore and left a detailed record of his experience. Hickman wrote that "she could see a person's past and future history. is a strong saint & has had the stone blessed. I blessed the stone and made it a matter of prayer before I had her look for me." Hickman then recorded nearly 1,200 words of blessing that Russell had given. Like Dame's blessing on Martineau mentioned earlier, Russell's blessing was saturated with the imagery and vernacular of the church and in many cases paralleled the language of patriarchal blessings. For example, Russell told Hickman, "You are through Ephraim and Isaac and Rebecca. You were a prophet and seer before you came here on earth and now possess the same power now, in part, it has not been given to you in full." Unlike a patriarchal blessing, however, much of what Russell pronounced was framed as what she saw: "I see two missions for you; one across the ocean and one in Eastern States." Russell provided details regarding Hickman's future marriages, education, and career. Forty years later Hickman went back through his journal and marked what had come to fruition—the majority of the text.[71]

Perhaps because of such pronouncements' similarity to the priesthood functions of patriarchs, by the time these two men had received their visions from Russell, the institutional tolerance for such activities had decidedly waned. Some church leaders appear to have always felt that popular seer stone usage was not desirable. When a woman brought a seer stone to the Heber C. Kimball household in 1858 that was "said to be one which formily belonged to Moses" and that "a great many people can see in it," Kimball remarked that "those were sacred things to be used only by the priesthood and when used by others were often led a stray."[72] The anonymous writer who published a criticism of seer stones in the 1885 *Deseret News* also declared: "The gift of prescience or the power to penetrate the future belongs to and [is] always accompanied the Melchisedek Priesthood. Whenever and wherever it was not this gift could not be found. Counterfeits have always existed, however, cotemporary [sic] with the genuine gift, and have succeeded in leading many of the unwary away."[73] In the years that followed, church leaders increasingly concurred with these sentiments.

When the bishop of Schofield, Utah, visited Sophia Russell in 1888, his counselors remonstrated. To quell their objections, the bishop wrote directly to the First Presidency. Wilford Woodruff responded incredulously to the letter, siding with the bishop's counselors: "That you, a Bishop of the Church and bearer of the Holy Priesthood, should subject yourself in this way to such an influence is very surprising and shows that your conception of the power of your priesthood is not what it should be."[74] In significant ways, Woodruff's response was consistent with the accommodation he had outlined in Britain over forty years earlier to "seek to be fed through the head and not through the feet."

Russell, however, claimed to have received the support of John Taylor and Joseph F. Smith. Taylor was by 1888 dead, but both Smith and Taylor's secretary, George Reynolds, only remembered condemning her practices.[75] With each decade that had passed, the institutional controls over revelation developed to a point that the early practices became superfluous. Though she continued to assert her right to use her gift to see "through seer stones in her possession," within the next five years the Salt Lake High Council tried Russell and forbade her from using the stone, "except as she was directed by the Priesthood."[76]

When James Talmage, the geologist, theologian, and confidant of the First Presidency mentioned earlier, expressed a desire to examine seer stones in 1893, Stake President Angus Cannon led him to Sophia Russell and Edwin Rushton, a British convert who had emigrated to Nauvoo and then to the

James Talmage in his geology laboratory. Original in the possession of Shannon Howells, Salt Lake City, Utah. Used with permission.

Great Basin. Both expressed faith in the utility of their seer stones, described the specifics of how they had used them, and related the types of visions possible through them. Rushton believed that his stone was one of the white stones promised in the Book of Revelation[77] and described the "day vision" that led him to finding it in Nauvoo, as well as how he had employed it to fulfill a mission that Joseph Smith had entrusted to him and others and how he subsequently lost the gift to use it. Talmage evaluated the stones as a scientist and even conducted chemical analyses on Rushton's stone, describing the rocks as mundane physical objects. While admitting that his evaluation did not negate the possibility of some supernatural character (he admitted to receiving neither visual nor aural manifestations from God himself), he observed that "the Lord could endow a piece of brick with the properties of a Seer Stone, and endow his chosen servants with power to use such." Despite this affirmation of the prophetic use of seer stones, Talmage concluded that Russell's "divination" was contrary to the order of the priesthood, a conclusion that he noted Wilford Woodruff reaffirmed.[78]

As a scientist, Talmage was an heir of the Enlightenment and the skepticism that had pushed cunning-folk traditions outside the boundaries of educated society, yet he was also wholly committed to the reality of Joseph Smith's Restoration. As such, he was emblematic of church members as a whole, who in the twentieth century grew to see the urim and thummim of Joseph Smith as completely dissociated from "seer stones" and any cunning-folk traditions, and as entirely under the auspices of the priesthood ecclesiology.

Healers and Healing

Through the nineteenth century, LDS Church leaders positioned Mormonism in a way that integrated practitioners of the attenuated cunning-folk traditions, and simultaneously channeled their impulses toward the orthodox liturgy. As mentioned earlier, cunning-folk practice was not entirely uncommon in colonial and antebellum Christianity. What was different about Mormons was that they integrated aspects of the cunning-folk traditions into their church. Joseph Smith, church leaders, and church members all incorporated seer stones into their cosmology and created liturgical and ecclesiastical outlets for prophecy. In both these cases—seership and prophecy—the church leaders exerted a tremendous governing influence to the increasing exclusion of nonbureaucratic manifestations. Healing is another area where attenuated cunning folk practice was common in the broader culture. The Mormon healing liturgy successfully channeled the hopes of its members. I have examined thousands of cases of Mormon healing and have found the standard liturgical and medical approaches to be normative;

still, folk healing remained within the culture, though largely on the periphery of the church and championed by "natural healers."

Early Latter-day Saint healing practice drew liturgically from the Bible and professionally from the botanic medicine popularized by Samuel Thomson. Throughout his life Joseph Smith and other church leaders engaged in a continual process of ritualization in which the salvific rituals of the church were adapted to the practice of healing. As the previous chapter demonstrated, Smith sought to equip all his people with rituals to channel the power of God to heal and authorized all men and women as administrators of the healing liturgy.[79] Thomsonianism was common among evangelical Christians of the period, as it appealed to anti-elite sentiments and offered readily available therapies that seemed less deleterious than standard cures such as toxic mercury-based compounds.

Mormons positioned their healing practice in contrast to Christian cessationism and traditional professional medicine.[80] As Oliver Cowdery wrote in 1835:

> We are a people who design living near the Lord, that our bodies may be healed when we are sick, for a general rule, though our faith is yet weak, being young, weak and surrounded by a wicked enticing world—When, however, we have need of an earthly physician, and in many instances we have, we call upon our highly esteemed friend and brother Dr. F. G. Williams [counselor to Joseph Smith], universally known through this country as an eminent and skilful man. I may say in short, he is also a Botanic Physician—which course of practice is generally approved by us.[81]

Cowdery's negotiation between faith and medicine was normative for Mormonism of the era. In practice, Mormons consistently applied for medical aid in addition to participating in the healing liturgy—the set of rituals church leaders and members employed in the name of Jesus Christ. Brigham Young was a staunch believer in healing blessings and botanic medicine, but as medical technology became more sophisticated, he began to support male and female medical students in eastern universities. He encouraged men and women to bless their children when ill and also sent his nephew to medical school. The Relief Society chartered the Deseret Hospital, where believers could be treated by professionally trained physicians and receive healing rituals from men and women.[82]

The healing liturgy and professional medicine were not exclusive in Mormonism, however, and folk healing practices remained. Hans de Waardt has argued that in a time when the belief in witchcraft had essentially disappeared but a robust belief in the "wonders of nature" persisted, the yearning for miraculous cures created space for cunning-folk to evolve into natural healers who retained many of the same techniques.[83] These healers functioned particularly well when medicine failed. With the Mormon healing liturgy already accommodating medical professionals, the Church indicated no impulse for exclusivity in healing. In consequence, alongside the Mormon healing liturgy and professional medicine, the "natural-healer" has been a regular feature of Mormon healing practice, even into the twenty-first century. Historically, many Mormons likely viewed folk practice as no different than their botanic remedies. While folk healing practice was not endorsed by the church, these practitioners have generally been Mormon, so their healing has often had a particular Mormon flavor.

The most prominent examples of cunning-folk healing practice are the few astrologers who existed on the outer fringes of Mormonism. John Sanderson prescribed herbal remedies for diphtheria[84] but also cured "bosom serpentry," an ailment believed to be caused by a snake or frog living in one's stomach.[85] Astrologer-patriarch John Steele acted as a traditional botanic physician but also engaged in urine diagnoses and charming, prescribed bacon poultices as a means of disease transference, and created astrological healing amulets.[86] There are also rare examples of the use of folk-healing techniques among the high church leadership. In the early church, Frederick Williams, the counselor to Joseph Smith referred to earlier, was a Thomsonian physician, but he also advertised urine scrying among his diagnostic abilities.[87] George Watt, who was blessed by Margaret Anderton in Preston, England, advertised the use of a bloodstone brooch as a hemostatic amulet in an early Utah newspaper. Watt became Brigham Young's secretary and gave the brooch to him.[88] Young then lent it or other bloodstones in his possession to stanch bleeding in others.[89]

Zina D. H. Young, the American convert, midwife, General Relief Society president, and wife to both Joseph Smith and Brigham Young who has been previously discussed, is perhaps the most documented performer of healing rituals in all of Mormonism.[90] Her papers include a few examples of folk-healing techniques and charms, including a verbal charm intended to quiet a burn that is most proximately documented in mid-eighteenth-century Cambria, England.[91] There are also some examples of what some scholars call "sympathetic magic." For example, to induce urination when a catheter was ineffectual, the remedy was "the penus of a Deer [in] one pint of whiskey." Hemorrhoids could be treated with "the last gut of a pig stewed in or with the white of hen dung stewed together."[92] Perhaps the most interesting folk treatment in Zina Young's papers is a hemostatic prayer[93] that appears to be based on the "in sanguine Adæ" charm, first found in English in Scot's *Discovery*.[94] Despite the inclusion of these examples in her papers, I have not found any documentation of her using these techniques in practice.

One particular folk-healing form involved the use of wooden canes.[95] The following two accounts highlight the difference in some British Mormons' approach to these folk practices in comparison to their American coreligionists. The first account describes the healing use of a cane in Winter Quarters before the vanguard company left for the Great Basin in 1847. According to his journal, John D. Lee suffered from a violent fever and vomiting. Brigham Young, Wilford Woodruff, and a few others came to his residence, whereupon Young "laid on my breast a cane built from one of the branches of the Tree of Life that stood in the garden in the Temple." The sick man described that "this as a matter to be expected, collected my thoughts and centered them on sacred and solemn things." Woodruff then anointed and blessed him.[96] In this case, the traditional folk use of the cane was grafted onto the symbolism of the Mormon temple. While the healing nature of the cane was reflected in its placement upon the chest of the afflicted, the implement itself was metaphorically understood to be a branch from the Tree of Life, a central image in the temple liturgy, and the ultimate remedy for the mortal and corruptible state of humanity. The cane was also a supplement to the regular healing liturgy of the church.

The second account can be found in an 1848 letter published in the *Millennial Star* in which John Albiston, a native elder in England, recounted several miraculous healings elicited by the use of his cane:

> While I was looking about me one day, I left my stick at the brothers in Old Swinford; the brother and father-in-law worked together as nailors, and the young man had a deep cut in his hand, caused by a piece of iron with which he had been at work. He went to my stick and rubbed his hand against it, and the wound immediately closed. Both father-in-law and mother-in-law were witnesses to this healing. The old man and woman had each wounds; they took the stick and rubbed, and were healed,—so there were three healed in that house, one after another.[97]

Albiston's cane was used again for healing when he visited the Cheltenham branch: "When I got to Cheltenham, there was a sister there greatly disfigured by two scurvy lumps on her top lip, I told the story of the stick, without thinking she would make use of it. I went to look through the town of Cheltenham, and some time after I again saw the sister, but the lumps were gone! She had made use of my stick. This is truth." These latter examples of healing by cane differ from the Winter Quarters example in that the cane itself was seen as the supernatural therapy, one that included no Christian allusions and lacked any connection to the healing liturgy. Still, church leaders were willing to publish accounts of these healings in the church periodical, reinforcing the understanding that such practitioners were welcome participants in Mormonism.

Folklorists Wayland D. Hand and Jeannine E. Talley have hypothesized that the large amount of unique folk traditions in Utah compared to other areas of the United States is due to the relatively high rate of international immigration to the area.[98] Despite the influx of folk-healing practice with successive waves of emigration, the church's emphasis on healing through the accessible liturgy of the church appears to have pushed Mormons away from such practices. For example, Claire Noall observed in her study of midwifery that Mormon midwives were extremely less likely than other American midwives to practice folk ritual or teach folk beliefs related to their labors. Instead, these women focused on the healing rituals of the church along with the standard medical therapies of the era.[99]

In the last decades of the nineteenth century and the first decades of the twentieth century, medicine became clinically viable, and hospitals became normative features in the American health care system. Church leaders consequently strengthened their support for professional medical treatments. They built hospitals and encouraged Mormons to use them. Church leaders grew to have a more rationalist and medicalized view of the body, modified the healing liturgy to reflect those perspectives, and also excluded female administrators in part of a process of liturgical reform that eliminated baptism for health, washings and anointings for health, anointing the area of affliction, and drinking consecrated oil.[100] As discussed in chapter 4, during the twentieth century the streamlined priesthood "ordinances" of anointing the head and sealing blessings became the universal healing liturgy in the church.

Folk healing remained in Mormonism as well as the broader society, but it changed in significant ways. While the urine scrying, textual amulets, and "sympathetic magic" of the cunning-folk are essentially absent in contemporary British, American, and Mormon healing practice, "complementary and alternative medicine" (CAM) is common to them all. CAM comprises a diverse set of health care approaches associated by their shared status of being outside the established and clinical mainstream of medicine. CAM is hardly a Mormon phenomenon—the shelves of upscale grocery stores are filled with CAM pills, compounds, and books, and it is extremely popular among conservative Protestant Christians.[101] Mormons nevertheless engage CAM in distinctively Mormon ways. Multilevel marketing enables women, who no longer participate in the healing liturgy and were discouraged in the twentieth century from entering medicine and other professional pursuits, to contribute economically to the household—and, in the case of products like essential oils or healing juices, medically to their families and communities. Moreover, healing techniques based on otherwise hidden aspects of nature allow Mormons to participate in healing in a manner analogous to that offered by the nineteenth-century natural healers in the church.

Though systematic sociological research is still needed to determine statistically relevant trends of CAM use among Mormons, one Mormon CAM practitioner described her work in a way that situated it in an explicitly Mormon context. As a practitioner of a type of energy healing, a therapy that employs the vernacular of quantum physics to describe a relationship between sensing and changing molecular vibrations, emotions, and healing,[102] she primarily focuses on areas such as chronic pain in which many patients have found clinical medicine to provide poor results. In the context of her work this practitioner described regularly praying for and receiving the "gift of healing," as described in Mormon scripture. She believed that healing by church ritual and energy healing functioned through similar mechanisms.[103]

Christ-centered energy healers draw large audiences for conventions and conferences in areas with significant Mormon populations,[104] but there are also limits to the institutional tolerance of such healers in the church. Julie Rowe is an energy healer based in Utah who has written several books related to prophetic gifts that allow her to see into the future. She has traveled around the country giving fireside talks and seminars relating to both her healing techniques and her apocalypticism. In September 2015, many associated her eschatological predictions with a "blood moon" that portended widespread financial, political, and sociological ruin.[105] She associated her predictions with the "prepper" movement, a social current that commercializes survival food and equipment. Church leaders responded by adding her book to a list of spurious literature and warning LDS educators against including her writings in their teaching.[106] The church also released a public statement disavowing "extreme efforts to anticipate catastrophic events" and the related "writings and speculations of individual Church members, some of which have gained currency recently."[107] Moreover, in response to questions about an alternative healer convention in Utah, a church public affairs representative urged "Church members to be cautious about participating in any group that promises—in exchange for money—miraculous healings or that claims to have special methods for accessing healing power outside of properly ordained priesthood holders."[108]

Conclusion

There is no Christian culture from antiquity to the present that is without charms and incantations, and, as David Gay has noted, the context of even the most non-Christian charm within a Christian culture is explicitly Christian.[109] However, how clerics have viewed these practices has varied greatly. In England, charms were first collected by monks, and clerics were popular exorcists and astrological healers before the modern era.[110] At the same time that Joseph Smith peered into his sacred stones to annunciate histories, sermons, and revelations, many people in England still believed that cunning-folk were doing God's work—what the church should have been doing[111]; however, such beliefs were also decidedly far outside the bounds of Christian orthodoxy. Churches had by then moved beyond the cunning-folk traditions.

When Joseph Smith fractured heaven's silence, the resulting space was chaotic. God and angels communed with believing men and women. The attenuated cunning-folk traditions on edge of society—divination, prophecy, and healing in the face of medical failure—all became, in some measure, normalized within the church. Joseph Smith translated some the fixtures and activities, such as seer stones, into the cosmology and liturgy of the church. More generally, however, the practitioners of the folk rituals were themselves integrated into the church, and translated into Mormons and equipped with the liturgy of the church. This process of translation highlights important distinctions between the highly textual traditions of many British converts and the oral tradition of their American coreligionists. Moreover, with increasing time and institutional control over divine media, healing has remained the primary locus of Mormonism's accommodation of such traditions, with alternative practitioners continuing to integrate their complementary systems into Mormonism. Despite their increasing level of control, church leaders have been remarkably consistent in their insistence that members "seek to be fed through the head and not through the feet"—that is, that folk practice is acceptable as long as it maintains deference to priesthood ecclesiology. However, the limits of that deference grew to only tolerate alternative healers.

Conclusion

*The churches of the world have a form of godliness, but they
deny the power thereof. It is in and through the authority of
the priesthood that the power of godliness is manifest. And we
are the only people on earth who have that priesthood, that
power to act in the Lord's name and have our acts approved
and acknowledged both on earth and in heaven.*[1]

BRUCE R. MCCONKIE, General Conference sermon, 1949

EACH CHAPTER OF this book has opened with a vignette—one or more
descriptions of Mormons ordering their lives and the cosmos that contains them.
Ultimately, the stale handbooks, liturgical texts, and instructional letters that
direct church members are meaningless absent the lived experience of the believers themselves. Their ritual acts are inherently ephemeral, only rarely and imper-
fectly captured in the memories and media close at hand. However, with sufficient
documentation and context, we can begin to perceive the meaning these people
found in their rituals and the work performed in their liturgies. In this way, and
in contrast with claims of exceptionalism, Mormons are every woman and man.

However, it is in the particular and localized acts of Latter-day Saints that
this book takes interest. What is priesthood? What do sealings accomplish? Why
are babies blessed? Who has the authority to perform sacred ordinances? What
authority exists outside of ecclesiology? In answering these questions this book
attempts to illuminate the cosmos in which Mormon women and men live and
perform their religion. A principal concept that appears in each chapter is the
idea of a cosmological priesthood—a priesthood constructed on the altars of
Mormon temples—that rose and fell in the history of Mormon belief.

The gender-inclusive priesthood language of the Nauvoo Temple contra-
dicted the exclusively male ecclesiastical priesthood language that developed in
the church; ultimately, the latter held sway. After the decline of the cosmological
priesthood as an active internal framework, Mormons spent the last one hundred
years working to understand how women fit into an increasingly vast priesthood
authority structure. Similarly, baby blessings, which once announced the place

of children in the cosmological priesthood, grew to be a performative act of a sacerdotal and ecclesiastical fatherhood. With regard to healing, cosmological priesthood language became an area of confusion as church leaders concentrated church liturgy and authority within the priesthood ecclesiastical structures of the church and created ordinances—sacred and venerable rituals performed by priesthood officers that became the basis of worship for millions. Any analysis of authority throughout Mormon history is consequently challenged by the changing lexical terrain. Over time, church leaders and members have used the term "priesthood" in reference to various aspects of liturgical, ecclesiastical, and priestly (temple) authorities. This framework is key to understanding how Mormons have tamed the chaotic heaven opened by an angel and a golden book.

The Power of Godliness

In the Bible, nested among Paul's litany of perils in the last days is a warning against traitors to the church "having a form of godliness, but denying the power thereof." Paul's godliness was piety, or lived religion. When Joseph Smith worked with his secretaries to produce his religious biography, he included in the account of his youthful vision of God the narration of his desire to know which church to join. The Lord responded to his inquiry by declaring that all existing churches were in error. "They teach for doctrines the commandments of men, having a form of Godliness but they deny the power thereof."[2] The charge of formalism was not uncommon to Christian leaders of the time who were interested in reform. John Wesley wrote from the outset that Methodist societies were to be "no other than a Company of Men having the Form and seeking the Power of Godliness."[3] As Christopher Jones has written, Methodists were not alone in their concern for both the form and the power of godliness, even if their focus was particularly intense; Mormons too sought for this power. However, what early Mormons and Methodists viewed as the power of godliness was not the same.[4]

As described in Chapter 1, Mormons viewed the power of godliness as the power of God manifest among the faithful in all its anticessationist splendor. This conception began to change in late September 1832, when the Saints in Kirtland, Ohio, held a two-day conference during which several traveling elders returned from and reported on their proselytizing efforts. During the proceedings, Joseph Smith dictated a revelation that addressed the future temple in Zion, evangelism, and his burgeoning priesthood cosmology. The revelation declared that the High Priesthood "administereth the gospel and holdeth the key of the misteries of the kingdom, even the key of the knowledge of God[,] therefore in the ordinences thereof the power of Godliness is manifest[,] and without the ordinences thereof, and the authority of the Priesthood, the power of Godliness is not manifest unto man in the flesh, for without this no man can see the face of God even the father and live."[5] As described in Chapter 4, ordinances in early Mormonism were laws, and at this point in history the High Priesthood was responsible for governing the church and for performing one ritual—the sealing of people up into eternal life. Only through a church governed by authorized high priests could the power of godliness be realized. Joseph Smith's continued revelations, both textual and oral, resulted in an evolution of Mormons' conception of priesthood. And the power of godliness grew in the hands of Mormon stewards from Paul's experience of genuine piety within the authorized church to a reality constructed, as Apostle Bruce McConkie declared in 1949, by priesthood "acts approved and acknowledged both on earth and in heaven."[6] In the twentieth century, as priesthood became the exclusive power of God, the power of godliness became the lived experience of Mormons as they participated in all of the venerable priesthood ordinances of the church.

Paintings and Plants

In a perspicacious essay explaining Mormon conceptions of revelation and the open canon, historian David Holland employed an extended metaphor that described the teachings of church leaders as strokes of a brush, which through generations and layers reveal an emergent and cohesive image. Holland readily acknowledged the tension between various pasts and presents yet suggested that resolution was to be found in the developmental harmony of the whole. In describing the limits upon possible revelation, he wrote that "a ham-fisted or incongruous effort to completely obliterate past images has the potential to damage the entire composition." In support of this statement he offered the hypothetical case of a church leader who decided to teach against the divinity of Jesus: "He would have to scribble over millennia of the most exquisite prophetic artistry while somehow preventing the ongoing devotional statements of his fellow ecclesiarchs and the irresistible witness in millions of Mormon souls."[7] Through this metaphor Holland described the inherent conservatism of Mormon revelation and, without fully articulating it, approached the role of tradition in the church.

In 2004, Joseph Cardinal Ratzinger wrote a remarkably self-aware introduction to a monograph on the "organic development" of Roman Catholic liturgy. Ratzinger situated himself and the book in between proponents and opponents of radical reform, championing a view of "the Liturgy as something living, and thus as growing" and noting that "proper development is possible only if careful attention is paid to the inner structural logic of this 'organism.'" Like Holland, Ratzinger demarcated the limits of ecclesiology by referencing the idea of a venerable tradition: "The pope is not an absolute monarch whose will is law; rather, he is the guardian of the authentic Tradition . . . . He cannot do as he likes." And absent the possibility of "arbitrary power," Ratzinger stated, he is not a painter, but a gardener; not a "technician who builds new machines and throws the old ones on the junk-pile," but a curator and nurturer.

Both Holland and Ratzinger recognized that many partisans would reject the metaphors they used to normalize a thoughtful and historically informed present. Holland outlined the possibility of schism when focused on isolated periods or styles of brushstrokes. Ratzinger outlined the historical dialogue between the "archaeological enthusiasm" often held by historians and other experts and the "pastoral pragmatism" of clerics. Both groups have long struggled, interweaving Holland's metaphor, to appreciate the whole painting. Where Holland was quick to demonstrate how an emphasis on isolated brushstrokes could lead to violence or racism, Ratzinger noted the importance of "distinguishing actions that are helpful and healing from those that are violent and destructive."[8]

Both Holland and Ratzinger were interested in holistic understandings of their respective traditions and advocated an evolutionary approach to church practice, both out of an appreciation for all antecedents and in a recognition of the inherent ecology of them. In situating this book in light of their respective metaphors, I make an effort to understand the brushstrokes of church leaders and members through time as they have contributed to the living system of Mormonism. It is my intention to complicate the facile or presentist reading, the proof-text, and the analytically lazy, whether academic or parochial. This book is not concerned with what Mormons should believe or teach. It is concerned with what Mormons have believed and taught as they have ordered their universe.

Notes

INTRODUCTION

1. Eliza R. Snow, excerpt from "The Ladies of Utah," in *Eliza R. Snow: The Complete Poetry*, ed. and comp. Jill Mulvay Derr and Karen Lynn Davidson (Provo/Salt Lake City: Brigham Young University Press/University of Utah Press, 2009), 558.

2. Brigham Young, "Pres. B. Young's dream Feb.y 17, 1847," Box 75, Folder 34, BYOF. On the broader context of this dream, see Jonathan A. Stapley, "Adoptive Sealing Ritual in Mormonism," *Journal of Mormon History* 37 (Summer 2011): 78–80.

3. Mimeograph of washing and anointing text from Panguitch, CR 11 304, Folder 2, Relief Society Washing and Anointing File, CHL.

4. Jan Shipps and John W. Welch, eds., *The Journals of William E. McLellin, 1831–1836* (Provo, Urbana, IL, and Chicago: BYU Studies and University of Illinois Press, 1994), 152.

5. Peter Cartwright, *Autobiography of Peter Cartwright*, with an introduction by Charles L. Wallis (Nashville, TN: Abingdon Press reprint, 1984), 225–226. See Christopher C. Jones, "'We Latter-day Saints Are Methodists': The Influence of Methodism on Early Mormon Religiosity" (M.A. thesis, Brigham Young University, 2009).

6. On popular anticreedalism, see Nathan O. Hatch, *The Democratization of American Christianity* (New Haven, CT: Yale University Press, 1989). See also Christopher C. Jones and Stephen J. Fleming, "'Except among That Portion of Mankind': Early Mormon Conceptions of the Apostasy," in *Standing Apart: Mormon Historical Consciousness and the Concept of Apostasy*, edited by Miranda Wilcox and John D. Young (New York: Oxford University Press, 2014).

7. Ryan G. Tobler, "'Saviors on Mount Zion': Mormon Sacramentalism, Mortality, and the Baptism for the Dead," *Journal of Mormon History* 39, no. 4 (Fall 2013): 182–238; Jonathan A. Stapley and Kristine Wright, "'They Shall Be Made Whole': A History of Baptism for Health," *Journal of Mormon History* 34 (Fall

2008): 69–112; D. Michael Quinn, "The Practice of Rebaptism at Nauvoo," *BYU Studies* 18 (Winter 1978): 226–232.

8. Samuel M. Brown, *In Heaven as It Is on Earth: Joseph Smith and the Early Mormon Conquest of Death* (New York: Oxford University Press, 2012), ch. 6.

9. Jonathan A. Stapley and Kristine Wright, "The Forms and the Power: The Development of Mormon Healing to 1847," *Journal of Mormon History* 35 (Summer 2009): 42–87.

10. Brown, *In Heaven as It Is*, chs. 7–8.

11. Jonathan A. Stapley, "Last Rites and the Dynamics of Mormon Liturgy," *BYU Studies* 50, no. 2 (2011): 97–128.

12. Richard E. Bennett, "'Line upon Line, Precept upon Precept': Reflections on the 1877 Commencement of the Performance of Endowments and Sealings for the Dead," *BYU Studies* 44, no. 3 (2005): 39–77.

13. Stapley, "Last Rites."

14. Stapley and Wright, "Female Ritual Healing," 11–19.

15. William G. Hartley, "The Priesthood Reform Movement, 1908–1922," *BYU Studies* 13 (Winter 1973): 137–156; William G. Hartley, "From Men to Boys: LDS Aaronic Priesthood Offices, 1829–1996," *Journal of Mormon History* 22 (Spring 1996): 115–117; Thomas G. Alexander, *Mormonism in Transition: A History of the Latter-day Saints, 1890–1930* (Urbana: University of Illinois Press, 1986), 93–115.

16. Dale C. Mouritsen, "A Symbol of New Directions: George F. Richards and the Mormon Church, 1861–1950" (Ph.D. diss., Brigham Young University, 1982), 203–210; Alexander, *Mormonism in Transition*, 302; Stapley and Wright, "Female Ritual Healing."

17. Stapley and Wright, "'They Shall Be Made Whole,'" 69–112; Stapley, "Last Rites."

CHAPTER 1

1. Ordination of Wilkins Jenkins Salisbury, Ordinations of the Seventy, March 1, 1835, Minute Book 1, 176, in JSP W.

2. Osmer D. Flake, diary, December 6–15, 1897, digital images of holograph, MSS 1564, LTPSC.

3. Seymour B. Young, diary, December 15, 1897, MS 1345, Seymour B. Young Papers, CHL.

4. For examples of seventies' ordination texts during this period, see the following texts at the CHL: Ordination of Jos. H. Goff, May 19, 1893, photocopy of type-script, MS 21735, J. H. Willard Goff Mission Papers; Ordination of Charles Homer Wentz, April 18, 1897, microfilm of typescript, MS 7960 1, Charles H. Wentz Papers; Ordination and Setting Apart of Heber Brooks Bryce, April 11, 1898, digital images of typescript, MS 20984, Box 1, Folder 1, Marden Elbert Alder Papers 1851–1978; Ordination of John Widtsoe, August 5, 1898, digital copy of typescript, MS 7692, Box 33, Folder 3, Susa Young Gates Papers.

5. Joseph Smith, et al., "Church History," *Times and Seasons* 3, no. 9 (March 1, 1842): 709. Smith and/or his scribes based this text on earlier documents by Orson and Parley Pratt. See JSP H1, xxxiv, 520, 540, 542.

6. Oliver Cowdery, "Articles of the Church of Christ," in JSP D1, 367–373.

7. Joseph Smith, "Articles and Covenants," in ibid., 116–126 [D&C 20].

8. Cessationist dissenters frequently viewed ordination by the laying on of hands as categorically similar to healing rituals and miracles, which had ceased after the death of the biblical apostles. Jane Shaw, *Miracles in Enlightenment England* (New Haven: Yale University Press, 2006), 46; Charles Buck, "Imposition of Hands," in *A Theological Dictionary, Containing Definitions of All Religious Terms; A Comprehensive View of Every Article in the System of Divinity, an Impartial Account of All the Principal Denominations Which Have Subsisted in the Religious World, from the Birth of Christ to the Present Day: Together with an Accurate Statement of the Most Remarkable Transactions and Events Recorded in Ecclesiastical History*, 4th American ed. (Philadelphia: A. Griggs & Dickinson, 1815), 216–217.

9. *The Book of Mormon: An Account Written by the Hand of Mormon, upon Plates Taken from the Plates of Nephi* (Palmyra, NY: Joseph Smith Jr., 1830), 519, 535, 580 [Ether 12:12–18; Mormon 1:13–14, 9:7–9; Moroni 7:37–38].

10. See, e.g., Parley P. Pratt, *A Voice of Warning and Instruction to All People, Containing a Declaration of the Faith and Doctrine of the Church of the Latter Day Saints, Commonly Called Mormons* (New York: W. Sanford, 1837), 204, 211–212; John Hardy, *Hypocrisy Exposed, or J. V. Himes Weighed in the Balances of Truth, Honesty and Common Sense, and Found Wanting; Being a Reply to a Pamphlet Put Forth by Him, Entitled Mormon Delusions and Monstrosities* (Boston: Albert Morgan, 1842), 3, 6–7; William I. Appleby, *A Few Important Questions for the Reverend Clergy to Answer, Being a Scale to Weigh Priestcraft and Sectarianism In* (Philadelphia: Brown, Bicking & Guilbert, 1843), 10–11; John Taylor, *Truth Defended and Methodism Weighed in the Balance and Found Wanting: Being a Reply to the Third Address of the Rev. Robert Heys, Wesleyan Minister to the Wesleyan Methodist Societies in Douglas and Its Vicinity, and Also an Exposure of the Principles of Methodism* (Liverpool: J. Tompkins, 1841), 12.

11. *The Book of Mormon*, 112–113, 534 [2 Nephi 28:5–6; Mormon 8:28].

12. *The Book of Mormon*, 186 [Mosiah 15:3].

13. *The Book of Mormon*, i, 548, 533, 110, 150 [Introduction; Ether 5:3–4; Mormon 8:16; 2 Nephi 27:12; Omni 1:20]; Joseph Smith, revelation, March 1829, in JSP D1, 18 [D&C 5].

14. *The Book of Mormon*, 264 [Alma 19:24–27].

15. *The Book of Mormon*, 327 [Alma 37:18–19].

16. *The Book of Mormon*, 28–32 [1 Nephi 13].

17. *The Book of Mormon*, 142, 276, 309 [Jacob 7:21; Alma 19:6, 30:52].

18. *The Book of Mormon*, 329, 389 [Alma 37:40; Alma 57:26].

19. *The Book of Mormon*, 577–580, 586 [Moroni 7; Moroni 10:7]. See also ibid., 264 [Alma 19:26–28].

20. With regard to healing, see Jonathan A. Stapley and Kristine Wright, "The Forms and the Power: The Development of Mormon Ritual Healing to 1847," *Journal of Mormon History* 35 (Summer 2009): 42–71.

21. First Theological Lecture on Faith, "Theology. Lecture First on the Doctrine of the Church of the Latter Day Saints," ca. Feb. 1835, digital image of broadside, JSP W.

22. *The Book of Mormon*, 476–479 [3 Nephi 11:18–12:2].

23. *The Book of Mormon*, 574 [Moroni 2].

24. *The Book of Mormon*, 575–576 [Moroni 3–6]. For an example of the distinction between "officers" and "members," see Orson Hyde, diary, December 2, 1832, digital images of holograph, MS 1386, CHL.

25. "Old Testament Manuscript 1," in Scott H. Faulring, Kent P. Jackson, and Robert J. Mathews, *Joseph Smith's New Translation of the Bible: Original Manuscripts* (Provo, UT: BYU Religious Studies Center, 2004), 127 [Joseph Smith Translation, Genesis 14:30–31].

26. Stapley and Wright, "Forms and the Power," 55–56.

27. Parley P. Pratt, *Autobiography of Parley Parker Pratt, One of the Twelve Apostles of the Church of Jesus Christ of Latter-Day Saints, Embracing His Life, Ministry and Travels, with Extracts, in Prose and Verse, from His Miscellaneous Writings*, edited by. Parley P. Pratt [his son] (New York: Russell Brothers, 1874), 325 (emphasis in original). For more sources relating to this event, see Stapley and Wright, "Forms and the Power," n. 1. The accusation that one had the forms without the power was a bitter critique that invoked Paul's biblical prophecy of apostasy.

28. Joseph Smith, sermon, April 28, 1842, in FFY, 55–57. See chapter 4 and Jonathan Stapley and Kristine Wright, "Female Ritual Healing in Mormonism," *Journal of Mormon History* 37 (Winter 2011): 6–7.

29. See extended discussion in Stapley and Wright, "The Forms and the Power."

30. Joseph Smith, revelation, January 2, 1831, and revelation, February 1831–A, in JSP D1, 232–233, 258 [D&C 38:32, 38; D&C 43:16].

31. Joseph Smith, sermon account, November 12, 1835, in JSP J1, 98. See also Joseph Smith, revelation, June 1, 1833 in JSP D3, 106–107 [D&C 95:9].

32. Samuel M. Brown, *In Heaven as It Is on Earth: Joseph Smith and the Early Mormon Conquest of Death* (New York: Oxford University Press, 2012), 157–162.

33. JSP J1, 215–216 [March 30, 1836].

34. Stapley and Wright, "Forms and the Power," 71–75. Brown, *In Heaven as It Is*, chs. 7–8.

35. Kathleen Flake, *The Politics of American Religious Identity: The Seating of Senator Reed Smoot, Mormon Apostle* (Chapel Hill: University of North Carolina Press, 2004), ch. 5.

36. Christopher C. Jones, "The Power and Form of Godliness: Methodist Conversion Narratives and Joseph Smith's First Vision," *Journal of Mormon History* 37, no. 2 (Spring 2011): 88–114.

37. See Robin Scott Jensen, "'Rely upon the Things Which Are Written': Text, Context, and the Creation of Mormon Revelatory Records" (MLIS thesis, University of Wisconsin–Milwaukee, 2009), 151–172.

38. William V. Smith, "Early Mormon Priesthood Revelations: Text, Impact, and Evolution," *Dialogue: A Journal of Mormon Thought* 46, no. 4 (Winter 2013): 1–84. See also Gregory A. Prince, "Mormon Priesthood and Organization," in *The Oxford Handbook of Mormonism*, edited by Terryl L. Givens and Philip L. Barlow (New York: Oxford University Press, 2015), 167–181.

39. *The Book of Mormon*, 575 [Moroni 3].

40. There is some evidence that the office of priest constituted the "lesser priesthood" in the first years of the church, and that deacons and teachers were not priesthood offices but were instead nonpriesthood ecclesiastical offices. Smith, "Early Mormon Priesthood Revelations."

41. Joseph Smith, revelation, June 1829b, in JSP D1, 72–73 [D&C 18:29–30].

42. While the Articles and Covenants of the church clearly delineated that the office of priest was required to ordain deacons, teachers, and priests, the offices that came to be organized under the Melchizedek Priesthood had no similar clarity. The result was that there remained some controversy for over one hundred years over which offices in the Melchizedek Priesthood had authority to ordain other offices. A prominent example of this confusion was the debate over whether seventies had the authority to ordain bishops. See, e.g., Edward Leo Lyman, ed., *Candid Insights of a Mormon Apostle: The Diaries of Abraham H. Cannon, 1889–1895* (Salt Lake City: Signature Books, 2010), 273 [November 19, 1891]. Joseph F. Smith largely solved the problem by ordaining officers to be high priests, as well as apostles, seventies, and patriarchs. Smith, "Early Mormon Priesthood Revelations."

43. The office of chief patriarch jumped from one descendant of the elder Smith to another for over 140 years before it became too incongruous with a church that had anchored itself to the 1835 priesthood texts. Irene Bates and E. Gary Smith, *Lost Legacy: The Mormon Office of Presiding Patriarch* (Urbana: University of Illinois Press, 2003).

44. JSP J1, 1:239 [D&C 113:5–8]. See also Joseph Smith, revelation, December 6, 1832, in JSP D2, 324–327 [D&C 8, 6:8–10].

45. Anne Taves, "History and the Claims of Revelation: Joseph Smith and the Materialization of the Golden Plates," *Numen: International Review for the History of Religions* 61, nos. 2/3 (2014): 182–207.

46. This sentiment was reiterated by Joseph Smith's comments on the fate of the unsealed as separate, single, and alone. Andrew F. Ehat and Lyndon W. Cook, ed., *Words of Joseph Smith: The Contemporary Accounts of the Nauvoo Discourses of the Prophet Joseph* (Provo, Utah: BYU Religious Studies Center, 1980), 232. See also George D. Smith, *An Intimate Chronicle: The Journals of William Clayton* (Salt Lake City: Signature Books, 1995), 104 [May 18, 1843]; Joseph Smith, revelation,

July 12, 1843, digital images of manuscripts, MS 4583, Box 1, Folder 75, Revelations Collection ca. 1831–1876, CHL [D&C 132:15–17].

47. On the perseverance bestowed by Mormon sealings, see chapter 2.

48. Jonathan A. Stapley, "Adoptive Sealing Ritual in Mormonism," *Journal of Mormon History* 37 (Summer 2011): 56–65; Laurel Thatcher Ulrich, *A House Full of Females: Plural Marriage and Women's Rights in Early Mormonism, 1835–1870* (New York: Alfred A. Knopf, 2017), 88–91.

49. Brigham Young, office journal, January 12, 1846, Box 71, Folder 4, BYOF. Joseph Smith spoke about church members receiving the "keys of the kingdom" through the temple liturgy. Joseph Smith, sermon, April 28, 1842, in FFY, 57; Joseph Smith, sermon, May 1, 1842, in JSP J2, 53.

50. Joseph Smith, revelation, July 27, 1842, Box 1, Folder 104, Revelations Collection ca. 1831–1876, CHL.

51. Ulrich, *House Full of Females*, 131.

52. Stephen Fleming, "The Fulness of the Gospel: Christian Platonism and the Origins of Mormonism" (Ph.D. diss., University of California, Santa Barbara, 2014), 351–385.

53. It is not immediately clear why Smith and Young waited for completion of the temple to perform child-to-parent sealings. See Stapley, "Adoptive Sealing Ritual in Mormonism," 59.

54. Ibid., 67–71.

55. The most comprehensive treatment of this shift is W. Paul Reeve, *Religion of a Different Color: Race and the Mormon Struggle for Whiteness* (New York: Oxford University Press, 2015), esp. chs. 3–5.

56. Historian's Office General Church Minutes, February 13, 1849, digital images of manuscript, CR 100 318, Box 2, Folder 8, CHL.

57. Brigham Young, "Pres. B. Young's dream Feb.y 17, 1847," Box 75, Folder 34, BYOF. See Stapley, "Adoptive Sealing Ritual in Mormonism," 79–81.

58. On Jane Manning James, see Quincy D. Newell, "'Is There No Blessing for Me?': Jane James's Construction of Space in Latter-day Saint History and Practice," in *New Perspectives in Mormon Studies: Creating and Crossing Boundaries*, edited by Quincy D. Newell and Eric F. Mason (Norman: University of Oklahoma Press, 2012), 41–68.

59. Stapley, "Adoptive Sealing Ritual in Mormonism," 99–115.

60. Wilford Woodruff, April 8, 1894, in CD, 4:67–75.

61. Stapley, "Adoptive Sealing Ritual," 113–115. See also discussion in later chapters.

62. Reeve, *Religion of a Different Color*, ch. 6.

63. Stapley, "Adoptive Sealing Ritual in Mormonism," 74–90.

64. Brigham Young, sermon, August 11, 1872, in JD, 126–128.

65. Smith, "Early Mormon Priesthood Revelations," 39–46.

66. An interesting antecedent ordination formula for bishops was produced by Brigham Young and George Cannon in which candidates were ordained as seventies and

then set apart as bishops. Form of ordinations of bishops, undated, Box 75, Folder 27, BYOF.

67. Lyman, *Candid Insights*, 592 [January 24, 1895]; example ordinances, ca. 1897, in Linn M. Davis mission priesthood ordinances [handwritten at the end of George Q. Cannon, *Ready References* (Salt Lake City: George Q. Cannon & Sons, 1891)], microfilm of holograph, MS 22494, CHL. For an example of a setting apart of a high priest, see Thomas Memmott, journal, January 24, 1903, microfilm of holograph, MS 8696, CHL.

68. George Q. Cannon, "Editorial Thoughts," *Juvenile Instructor* 29 (February 15, 1894): 114.

69. John Taylor, letter to Thomas Memmott, January 8, 1887, FPL; Thomas Memmott, journal, January 8, 1887. In 1896 George Q. Cannon published an argument for following the ordination text in the Book of Mormon and keeping the ritual simple. George Q. Cannon, "Editorial Thoughts," *Juvenile Instructor* 31 (March 15, 1896): 174–175.

70. William B. Smart, ed., *Mormonism's Last Colonizer: The Journals of William H. Smart, April 11, 1898–October 24, 1937*, CD-ROM, April 2, 1901, 469, included with William B. Smart, *Mormonism's Last Colonizer: The Life and Times of William H. Smart* (Logan: Utah State University Press, 2008). Two decades later, Apostle James Talmage sustained this same argument but determined that conferring the entire priesthood was nevertheless appropriate. James E. Talmage, letter to Ralph P. Morgan, February 9, 1923, MS 1232, Box 6, Folder 28, James E. Talmage Collection, CHL.

71. Joseph F. Smith, "Answers to Questions," *Improvement Era* 4 (March 1901): 394. See also Joseph F. Smith, "Restoration of the Melchisedec Priesthood," *Contributor* 10 (June 1899): 307–311.

72. Minutes of weekly meeting of the First Presidency and Twelve, April 24, 1902, in JH, April 24, 1902, 11–12.

73. Rudger Clawson, letter to J. S. McCann, December 9, 1911, in London Conference, British Mission, Book of Instructions, 53, LR 5006 34, CHL. An ordination text used in France and Switzerland during this same period employed the new form. French ordination text, ca. 1913, unpaginated journal, MS 18330, Box 1, Folder 3, Hans A. Davidson Papers, 1913–1915, CHL.

74. Dale C. Mouritsen, "A Symbol of New Directions: George Franklin Richards and the Mormon Church, 1861–1950" (Ph.D. diss., Brigham Young University, 1982), 152. Mouritsen cites Richards's diary as the source of this instruction, a document that is currently restricted from use in the CHL.

75. John P. Hatch, *Danish Apostle: The Diaries of Anthon Lund, 1890–1921* (Salt Lake City: Signature Books, 2006), 750 [September 10, 1919].

76. Heber J. Grant, Anthon H. Lund, and Charles W. Penrose, "Addenda," in *Gospel Doctrine: Selections from the Sermons and Writings of Joseph F. Smith*, 2nd ed. (Salt Lake City: Deseret News, 1919 [1920]), 686–687. The source for these statements

is likely First Presidency and Quorum of the Twelve Minutes, April 13, 1899, in JH, April 13, 1899. Heber J. Grant later attributed similar language to Joseph F. Smith. Heber J. Grant, letter to Burton Dye, August 30, 1935, in FPL. This position is similar to that taken by George Q. Cannon, in "Editorial Thoughts," *Juvenile Instructor* 29 (February 15, 1894): 114.

77. Hatch, *Danish Apostle*, 751.

78. Devery S. Anderson, *Development of LDS Temple Worship, 1846–2000: A Documentary History* (Salt Lake City: Signature Books, 2011), 181–182. As an example of apostolic support for Joseph F. Smith's ordination pattern at this time, see James E. Talmage, letter to J. W. Nixon, April 18, 1918, Box 6, Folder 31, James E. Talmage Collection. On the shift away from the pattern, see John A. Widtsoe, Letter to Preston D. Richards, June 1, 1939, John A. Widtsoe papers, CHL.

79. See, e.g., minutes of the Council of the First Presidency and Quorum of the Twelve, February 24, 1898, in JH, February 24, 1898, 2; "Ordinances and Ceremonies," *Improvement Era* 51 (November 1948): 731.

80. See, e.g., *The Elders' Manual* (Independence, MO: Press of Zion's Printing and Publishing Company, [191?]), 39–40; George S. Romney, *The Missionary Guide: A Key to Effective Missionary Work* (Independence, MO: Zion's Printing and Publishing Company, [193?]), 101–102; Church of Jesus Christ of Latter-day Saints, *The Missionary Hand Book* (Independence, MO: Zion's Printing and Publishing Company, 1937, 1940, 1944, 1946 [rev. ed.]), 137 [141, 1946 ed.]. It appears that missionaries began circulating ritual texts in the late 1890s, before these official publications became available. Minutes of the Council of the First Presidency and Quorum of the Twelve, February 24, 1898, in JH, February 24, 1898, 2.

81. *Handbook of Instructions for Bishops and Counselors Stake and Ward Clerks*, no. 14 (n.p., 1928), 14; *Handbook of Instructions for Stake Presidencies, Bishops and Counselors, Stake and Ward Clerks*, no. 15 (n.p., 1934), 15; *Handbook of Instructions for Stake Presidencies, Bishops and Counselors, Stake and Ward Clerks and Other Church Officers*, no. 16 (n.p., 1940), 17–18; *Aaronic Priesthood Handbook* (Salt Lake City: Presiding Bishopric, 1941), 27. See also David O. McKay, letter to James M. Kirkham, December 7, 1934, in FPL.

82. See, e.g., Bruce R. McConkie, "Ordination," in *Mormon Doctrine* (Salt Lake City: Bookcraft, 1958), 496–497. McConkie also served on the Priesthood Correlation Committee that added the new ordination text to the handbooks.

83. Council Meeting Minutes, January 31, 1957, in Items for Meeting with Temple Presidents, in David O. McKay, diary, April 7, 1957, MS 668, David Oman McKay Papers, JWML.

84. *Melchizedek Priesthood Handbook* (Salt Lake City: Church of Jesus Christ of Latter-day Saints, 1964), 43; *General Handbook of Instruction*, no. 20 (Salt Lake City: First Presidency of the Church of Jesus Christ of Latter-day Saints, 1968), 88.

85. See chapter 4.

86. For example, the high priest quorums and their presidencies were dissolved in 1968, with the stake presidency taking the de facto role of the presidency over the high priests. Before this time, the stake president had not had "keys" in the sense of being a quorum president.

87. Vandenberg had stated that God had given the Aaronic Priesthood holders "his power on earth, the same power by which this earth and other worlds were created; the same power by which the waters of the Red Sea were parted; the same power by which Elijah sealed the heavens so that no rain fell upon the earth; the same power by which Jesus gave sight to the blind, legs to the lame, and new life to the dead." *Conference Report* (April 1970), 59.

88. N. Eldon Tanner, *Conference Report* (April 1970), 61.

89. *True to the Faith: A Gospel Reference* (Salt Lake City: Church of Jesus Christ of Latter-day Saints, 2004), 124; *Handbook 2: Administering the Church* (Salt Lake City: Church of Jesus Christ of Latter-day Saints, 2010), 8; *Doctrinal Mastery: Core Document* (Salt Lake City: Church of Jesus Christ of Latter-day Saints, 2016), 9.

90. Martha Sontag Bradley, *Pedestals and Podiums: Utah Women, Religious Authority, and Equal Rights* (Salt Lake City: Signature Books, 2005).

91. Kristen Moulton, "Mormon women shut out of all-male priesthood meeting," *Salt Lake Tribune*, October 18, 2013, http://archive.sltrib.com/story.php?ref=/sltrib/news/56963037-78/women-mormon-church-priesthood.html.csp; Joseph Walker, "LDS Church responds to priesthood meeting request by activists," *Deseret News*, September 24, 2013, http://www.deseretnews.com/article/865586996/LDS-Church-responds-to-priesthood-meeting-request-by-activists.html?pg=all.

92. Carolyn J. Rasmus, "Mormon Women: A Convert's Perspective," *Ensign* (August 1980), 66–70.

93. Sheri Dew, *Women and the Priesthood: What One Mormon Woman Believes* (Salt Lake City: Deseret Book, 2013), 109.

94. Ibid., 109. In this article Dew makes a number of other suggestions foreign to the context of early Mormonism and the historical record: "Was the prophet's reference to 'administering to the sick' referring to prayers of faith and comfort rather than a priesthood ordinance? Had issues regarding women and the priesthood not yet been fully revealed? Was he anticipating women officiating in priesthood ordinances in the temple? Were there reasons the Lord allowed women to give blessings of healing—as distinct from performing actual ordinances—during those turbulent days in Nauvoo when illness threatened the Saints constantly, priesthood bearers were frequently away from the home, and women often found themselves caring for their families alone? I don't know if any of these explanations are correct, though all would seem to be possibilities." Ibid, 109–110.

95. See, e.g., D. Michael Quinn, "Mormon Women Have Had the Priesthood Since 1843"; Linda King Newell, "The Historical Relationship of Mormon Women and Priesthood"; and Margaret Merrill Toscano, "Put on Strength O Daughters of Zion:

Claiming Priesthood and Knowing the Mother," all in *Women and Authority: Re-emerging Mormon Feminism*, edited by Maxine Hanks (Salt Lake City: Signature Books, 1992), 23–48, 365–410, 411–438.

96. Maxine Hanks, "Introduction," in Hanks, *Women and Authority*, xxvii; and Maxine Hanks, "Sister Missionaries and Authority," in Hanks, *Women and Authority*, 324.

97. M. Russell Ballard, "'This Is My Work and My Glory,'" *Ensign* (May 2013), 18.

98. Robert D. Hales, "Blessings of the Priesthood," *Ensign* (November 1995), 32–34; *True to the Faith*, 9; Council of the First Presidency and Quorum of the Twelve Apostles of the Church of Jesus Christ of Latter-day Saints, circular letter, June 28, 2014, https://www.lds.org/bc/content/ldsorg/prophets-and-apostles/recent-messages/june-first-presidency-statement.pdf.

99. "Transcript: Top Mormon Women Leaders Provide Their Insights into Church Leadership," Mormon Newsroom, n.d., http://www.mormonnewsroom.org/article/transcript-mormon-women-leaders-insights-church-leadership.

100. M. Russell Ballard, "Let Us Think Straight," August 20, 2013, https://speeches.byu.edu/talks/m-russell-ballard_let-us-think-straight-2/.

101. Dallin H. Oaks, sermon, August 18, 2013, Ben Lomand Stake Conference, Ogden High School Auditorium, recording and transcript in my possession.

102. Joseph Fielding Smith, "Relief Society—an Aid to the Priesthood," *Relief Society Magazine* 46 (January 1959): 4. In this sermon he also references the temple cosmology: "It is within the privilege of the sisters of this Church to receive exaltation in the kingdom of God and receive authority and power as queens and priestesses, and I am sure if they have that power they have some power to rule and reign. Else why would they be priestesses?" Ibid., 5–6. Smith was particular about distinguishing between priesthood and other authority in the church. For example, he suggested that setting apart teachers was not desirable because that would open the door to the conflation of priesthood and the authority to teach. Bruce R. McConkie, comp., *Doctrines of Salvation: Sermons and Writings of Joseph Fielding Smith*, 3 vols. (Salt Lake City: Bookcraft, 1954–1956), 3:106–107.

103. Dallin H. Oaks, "The Keys and Authority of the Priesthood," *Ensign* (May 2014), 49–52. An interesting developmental contrast with this sermon is the address Oaks delivered at the October 2005 General Conference, "Priesthood Authority in the Family and the Church," *Ensign* (November 2005), 24–27.

104. Church of Jesus Christ of Latter-day Saints, "June: Priesthood and Priesthood Keys," (accessed May 9, 2013) and "What are my responsibilities in the work of the priesthood," (accessed January 15, 2015) https://www.lds.org/youth/learn/yw/priesthood-keys?lang=eng. For a comparison of the changes, see Laura Compton, "YW Lesson Comparisons June 2013 to June 2014," https://drive.google.com/file/d/0B5IILxCHTVLueHpLbld5SVU5N0E/.

105. David Dickson, "A Great Work—and You're Doing It," *New Era* (June 2016), 15.

106. Linda K. Burton, "Priesthood Power—Available to All," *Ensign* (June 2014), 38.

107. Dew, *Women and the Priesthood*, 102, 104, 105, 121, 125–126, 101.

108. "Priesthood Power through Keeping Covenants," *Ensign* (June 2017), 7.

109. Church of Jesus Christ of Latter-day Saints, "Joseph Smith's Teachings on Women, the Temple, and Priesthood," https://www.lds.org/topics/joseph-smiths-teachings-about-priesthood-temple-and-women?lang=eng. See also Jennifer Reeder and Kate Holbrook, eds., *At the Pulpit: 185 Years of Discourses by Latter-day Saint Women* (Salt Lake City: Church Historian's Press, 2017), xxiii, n. 53.

110. Tally S. Payne, "'Our Wise and Prudent Women': Twentieth-Century Trends in Female Missionary Service," in *New Scholarship on Latter-day Saint Women in the Twentieth Century*, edited by Carol Cornwall Madsen and Cherry B. Silver (Provo, UT: Joseph Fielding Smith Institute for Latter-day Saint History, 2005), 125–140.

111. For an example setting-apart text for a female missionary in 1903, see Hyrum M. Smith, "Setting Apart Blessing," digital images of typescript, MS 26203, Image 39, Adams Family Scrapbook, 1903–1960, CHL.

CHAPTER 2

1. Joseph Smith, revelation, July 12, 1843, digital copy of manuscripts, MS 4583, Box 1, Folder 75, Revelations Collection, ca. 1829–1876, CHL.

2. Mary Glover Johnson, "The Life Story of Mary Glover Johnson," ca. 1940, typescript in author's possession. European Mission emigration records, 1849–1925, microfilm of manuscript, Book 1042, 251, 305, CR 271 25, CHL.

3. Mary Glover and Jane C. Johnson, letter to the First Presidency, June 18, 1884, holograph, Vault MSS 790, Box 3, Folder 9, L. John Nuttall Papers, LTPSC; W. D. Johnson, Jr., letter, February 4, 1884, Box 3, Folder 8, L. John Nuttall Papers.

4. L. John Nuttall, letter to Jane C. Johnson and Mary Glover Johnson, November 22, 1884, holograph, Box 4, Book 3, 245, L. John Nuttall Papers. For similar examples, see Wilford Woodruff and Joseph F. Smith, letter to J.D.T. McAllister, April 26, 1894, FPL.

5. On LDS funerary rituals, see Jonathan A. Stapley, "Last Rites and the Dynamics of Latter-day Saint Liturgy," *BYU Studies* 50, no. 2 (2011): 97–128.

6. Account in author's possession.

7. Samuel M. Brown, *In Heaven as It Is on Earth: Joseph Smith and the Early Mormon Conquest of Death* (New York: Oxford University Press, 2012), 146–149, 164–169; William V. Smith, *Textual Studies of the Doctrine and Covenants: The Plural Marriage Revelation* (Salt Lake City: Kofford Books, forthcoming).

8. Smith stated that "the power of Elijah is sufficient to make our calling & Election sure." Andrew F. Ehat and Lyndon W. Cook, *Words of Joseph Smith: The Contemporary Accounts of the Nauvoo Discourses of the Prophet Joseph* (Orem, UT: Religious Studies Center, 1980), 330 [March 10, 1844].

9. Ibid., 318 [January 21, 1844], 334 [March 10, 1844].

10. Ibid., 232 [July 16, 1843]. See also George D. Smith, *An Intimate Chronicle: The Journals of William Clayton* (Salt Lake City: Signature Books, 1995), 104 [May 18, 1843]; Joseph Smith, revelation, July 12, 1843 [D&C 132].

11. Joseph F. Smith, comp., "Sealings and Adoption, 1846–1857," ca. 1869–1870, microfilm 183374, Special Collections, FHL; Donald G. Godfrey and Brigham Y. Card, eds., *The Diaries of Charles Ora Card: The Canadian Years 1886–1903* (Salt Lake City: University of Utah Press, 1993), 573; Jean Bickmore White, ed., *Church, State, and Politics: The Diaries of John Henry Smith* (Salt Lake City: Signature Books, 1990), 258; Stan Larson, ed., *A Ministry of Minutes: The Apostolic Diaries of Rudger Clawson* (Salt Lake City: Signature Books, 1993), 411, 430; First Presidency and Quorum of the Twelve Meeting Minutes, September 29, 1904, in JH, September 29, 1904, 12.

12. *The Humble Advice of the Assembly of Divines, Now by Authority of Parliament Sitting at Westminster, Concerning a Confession of Faith: With the Quotations and Texts of Scripture Annexed. Presented by Them Lately to Both Houses of Parliament* (Edinburgh: Evan Tyler, 1647), 636.

13. Orson Spencer, *Letters Exhibiting the Most Prominent Doctrines of the Church of Jesus Christ of Latter-day Saints . . . In Reply to the Rev. William Crowell, A. M., Boston, Massachusetts, U.S.A.* (Liverpool: Orson Spencer, 1848), 169–171. Though employed to describe the cosmological priesthood here, this phrase was not uncommon among other Christian groups during this period and was likely drawn from 1 Samuel 25:29.

14. Ehat and Cook, *Words of Joseph Smith*, 241–242 [August 13, 1843]. See also the account in Howard Coray and Martha Jane Knowlton Coray, "Notebook," in ibid., 240–241.

15. Joseph Smith, revelation, July 27, 1842, Box 1, Folder 104, Revelations Collection, ca. 1831–1876.

16. Smith, *Textual Studies*.

17. "Antinomianism" is generally employed as an epithet signaling heresy in the broader Christian community. The term has various meanings, but the root idea is the proposition that if one is saved by (typically irresistible) grace, then one's actions cannot be held to any other standard or laws. The caricature of this proposition is that those who are saved do not need to live by rules in order to retain that salvation.

18. Joseph Smith, sermon account, between ca. 26 June and ca. 2 July 1839, reported by Willard Richards, JSP W; Joseph Smith, revelation, January 19, 1841, in "Book of the Law of the Lord," JSP W [D&C124:124]; Joseph Smith, revelation, July 12, 1843 [D&C 132:18]; Smith, *Textual Studies*. These excerpts evoke Ephesians 1:13 and Matthew 23:31–32. For later consistent readings on the idea of the "Holy Spirit of Promise," as the sealing power see "Editorial," *Elders' Journal* 3, no. 2 (September 15, 1905): 26; Charles R. Brashear, letter to James Talmage, November 13, 1922; and James Talmage, letter to Charles R. Brashear, November 27, 1922, both digital images of manuscripts, MS 1232, Box 23, Folder 11, James E. Talmage Collection, CHL.

19. Joseph Smith, revelation, July 12, 1843, 4 [D&C 132:19].

20. Vilate Kimball, letter to Heber C. Kimball, June 8, 1844, in *Life of Heber C. Kimball, an Apostle; the Father and Founder of the British Mission* (Salt Lake City: Kimball Family, 1888), 345; Stanley B. Kimball, *Heber C. Kimball: Mormon Patriarch and Pioneer* (Urbana and Chicago: University of Illinois Press, 1986), 100.

21. Ronald O. Barney, ed., *The Mormon Vanguard Brigade of 1847: Norton Jacob's Record* (Logan: Utah State University Press, 2005), 64.

22. Smith, "Sealings and Adoption," 517–518, 561–562.

23. See Smith, *Textual Studies*. Church leaders have interpreted the sin against the Holy Ghost variously, but in Nauvoo it appears to have been linked to an ultimate betrayal of Christ, i.e., "crucifying the Son of God afresh & putting him to an open shame," as well as to murder.

24. Ronald W. Walker, Richard E. Turley, and Glen M. Leonard, *Massacre at Mountain Meadows* (New York: Oxford University Press, 2008), 61.

25. Brigham Young, office journal, January 10, 1857, Box 72, Folder 3, BYOF. Young later described the grave as a "purifying place for mortals." Ibid., March 7, 1857.

26. Jonathan A. Stapley, "Adoptive Sealing Ritual in Mormonism," *Journal of Mormon History* 37 (Summer 2011): 85.

27. Brigham Young, office journal, December 4, 1860, Box 72, Folder 5, BYOF.

28. Brigham Young, sermon, April 29, 1866, in JD, 11:215.

29. Lisle G. Brown, *Nauvoo Sealings, Adoptions, and Anointings: A Comprehensive Register of Persons Receiving LDS Temple Ordinances 1841–1846* (Salt Lake City: Signature Books, 2006), 361.

30. Stapley, "Adoptive Sealing Ritual," 66.

31. Brigham Young, quoted in Scott G. Kenney, ed., *Wilford Woodruff's Journal, 1833–1898*, 9 vols. (Midvale, Utah: Signature Books, 1983–85), 3:134–137. See also Charles Kelly, ed., *The Journal of John D. Lee, 1846–47 and 1859* (Salt Lake City: University of Utah Press, 1984), 86–89.

32. Orson Pratt, "Celestial Marriage," *Seer* 1 (February 1853): 31–32. On the publication of this text, see Brigham Young, letter to Orson Pratt, June 1, 1853, Box 17, Folder 8, BYOF; and Orson Pratt, letter to Brigham Young, September 10, 1853, Box 41, Folder 2, BYOF.

33. Wilford Woodruff, letter to Samuel Roskelley, June 8, 1887, typescript, MSS 65, Box 2, Book 4, Samuel Roskelley Collection, MCL. Woodruff also instructed that proxy marriage sealings not be made to deceased sisters or aunts. Wilford Woodruff, letter to John Steele, May 9, 1889, MS 2683, Folder 3, John Steele Collection, CHL.

34. Robert Campbell and John M. Bernhisel, entry, July 29, 1868, in JSP J3, 120–121.

35. A. Karl Larson and Katherine Miles Larson, eds., *Diary of Charles Lowell Walker*, 2 vols. (Logan: Utah State University Press, 1980), 1:464–465 [August 15–17, 1877]; Donald G. Godfrey and Rebecca S. Martineau-McCarty, eds., *An Uncommon Common Pioneer: The Journals of James Henry Martineau, 1828–1918* (Provo, UT: Religious Studies Center, 2008), 296, 298, 300, 321–322 [June 6, July 14 and

August 20, 1884]; George Q. Cannon, journal, April 13, 1877, Church Historian's Press, https://www.churchhistorianspress.org/george-q-cannon/.

36. L. John Nuttall, letter to Samuel Claridge, January 23, 1880, Box 4, Book 1, 115–116, L. John Nuttall Papers.

37. Wilford Woodruff and George Q. Cannon, April 8, 1894, in CD, 4:67–75; Wilford Woodruff and George Q. Cannon, "The Law of Adoption," *Deseret Weekly*, April 21, 1894, 541–545; George Q. Cannon, "The Linking of Generations by the Law of Adoption—Equality in Temporal Affairs and How to Attain It," *Deseret Weekly*, May 26, 1894, 701–704.

38. James J. Farrell, *Inventing the American Way of Death, 1830–1920* (Philadelphia: Temple University Press, 1980), 84–85. The theological controversy over "future probations" also influenced Protestant missiology. William R. Hutchison, *The Modernist Impulse in American Protestantism* (Durham, NC: Duke University Press, 1992), 132–140.

39. Wilford Woodruff, April 8, 1894, in CD, 4:67–75.

40. Edward Leo Lyman, ed., *Candid Insights of a Mormon Apostle: The Diaries of Abraham H. Cannon, 1889–1895* (Salt Lake City: Signature Books, 2010), 491–492 [April 5, 1894]. See also George Q. Cannon, journal, April 5, 1894, CHL. On unmarried women and sealing, see Smith, *Textual Studies*.

41. George Q. Cannon, journal, April 5, 1894; cf. Lyman, *Candid Insights*, 491–492.

42. Stapley, "Adoptive Sealing Ritual in Mormonism," 83.

43. William V. Smith, *Every Word Seasoned with Grace: A Textual Study of the Funeral Sermons of Joseph Smith* (Salt Lake City: Kofford Books, forthcoming).

44. Lorenzo Snow, sermon, May 8, 1899, *Deseret News*, June 3, 1899.

45. For example, Joseph Fielding Smith sealed Ezra Taft Benson to his recently deceased and never-married cousin at the instigation of Benson's wife. See Gary Bergera, "'Weak-Kneed Republicans and Socialist Democrats': Ezra Taft Benson as U.S. Secretary of Agriculture, 1953–61, Part 2," *Dialogue: A Journal of Mormon Thought* 41 (Winter 2008): 83, n. 6.

46. Marybeth Raynes and Erin Parsons, "Single Cursedness: An Overview of LDS Authorities' Statements about Unmarried People," in *Multiply and Replenish: Mormon Essays on Sex and Family*, edited by Brent Corcoran (Salt Lake City: Signature Books, 1994), 217–227.

47. In a 2006 interview, Apostle Jeffrey R. Holland described this principle in relation to those not able to have children and lesbian, gay, bisexual, and transgender individuals, noting that "these conditions will not exist post-mortality." Jeffrey R. Holland, interview with Helen Whitney, March 4, 2006, http://www.pbs.org/mormons/interviews/holland.html.

48. Ezra Taft Benson, "To the Single Adult Sisters of the Church: An Address by President Ezra Taft Benson Delivered in the General Women's Meeting 24 September 1988" [pamphlet] (Salt Lake City: Church of Jesus Christ of Latter-day Saints, 1988).

49. Ezra Taft Benson, "To the Single Adult Brethren of the Church: An Address Given by President Ezra Taft Benson Delivered in the Priesthood Session of General Conference on 2 April 1988" [pamphlet] (Salt Lake City: Church of Jesus Christ of Latter-day Saints, 1988).

50. James Allen, Kahlile Mehr, and Jessie Embry, *Hearts Turned to the Fathers: A History of the Genealogical Society of Utah, 1894–1994* (Provo: BYU Studies Press, 1995), 44–47.

51. Stapley, "Adoptive Sealing Ritual in Mormonism," 96.

52. Council of the Twelve Meeting Minutes, May 5, 1954, photocopy of original typescript, MS 447, Box 18, Folder 12, Linda King Newell Papers, JWML. Bruce R. McConkie of the Quorum of the Twelve taught that polygamy would be reinstated during the Millennium. See McConkie, "Plural Marriage," in *Mormon Doctrine*, 2nd ed. (Salt Lake City: Bookcraft, 1966), 578.

53. President David McKay approved of the sealing of two single women to a deceased man in 1956 and affirmed the practice as a policy in 1966. David O. McKay, diary, October 30, 1956, and July 6, 1966, MS 668, David Oman McKay Papers, 1897–1983, JWML. For examples of a church leader being sealed to multiple deceased women in the first decade of the twentieth century, see Dale C. Mouritsen, "A Symbol of New Directions: George Franklin Richards and the Mormon Church, 1861–1950" (Ph.D. diss., Brigham Young University, 1982), 256–258.

54. Jake Garn, *Why I Believe* (Salt Lake City: Aspen Books, 1992), 13, quoted in Robert E. Wells, "Uniting Blended Families," *Ensign* (August 1997), 24–29.

55. Dallin H. Oaks, interview with Helen Whitney, http://www.mormonnewsroom.org/article/elder-oaks-interview-transcript-from-pbs-documentary. In 2011, Oaks published similar statements in a devotional volume advising Latter-day Saints on the subject of remarriage. Dallin H. Oaks, *Life's Lessons Learned* (Salt Lake City: Deseret Book, 2011), 143–148.

56. See, e.g., Carol Lynn Pearson, *The Ghost of Eternal Polygamy: Haunting the Hearts and Heaven of Mormon Women and Men* (n.p.: Pivot Point Books, 2016).

57. See, e.g., Edwin B. Firmage, *An Abundant Life: The Memoirs of Hugh B. Brown* (Salt Lake City: Signature Books, 1988), 117–120.

58. Ibid.; David O. McKay, diary, May 8, 1859, and October 21, 1968. As a potential antecedent, see Brigham Young, letter to Cooper, March 9, 1877, Box 11, Volume 16, BYOF.

59. Allen, Embry, and Mehr, *Hearts Turned to the Fathers*, 178–185.

60. Ibid., 304–305.

61. Minutes of the Meeting of the First Presidency, January 14, 1969, in David O. McKay, diary.

62. Allen, Embry, and Mehr, *Hearts Turned to the Fathers*, 305.

63. Minutes of the Meeting of the First Presidency, January 14, 1969. Hunter continued that "it was perfectly proper that in life a woman be sealed to only one husband, but after death and many years have passed and there are posterity from the lines of several husbands, it becomes a different situation." See also David O. McKay, diary, February 3, 1969, March 6, 1969.

64. *General Handbook of Instructions*, no. 21 (n.p.: Church of Jesus Christ of Latter-day Saints, 1976), 61–62.

65. First Presidency, circular letter, December 8, 1988, First Presidency Circulars, CHL.

66. *General Handbook of Instructions* (Salt Lake City: Church of Jesus Christ of Latter-day Saints, 1989), 6–5, 6–6.

67. *Handbook 1: Stake Presidents and Bishops* (Salt Lake City: Church of Jesus Christ of Latter-day Saints, 2010), 20–21.

68. For an example of sealing perseverance between couples in official church publications, see Hyrum M. Smith, *The Doctrine and Covenants, Containing Revelations Given to Joseph Smith, Jr., the Prophet with an Introduction and Historical and Exegetical Notes by Hyrum M. Smith, of the Council of the Twelve Apostles; Divided into Verses by Orson Pratt, Sen.* (Liverpool: George F. Richards, 1919), 1021. This commentary was redacted and replaced with comments to the contrary when the revised edition was published in 1957. Hyrum M. Smith and Janne Mattson Sjodahl, *The Doctrine and Covenants Containing Revelations Given to Joseph Smith, Jr., the Prophet: With an Introduction and Historical and Exegetical Notes* (Salt Lake City: Deseret Book, 1951), 829. See also Charles R. Brashear, letter to James Talmage, June 9, 1922; and James Talmage, letter to Charles R. Brashear, June 13, 1922, both in MS 1232, Box 23, Folder 11, James E. Talmage Collection, CHL.

69. Orson F. Whitney, sermon, April 7, 1829, *Conference Report* (April 1929), 110.

70. Joseph Fielding Smith, "The Blessing of Being Born under the Covenant," *Church News*, March 13, 1948, 8.

71. Bruce R. McConkie, comp., *Doctrines of Salvation: Sermons and Writings of Joseph Fielding Smith*, 3 vols. (Salt Lake City: Bookcraft, 1955), 2:91. McConkie later claimed in a controversial speech at Brigham Young University that perseverance of sealing relationships and second chances for salvation were "deadly heresies." Bruce McConkie, "Seven Deadly Heresies," June 1, 1980, https://speeches.byu.edu/talks/bruce-r-mcconkie_seven-deadly-heresies/.

72. Lee May, letter to John A. Widtsoe, January 21, 1946, John A. Widtsoe Papers, CHL.

73. John A. Widtsoe, letter to Lee May, January 24, 1946, John A. Widtsoe Papers.

74. See, e.g., Henry B. Eyring, "Our Perfect Example," *Ensign* (November 2009), 70–73; James E. Faust, "Dear Are the Sheep That Have Wandered," *Ensign* (May 2003), 61; "Hope for Parents of Wayward Children," *Ensign* (September 2002), 11; Gordon B. Hinckley, *Teachings of Gordon B. Hinckley* (Salt Lake City: Deseret Book, 1997), 54; Boyd K. Packer, "Our Moral Environment," *Ensign* (May 1992), 66.

75. David A. Bednar, "Faithful Parents and Wayward Children: Sustaining Hope While Overcoming Misunderstanding," *Ensign* (March 2014), 31.

76. McConkie, *Doctrines of Salvation*, 2:92. This statement was discussed by members of the First Presidency when they debated proxy sealings for one woman to multiple men. David O. McKay, diary, February 3, 1969. See also, ibid., February 14, 1964.

77. James A. Cullimore, "Q&A: Questions and Answers," *New Era* (December 1975), 14–15.

78. Thomas E. Daniels, who worked for the Genealogical Society, employed the term "eternal parentage" in the earliest publication of which I am aware. "I Have a Question," *Ensign* (March 1974), 22–24. See also *General Handbook of Instructions,* no. 21 (n.p.: Church of Jesus Christ of Latter-day Saints, 1976), 62; *Teachings of Presidents of the Church: Ezra Taft Benson* (Salt Lake City: Church of Jesus Christ of Latter-day Saints, 2014), 172; *Handbook 1: Stake Presidents and Bishops* (Salt Lake City: Church of Jesus Christ of Latter-day Saints, 2010), 21–22.

79. Ezra Taft Benson, letter to Milne family, February 19, 1988, quoted in Deborah Milne, *Reflections from a Broken Mirror: Spiritual Values I Learned as an LDS Child of Divorce* (Salt Lake City: Deseret Book, 1998), 146–147; Spencer W. Kimball, Marion G. Romney, and Gordon B. Hinckley, letter [date and recipient redacted], http://emp.byui.edu/ANDERSONR/itc/Doctrine_and_Covenants/sections101-138/section127-128/127_07templedivorce_tfp.htm.

80. *Handbook 1: Stake Presidents and Bishops* (Salt Lake City: Church of Jesus Christ of Latter-day Saints, 2010), 21–22.

81. Gordon B. Hinckley, Thomas Monson, and James E. Faust, letter, January 21, 1999, copy in author's possession.

82. See also the discussion in Smith, *Textual Studies.*

83. David O. McKay, diary, May 6, 1965, and February 10, 1966.

84. *General Handbook of Instructions,* no. 20 (Salt Lake City: First Presidency of the Church of Jesus Christ of Latter-day Saints, 1968), 102.

85. *General Handbook of Instructions* (n.p.: Church of Jesus Christ of Latter-day Saints,1983), 41, 64.

86. *General Handbook of Instructions: Book 1. Stake Presidencies and Bishoprics* (Salt Lake City: Church of Jesus Christ of Latter-day Saints, 1998), 74–76, 130.

87. *Handbook 1* [2010], 21.

88. Henry B. Eyring, Facebook post, August 7, 2016, https://www.facebook.com/lds.henry.b.eyring/.

89. See, e.g., Kerril Sue Rollins, "'Families Are Forever': New Church Film for Sharing the Gospel," *Ensign* (October 1982), 79–80; Church of Jesus Christ of Latter-day Saints, *Together Forever* [videocassette] (Bonneville Media Communications, 1988); Gordon B. Hinckley, "The Marriage That Endures," *Ensign* (July 2003), 2–7.

90. "Jennifer in GA," comment on Aaron R., "Temple Annulments and Temple Divorces," *By Common Consent,* March 30, 2016, https://bycommonconsent.com/2016/03/30/temple-annulments-and-temple-divorces/#comment-368813.

91. Email in my possession, April 3, 2016.

CHAPTER 3

1. Eliza R. Snow, excerpt from "Line's on the Death of Leonora Agnes," in Jill Mulvay Derr and Karen Lynn Davidson, edited and compiled by *Eliza R. Snow: The Complete Poetry* (Provo and Salt Lake City: Brigham Young University Press/

University of Utah Press, 2009), 357. On the idea that the resurrection was to be effected through familial lines, see Jonathan A. Stapley, "Adoptive Sealing Ritual in Mormonism," *Journal of Mormon History* 37 (Summer 2011): 73.

2. Scott G. Kenney, ed., *Wilford Woodruff's Journal, 1833–1898*, 9 vols. (Midvale, UT: Signature Books, 1983–1985), 5:109.

3. This idea has persisted through liturgical history to the present: families are currently allowed to name stillborn children and include them in personal genealogy, but these children are not to be included on church records and may not receive proxy temple rituals. See First Presidency, letter to Jed Tomlinson, January 8, 1894, FPL; "I Want to Know," *Church News*, July 11, 1948, 20C; *Handbook 2: Administering the Church* (n.p.: Church of Jesus Christ of Latter-day Saints, 2010), 21.3.10, 194.

4. Brian D. Spinks, *Early and Medieval Rituals and Theologies of Baptism: From the New Testament to the Council of Trent* (Burlington, VT: Ashgate, 2006), 129; Brian D. Spinks, *Reformation and Modern Rituals and Theologies of Baptism: From Luther to Contemporary Practices* (Burlington, VT: Ashgate, 2007), 18–19; Maxwell E. Johnson, *The Rites of Christian Initiation: Their Evolution and Interpretation*, 2nd rev. ed. (Collegeville, MN: Liturgical Press, 2007), esp. 265, 311, 329. Note that some pre-Reformation traditions required an individual to hold a Christian name, and thus in some instances renaming was required.

5. Anne S. Brown and David D. Hall, "Family Strategies and Religious Practice: Baptism and the Lord's Supper in Early New England," in *Lived Religion in America: Toward a History of Practice*, edited by David D. Hall (Princeton, NJ: Princeton University Press, 1997), 41–68.

6. E. Brooks Holifield, *The Covenant Sealed: The Development of Puritan Sacramental Theology in Old and New England, 1570–1720* (New Haven, CT: Yale University Press, 1974), 169–186; Edmund S. Morgan, *Visible Saints: The History of a Puritan Idea* (New York: New York University Press, 1963), 113–138. See also George M. Marsden, *Jonathan Edwards: A Life* (New Haven, CT: Yale University Press, 2003), 30–33.

7. Marsden, *Jonathan Edwards*, 354. Edwards's removal was also influenced by other conflicts with church member families.

8. Methodist Episcopal Church, *The Doctrines and Disciplines of the Methodist Episcopal Church* (New York: Methodist Episcopal Church, 1829), 102–103.

9. Janet Moore Lindman, *Bodies of Belief: Baptist Community in Early America* (Philadelphia: University of Pennsylvania Press, 2008), 117.

10. L. F. Greene, ed., *Writings of the Late Elder John Leland, Including Some Events in His Life, Written by Himself, with Additional Sketches, &c.* (New York: G. W. Wood, 1845), 120. See also John Sparks, *The Roots of Appalachian Christianity: The Life and Legacy of Elder Shubal Stearns* (Lexington: University Press of Kentucky, 2005), 44–45, 234; Lindman, *Bodies of Belief*, 73–74. For one example see John S. Moore, "John William's Journal," *Virginia Baptist Register* 17 (1978): 806 [July 23, 1771].

11. Lindman, *Bodies of Belief,* 89; David Benedict, *Fifty Years among the Baptists* (New York: Sheldon & Company, 1860), 163.

12. Today many churches that profess believer's baptism perform "baby dedication" rituals. The Woodland Hills Church in St. Paul, Minnesota, for example, holds regular child dedication services, professing "that all infants are destined for heaven should they die before they are old enough to enter into a personal relationship with Jesus Christ. We also believe the Bible teaches that baptism should take place after a person has made a personal choice to follow Jesus Christ." Woodland Hills Church, St. Paul, MN, http://whchurch.org/ministries/heroes-gate/baby-child-dedication.

13. "Articles and Covenants," in JSP D1, 125 [D&C 20:70].

14. "Articles of the Church of Christ," in JSP D1, 370–374.

15. Hyrum Smith, diary, 45–46, digital copy of holograph, MSS 774, LTPSC. Joseph Smith Sr. may have also given Joseph F. Smith an eighth-day blessing in 1838 while Hyrum was incarcerated. Caroline Fransis Angell Holbrook, "Autobiography," ca. 1905, 5, microfilm of typescript, MS 20168, CHL. On the provenance of this document, see Mary Diana Beach Willie, "Caroline Fransis Angell Davis Holbrook," ca. June 1953, microfilm of typescript, MS 20168, Folder 2, CHL.

16. This position was later made explicit in the last quarter of the nineteenth century. Hannah T. King, "The Three Eras," *Juvenile Instructor* 14 (October 15, 1879): 230; "[First Grade] Lesson II. Blessing Children," *Children's Friend* 1 (January 1902): 9–10. Eighth-day blessings may also be evocative of a revelation indicating that John the Baptist was ordained to the priesthood at eight days old. Joseph Smith, revelation, September 22–23, 1832, in JSP D2, 296 [D&C 84:28].

17. "Old Testament Manuscript 1," in *Joseph Smith's New Translation of the Bible: Original Manuscripts,* edited by Scott H. Faulring, Kent P. Jackson, and Robert J. Mathews (Provo, UT: BYU Religious Studies Center, 2004), 132 [Genesis 17:11].

18. Brown and Hall, "Family Strategies and Religious Practice," 41–68; Holifield, *Covenant Sealed,* esp. 143–159, 169–196.

19. Oliver Cowdery, letter to John Whitmer, January 1, 1834, microfilm of holograph, MS 8144 2, Oliver Cowdery Letters, CHL.

20. Ibid.; see also Joseph Smith, "Let Every Man Learn His Duty," *Evening and the Morning Star* 1, no. 8 (January 1833): 61.

21. Joseph Smith, letter to William W. Phelps, November 27, 1832, 3, in JSP D2, 320 [D&C 85]. In this same letter, Smith wrote that those who could not commit fully to Zion should not "have there names enrolled with the people of God, neithe[r] is the geneology to be kept or to be had where it may be found on any of the reccords or hystory of the church there names shall not be found neithe[r] the names of ther fathers or the names of the children writen in the book of the Law of God saith the Lord of hosts." He explained further that those "whose names are found and the names of their fathers and of their children enroled in the Book of the Law of God" were to receive a lot in Zion as an inheritance.

22. Note as well that a "book of remembrance" is mentioned in Malachi 3:16, and that the entirety of Malachi 3 is included in the Book of Mormon as being quoted by Jesus; see 3 Nephi 23.

23. "Old Testament Manuscript 1," 97, 100 [Moses 6:5, 6:46].

24. Mark Ashurst-McGee, "Zion Rising: Joseph Smith's Early Social and Political Thought" (Ph.D. diss., Arizona State University, 2010), 197–203.

25. Alex D. Smith, "The Book of the Law of the Lord," *Journal of Mormon History* 38 (Fall 2012): 131–163.

26. See Samuel Morris Brown, *In Heaven as It Is on Earth: Joseph Smith and the Early Mormon Conquest of Death* (New York: Oxford University Press, 2012), 124–128; Samuel Brown, "Joseph (Smith) in Egypt: Babel, Hieroglyphs, and the Pure Language of Eden," *Church History* 78, no. 1 (March 2009): 26–65. On sacred record keeping more broadly, see Robin Scott Jensen, "'Rely upon the Things Which Are Written': Text, Context, and the Creation of Mormon Revelatory Records" (MLIS thesis, University of Wisconsin-Milwaukee, 2009).

27. Joseph Smith, revelation, January 2, 1831, in JSP D1, 231–232 [D&C 38; note as well the changes introduced to the 1833 printing]. See also Joseph Smith, revelation, August 30, 1831, in JSP D2, 53 [D&C 63:49].

28. Ashurst-McGee, "Zion Rising," 201.

29. In his history, John Whitmer twice gave totals for church membership in Zion in 1832. The *Evening and Morning Star* in its November 1832 issue gave the number of members as 465 and the number of children and nonmembers as 345. Such precise figures would have likely been drawn from records that are no longer extant. "Book of John Whitmer," in JSP H2, 50–51, n. 153.

30. John Corrill, *A Brief History of the Church*, in JSP H2, 194.

31. See JSP J1, 84. The early Saints frequently counted the day the child was born as day one of its life. The performance of baby blessings at a patriarchal blessing meeting may also indicate that the purposes of the blessings were similar.

32. Minute Book 2, April 21, 1834, and April 6, 1838, both in JSP W; Kenney, *Wilford Woodruff's Journal*, 1:459, 465 [June 14 and 21, 1840]; *Times and Seasons* 1, no. 2 (December 18, 1839): 31; *Times and Seasons* 4, no. 1 (November 15, 1842): 14; *Times and Seasons* 4, no. 3 (December 15, 1842): 39; *Times and Seasons* 6, no. 7 (April 15, 1845): 869; *Times and Seasons* 6, no. 12 (July 1, 1845): 953. These blessings may have been very short. For an example of blessing texts produced around this time, see Ambrosia Branch, record book, 30–36, LR 11408 21, Folder 1, CHL.

33. Minute Book 2, April 6, 1838, in JSP W.

34. Elden Jay Watson, ed., *The Orson Pratt Journals* (Salt Lake City: Elden Jay Watson, 1975), 25.

35. Kenney, *Wilford Woodruff's Journal*, 1:56.

36. Joseph Fielding, journal, June 14, 1837, 25, digital image of holograph, MS 1567, Folder 2, Image 27, CHL. Note that missionaries had previously blessed children in Britain. This was the first blessings in this locality.

37. Fielding, journal, December 27, 1837, 48.

38. See, e.g., Parley P. Pratt, *A Voice of Warning and Instruction to All People, Containing a Declaration of the Faith and Doctrine of the Church of the Latter Day Saints, Commonly Called Mormons* (New York: W. Sanford, 1837).

39. Patriarchal blessings are also an important antecedent to the recording of blessings. Some early examples of "father's blessing" texts exist, but they appear to relate to a situation in which the father is acting as a patriarch. John Taylor, "Patriarchal," *Times and Seasons* 6 (June 1, 1845): 921. For examples of such texts, see William Huntington, blessing on Zina Huntington, September 8, 1836, MS 4780, Box 3, Folder 8, Zina Card Brown Family Collection 1806–1972, CHL; Heber C. Kimball, blessing on Helen Mar Kimball, May 28, 1843, digital image of holograph, MS 23826, Folder 2, Images 1–2, Heber C. Kimball Family Collection, CHL.

40. JSP J1, 72–73, 81.

41. See William V. Smith, *Textual Studies of the Doctrine and Covenants: The Plural Marriage Revelation* (Salt Lake City: Kofford Books, forthcoming).

42. Kenney, *Wilford Woodruff's Journal*, 2:584–586 [January 25, 1845].

43. Stanley B. Kimball, *On the Potter's Wheel: The Diaries of Heber C. Kimball* (Salt Lake City: Signature Books, 1987), 125 [June 26, 1845]. Brigham Young later vested a significant amount of importance on his first child born after having been sealed. George Q. Cannon, diary, October 9, 1880, Church Historian's Press, https://www.churchhistorianspress.org/george-q-cannon/.

44. In Utah during the inter-temple period, Heber C. Kimball declared: "I am preaching these things to my brethren and sisters, that they may know, if they have not dedicated and consecrated their children to the Lord, that it has to be done. But you may inquire, 'How shall we do it?' You will have to do it as brother Brigham and others have done when in Nauvoo. We had to take our children and wash and anoint them, and place the birthright and father's blessing upon them in the house of God, and then have them sealed to us; and you will have to do just so." Heber C. Kimball, December 27, 1857, in JD, 6:191. See also Joseph F. Smith, comp., "Sealings and Adoption, 1846–1857," ca. 1869–1870, 561–562, microfilm 183374, FHL; Joseph Fielding, diary, January 26, 1846, Image 81; George A. Smith, "History of George A. Smith, circa 1857–1875," January 25, 1846, digital images of holograph, MS 1322, Box 2, Folder 1, CHL.

45. John Taylor, blessing upon George John Taylor, Joseph James Taylor, and Mary Ann Taylor, January 17, 1846, digital image of holograph, MS 1346, Box 1, Folder 22, Images 6–9, John Taylor Collection, 1829–1894, CHL.

46. On natural heirs, see Stapley, "Adoptive Sealing Ritual in Mormonism," 64.

47. John Taylor, eighth-day blessing, February 11, 1848, Box 1, Folder 22, Images 10–13, John Taylor Collection, 1829–1894.

48. Heber C. Kimball, eighth-day blessing on Moroni Young, January 15, 1847, Box 170, Folder 27, BYOF. See also Willard Richards, diary, January 15, 1847, digital image of manuscript, MS 1490, CHL. Brigham Young blessed Kimball's children the following month.

49. S. F. Kimball, "A Brand Plucked from the Burning," *Improvement Era* 9 (1906): 686.

50. Brigham Young, blessing on Sarah Helen Kimball, February 9, 1847, digital images of holograph, MS 23826, Folder 1, Heber C. Kimball Family Collection, 1840–1890, CHL; Brigham Young, blessing on David Kimball, February 9, 1847, microfilm of holograph, MS 5855, CHL; cf. digital image of copy, Folder 1, Heber C. Kimball Family Collection.

51. Samuel M. Brown, "Early Mormon Adoption and the Mechanics of Salvation," *Journal of Mormon History* 37 (Summer 2011): 15–27; John Taylor, "Patriarchal," *Times and Seasons* 10 (June 1, 1845): 921.

52. Bishop's Meeting Minutes, March 22, 1847, CR 100 318, Box 1, Folder 52, Images 19–20, Historian's Office General Church Minutes, 1839–1877, CHL; Kenney, *Wilford Woodruff's Journal*, 3:142–143. On June 27, 1847, and October 3, 1847, Patriarch Isaac Morley held meetings in Winter Quarters to bless children. Charles Kelly, ed., *The Journal of John D. Lee, 1846–47 and 1859* (Salt Lake City: University of Utah Press, 1984), 181–182; Minutes, October 3, 1847, LR 6359 21, Box 1, Folder 6, Winter Quarters Municipal High Council Records, 1846–1848, CHL. Lee refers to Morley as "Pres[iden]t" in his record.

53. Child blessing meeting minutes, January 6, 1850, digital image of holograph, Box 2 Folder 17, Images 1–2, Historian's Office General Church Minutes, 1839–1877. See also Zina D. H. Young, diary, January 6, 1850, digital image of holograph, MS 4780, Box 1, Folder 1, Image 19, Zina Card Brown Family Collection 1806–1972, CHL.

54. See, e.g., J. Cecil Alter, ed., "Extracts from the Journal of Henry Bigler," *Utah Historical Quarterly* 5 (October 1932): 141; George Henry Abbott Harris, "Autobiography, 1854–1892," 200–201, digital images of holograph, MSS 415, LTPSC; Cedar Stake Journal, 1856–1859, May 3, 1857, October 5, 1858, and February 3, 1859, all in MS 1, Box 89, Folder 12, William Rees Palmer and Kate Vilate Isom Palmer Western History Collection, Special Collections, Gerald R. Sherratt Library, Southern Utah University, Cedar City, Utah; Laura Pitkin Kimball, diary, March 3, 1859, digital images of holograph, MS 1775, CHL; Frederick Kesler, diary, 1859–1874, "Journal Nook No. 3," 26, 42, 45, 67, 77, 81, 166, digital copy of holograph, MS 0049, Box 1, Item 1, JWML.

55. Early settlements in Utah were considered stakes. Often a presiding elder or president was called to administer the spiritual aspects of a church, while a bishop handled its judicial and financial matters. William Pace was Palmyra's bishop, but Markham as the stake's president pronounced the blessings. William G. Hartley, *Another Kind of Gold: The Life of Albert King Thurber, a Utah Pioneer, Explorer, and Community Builder* (Troy, ID: C. L. Dalton Enterprises, 2011), 105.

56. "Record of Members, 1851–1856, Palmyra Branch, Palmyra, Utah Co., Utah," microfilm of manuscript, Film 7794, Item 3, FHL.

57. Ibid., 86.

58. Eliza S. Keeler, autobiography and journal, circa 1886–1898, digital images of holograph, MS 188, CHL.

59. Craig L. Dalton, ed., "Autobiography and Journal of Albert King Thurber," February 8, 1863; February 15 and 18, 1863; February 28, 1863; March 22, 1863; April 1 and 2, 1863; and April 19, 1863, all digital typescript, 33–35, 38–39, 41, in DVD-ROM included with Hartley, *Another Kind of Gold*; Spanish Fork Ward bishop's blessing records, 1860–1866, microfilm of manuscript, LR 8611 26, CHL.

60. Stephen S. Taysom, *Shakers, Mormons, and Religious Worlds: Conflicting Visions, Contested Boundaries* (Bloomington and Indianapolis: Indiana University Press, 2011); Paul H. Peterson, "The Mormon Reformation of 1856–1857: The Rhetoric and the Reality," *Journal of Mormon History* 15 (1989): 59–88.

61. Cedar City Stake Record of Children Blessed, microfilm of manuscript, LR 16635 22, CHL. For a similar register of blessings, see East Bountiful Ward Record of Children Blessed, microfilm of manuscript, LR 2399 22, CHL.

62. Advertisement, *Deseret News*, February 19, 1853, 27.

63. Shorthand baby blessings, September 1, 1853, Box 170, Folder 27, BYOF.

64. Brigham Young, office journal, March 3, 1859, Box 72, Folder 5, BYOF.

65. Brigham Young blessed his son Feramorz at the meeting. Brigham Young blessing for Feramorz Young, March 3, 1859, Box 170, Folder 27, BYOF.

66. For later recapitulations for this policy, see Joseph Fielding Smith, *Answers to Gospel Questions*, 3 vols. (Salt Lake City: Deseret Book, 1957–1966), 3:199–200; *General Handbook of Instructions*, no. 21 (n.p., 1976), 50.

67. For examples, see Elijah Funk Sheets, journal, April 20, 1848; September 10, 1858; June 29, 1860; May 3, 1861; March 13, 1862; December 27, 1863; October 14, 1867; June 20, 1872; and April 1, 1874, all microfilm of holograph, MS 1314, CHL; Joseph Holbrook, autobiography and journal, February 8, 1854, MS 5004, microfilm of holograph, CHL; Isaiah M. Coombs, diary, August 29, 1861; September 25, 1870; November 2, 1872; Friday 21, 1875; March 29, 1876; September 4, 1879; January 22, 1880; September 12, 1880; November 28, 1881; and October 24, 1882, all microfilm of holograph, MS 1198, Isaiah M. Coombs Collection 1835–1938, CHL; Kenney, *Wilford Woodruff's Journal*, 6:136 [November 11, 1863]; Robert Glass Cleland and Juanita Brooks, eds., *A Mormon Chronicle: The Diaries of John D. Lee, 1848–1876*, 2 vols. (San Marino, CA: Huntington Library, 1955), 2:24–25. For examples of eighth-day blessings pronounced by fathers during this period, see Joseph Horne, eighth-day blessing on Leonora T. Horne, January 23, 1849, microfilm of holograph, MS 7122, CHL; Harrison Burgess, eighth-day blessing on Benjamin Hammon Burgess, June 21, 1851, image of holograph, in Delbert E. Roach and Barbara B. Roach, *A Heritage of Faith and Courage: William and Violate Burgess and Their Family* (Murray, UT: Family Heritage Publishers, 2006), 205. Note that sometimes babies were also blessed on the day of their birth or other days. See, e.g., Donald G. Godfrey and Rebecca S. Martineau-McCarty, eds., *An Uncommon Common Pioneer: The Journals of James Henry Martineau, 1828–1918* (Provo, UT: Religious Studies Center, Brigham Young University, 2008), 19, 75, 99, 133, 135; Kenney, *Wilford Woodruff's Journal*, 6:572 [September 28, 1870].

68. David Moffat, "The Child's Ladder, or a Series of Questions Adapted for the Use of Children of the Latter-day Saints," *Millennial Star* 11, no. 5 (March 1, 1849): 74. See also David Moffat, *The Latter-day Saints' Catechism: Or, Child's Ladder. By Elder David Moffat. Being a Series of Questions Adapted for the Use of the Children of Latter-day Saints* (London: Thos. C. Armstrong, 1851), 3.

69. This situation appears to have endured quite late into the twentieth century in England, where in 1960 the majority of babies were not blessed by their fathers. "British Statistics," *Millennial Star* 122, no. 9 (September 1960): 416–417.

70. Kate B. Carter, "Pioneer Men's and Children's Clothing," *Heart Throbs of the West* 8 (1947): 69; Daughters of Utah Pioneers Lesson Committee, "The Pioneer Memorial Museum and Saramarie J. Van Dyke Carriage House," *An Enduring Legacy* 1 (1978): 64.

71. Salt Lake School of the Prophets Meeting Minutes, January 20, 1873, digital images of manuscript, CR 390 7, Box 1, Folder 4, CHL.

72. John Taylor, "The Blessing of Children," in *Messages of the First Presidency*, edited by James R. Clark, 6 vols. (Salt Lake City: Bookcraft, 1965–1976), 2:311–313. For an example of a church elder stating that eighth-day blessings were the only standard ritual for children, see A. Milton Musser, *The Fruits of "Mormonism"* (Salt Lake City: Deseret News, 1878), 31.

73. George Henry Abbott Harris, "Autobiography, 1854–1892," March 1, 1867, and March 6, 1867.

74. Florence A. Merriam, *My Summer in a Mormon Village* (Boston and New York: Houghton, Mifflin and Company, 1894), 117. For official statements indicating the same, see George Q. Cannon, "Editorial Thoughts," *Juvenile Instructor* 30 (March 1, 1895): 151; Albert Jones, "Theological Department," *Young Woman's Journal* 7 (February 5, 1896): 238. "Lesson II: Blessing Children," *Children's Friend* 1 (January 1902): 9–10. See also Hubert Howe Bancroft, *History of Utah, 1540–1886* (San Francisco: History Company, 1889), 343, n. 7. For examples of the practice of double blessings, see Eugene M. Cannon, diary, vol. 6, 193–194, digital images of holograph, MSS 1002, LTPSC; Charles M. Hatch and Todd M. Compton, eds., *A Widow's Tale: The 1884–1896 Diary of Helen Mar Kimball Whitney* (Logan: Utah State University, 2003), 273, 298; Emma H. Adams, *George Mason Adams and Martha Louise Devey, Descendants and Ancestors* (Mesa, AZ: Hogue Printing, 1972), 85. Note as well that single blessings were also common during this time.

75. For examples of mission statistics that include baby blessings of both members and nonmembers, see "Report of the Mission Conferences for Week Ending November 26, 1898," *Latter Day Saints Southern Star* 1, no. 3 (December 17, 1898): 24; Edward Sutton, "Newcastle Conference," *Latter Day Saints Southern Star* 1, no. 3 (December 17, 1898): 24; Nels P. Nelson, "Known by Their Fruits," *Latter Day Saints Southern Star* 1, no. 1 (December 3, 1898): 6; N. Johnston, "Irish Conference," *Latter Day Saints Southern Star* 1, no. 5 (December 31, 1898): 40. Edje Jeter collected several diary accounts of missionaries serving in the Southern States Mission blessing non-Mormon babies. See Edje Jeter, "Southwestern States Mission: The Naming and

Blessing of Children," *Juvenile Instructor*, October 27, 2013, http://juvenileinstructor.org/southwestern-states-mission-the-naming-and-blessing-of-children/.

76. Kenney, *Wilford Woodruff's Journal*, 8:239.
77. John Taylor, letter to R. L. Bybee, December 1, 1886, FPL. Bybee had written Taylor asking what to do, as "there are a great many children in this stake whose parents have forgotten the date of the naming and blessing of their children as no records were kept." Robert L. Bybee, letter to John Taylor, October 13, 1886, digital image of holograph, CR 1 180, First Presidency (John Taylor) Correspondence, CHL. For an example of an underground blessing, see Abraham H. Cannon, diary, March 25, 1895, MSS 62, LTPSC. This portion of his entry was not included in Edward Leo Lyman, ed., *Candid Insights of a Mormon Apostle: The Diaries of Abraham H. Cannon, 1889–1895* (Salt Lake City: Signature Books, 2010).
78. George Q. Cannon, "Editorial Thoughts," *Juvenile Instructor* 30 (March 1, 1895): 151. This counsel was reiterated by local leaders; see, e.g., the May 22, 1897, entry in *Charles P. Anderson Journal* (n.p.: Gilbert Publishing Company, 1975), 22.
79. Report of the March 18, 1900, quarterly conference of the Davis Stake in John J. Smith, "Stake Conferences," *Deseret Evening News*, March 24, 1900, 23; Stan Larson, ed., *A Ministry of Meetings: The Apostolic Diaries of Rudger Clawson* (Salt Lake City: Signature Books, 1993), 140.
80. Example ordinances, ca. 1897, in Linn M. Davis mission priesthood ordinances (handwritten at the end of George Q. Cannon, *Ready References* [Salt Lake City: George Q. Cannon and Sons, 1891]), microfilm of holograph, MS 22494, CHL.
81. Joyce Kinkead, *"A Schoolmarm All My Life": Personal Narratives from Frontier Utah* (Salt Lake City: Signature, 1996), 212.
82. Lorenzo Snow, blessing on Lorenzo S. Clawson, September 7, 1899, typescript, MS 24808, CHL; Larson, *Ministry of Meetings*, 233–234. Note that President Snow performed the ritual, as the child was his namesake, while Rudger Clawson blessed his other children; ibid., 556. The earliest example of language to "bestow upon him (her) the name of (name), by which he (she) shall be known here upon the earth, and upon the records of Thy Church" is in an unofficial ritual guide from around 1929. *Instructions in Ordinance Work* (n.p., 1929), M255 I59 1929, CHL.
83. George Q. Cannon, "Topics of the Times," *Juvenile Instructor* 34 (March 1, 1899): 137–138; reprinted in *Latter-day Saints' Millennial Star* 61 (March 30, 1899): 198–199; *Latter-day Saints Southern Star* 1 (April 29, 1899): 170. Church leaders also encouraged missionaries to bless the children of non-Mormons. See Osmer Flake, diary, December 15, 1897, digital images of holograph, LTPSC. See also "Being a Mormon," *The Independent* [New York] 59 (October 19, 1905): 908.
84. Charles Penrose[?], untitled item, *Deseret Evening News*, September 15, 1900, 4.
85. Larson, *Ministry of Meetings*, 16.
86. George Q. Cannon, "Editorial Thoughts," *Juvenile Instructor* 30 (February 1, 1895): 98; cf. First Presidency, letter to W. J. Conger, February 6, 1903, FPL; "Editors Table," *Improvement Era* 10 (November 1906): 67.

87. George Q. Cannon, "Topics of the Times," *Juveline Instructor* 26 (May 1, 1891): 276.

88. See, e.g., "Women's Sphere: Our Children. Christening Babies," *Deseret Weekly*, January 21, 1893, 145.

89. Report of the monthly priesthood meeting of the Salt Lake Stake in "Priesthood Meeting," *Deseret Weekly*, November 13, 1897, 698.

90. For examples of Joseph F. Smith performing eighth-day blessings for his own children, see Joseph F. Smith, diary, February 6, 1871; March 28, 1872; September 25, 1872; March 2, 1873; and May 8, 1880, all digital images of holographs, MS 1325, Joseph F. Smith Papers, 1854–1918, CHL. On at least one occasion, a second blessing was performed at church. Julina L. Smith, diary, July 1, 1886, digital image of holograph, MS 4364, Folder 4, CHL.

91. Joseph F. Smith, "The Repetition of Sacred Ordinances," *Juvenile Instructor* 38 (January 1, 1903): 19.

92. Nephi Anderson, "Stake Conferences: Boxelder Stake," *Deseret Evening News*, February 18, 1899, 11.

93. Francis M. Lyman[?], "Editorial," *Latter-day Saints' Millennial Star* 65 (March 26, 1903): 200. Forty years later, Matthew Cowley gave similar instructions, although he noted that a father in good standing did not need permission before performing the ritual. Matthew Cowley, "Notice to All Branch Presidents," *Te Karere* 36 (December 1942): 354.

94. In 1917, the *Improvement Era* printed an unsigned editorial responding to the question of whether babies who had received eighth-day blessings at home still needed to be blessed at church. The editorial stated: "We believe that it is not only the privilege but the duty of the father to so bless his child, also to record the blessing in his family record." However, it continued, "the blessing of which the Church takes cognizance is the blessing that is given when the child is brought 'unto the elders before the Church.' It becomes the blessing of public record." "Editor's Table: The Blessing of Children," *Improvement Era* 20 (March 1917): 451–452. See also Susa Young Gates, *Surname and Racial History: A Compilation and Arrangement of Genealogical and Historical Data for Use by the Students and Members of the Relief Society of the Church of Jesus Christ of Latter-day Saints* (Salt Lake City: General Board of the Relief Society, 1918), 68.

95. Charles Penrose, ed., "Blessing of Children," *Deseret Evening News*, March 13, 1906, 4.

96. *Circular of Instructions: To Presidents of Stakes and Counselors, Presidents of Missions, Bishops and Counselors, Stake, Mission and Ward Clerks and All Church Authorities, 1913* (n.p., 1913), 26.

97. *Handbook of Instructions for Bishops and Counselors, Stake and Ward Clerks* (n.p., 1928), 70; *Handbook of Instructions for Stake Presidencies, Bishops and Counselors, Stake and Ward Clerks* (n.p., 1934), 90. See also George S. Romney, *The Missionary Guide: A Key to Effective Missionary Work* (Independence, MO: Press of Zion's Printing and Pub. Co., [1934?]), 97.

98. "Third Sunday, October 15, 1933, Lesson 71. The Presentation in the Temple," *Instructor* 68 (August 1933): 378.

99. *Handbook of Instructions for Stake Presidencies, Bishops and Counselors, Stake and Ward Clerks and Other Church Officers* (n.p., 1940), 116.

100. Orson Pratt, "Prospectus of 'The Seer,'" *Seer* 1 (January 1853): 1, 7; Jedediah M. Grant, sermon, February 19, 1854, in JD, 2:13; Heber C. Kimball, sermon, October 6, 1855, in JD, 3:125; Wilford Woodruff, sermons, December 12, 1869; April 3, 1882; May 14, 1882, all in JD, 13:167, 22:147, 23:131; Kenney, *Wilford Woodruff's Journal*, 5:321, 6:452, 6:518, 7:251, 7:623, 8:188, and 9:112 [March 31, 1859; January 22, 1869; January 9, 1870; October 9, 1875; ca. 1880; July 22, 1883; September 25, 1890].

101. Joseph F. Smith, "The Rights of Fatherhood," *Juvenile Instructor* 37 (March 1, 1902): 146–147.

102. Irene Bates and E. Gary Smith, *Lost Legacy: The Mormon Office of Presiding Patriarch* (Urbana: University of Illinois Press, 2003), 140, 204; John W. Taylor, *Conference Report* (October 1900), 30; Eldred G. Smith, *Conference Report* (April 1952), 40.

103. Stephen L. Richards, *Conference Report* (April 1954), 33–34; Alvin R. Dyer, *Conference Report* (April 1963), 51; Bruce R. McConkie, *Mormon Doctrine*, 2nd ed. (Salt Lake City: Bookcraft, 1966), 844; Brent Barlow, "Strengthening the Patriarchal Order in the Home," *Ensign* (February 1973), 20–33; Dean L. Larson, "Marriage and the Patriarchal Order," *Ensign* (September 1982), 6–13.

104. See "Containment at Home: Cold War, Warm Hearth," in *Homeward Bound: American Families in the Cold War Era*, edited by Elaine Tyler May (New York: Basic Books, 2008), 19–38; Kate Holbrook, "Housework: The Problem That Does Have a Name," in *Out of Obscurity: Mormonism since 1945*, edited by Patrick O. Mason and John G. Turner (New York: Oxford, 2016), 198–213.

105. William R. Palmer, "A Father's Blessing," *Improvement Era* 58 (March 1955): 150–151, 170. The practice of not saying the surname is attested in responses to questions written at the turn of the century. See note 86 in this chapter.

106. Paul Cracroft, "The Blessings I Give My Child Bless Me," *Instructor* (July 1963), 262–263.

107. Sherman M. Crump, "The Baby: An Official Member," *Instructor* (June 1966), 243–245.

108. *Handbook of Instructions for Stake Presidencies, Bishops and Counselors, Stake and Ward Clerks and Other Church Officers* (n.p., 1940), 116; "I Want to Know," *Church News*, June 27, 1948, Twenty-C. While race may have been a consideration in the deliberations of church leaders, there were far fewer African Americans in the church than there were non-Melchizedek Priesthood office–holding men, who were common in most wards.

109. "Priesthood Bearers Only to Stand in Circle," *Messenger*, no. 14 (February 1957): 2.

110. Council minutes excerpts, March 27, 1957, holograph note, CR 601 5, Box 9, Folder 14, Delbert L. Stapley Files, 1951–1976, CHL.

111. "Only Melchizedek Priesthood to Assist in Blessing Babies and Performing Confirmations," *Messenger*, no. 14 (March 1957): 1.

112. "Fathers May Hold Their Babies While Being Blessed by the Melchizedek Priesthood," *Messenger*, no. 35 (January–February 1959): 1.

113. Church of Jesus Christ of Latter-day Saints, *General Handbook of Instructions*, no. 19 (n.p., 1963), 63. See also "News of the Church," *Ensign* (August 1975), 90–96. The 1983 *Handbook* changed the emphasis, stating that "if a father, whether he is a member or not, insists on holding his child while the child receives the blessing, he may do so."

114. "News of the Church," *Ensign* (August 1975), 94.

115. *General Handbook of Instructions*, no. 21 (n.p., 1976), 50; James Faust, "Patriarchal Blessings," fireside address at Brigham Young University, Provo, Utah, March 30, 1980, https://speeches.byu.edu/wp-content/uploads/pdf/Faust_James_1980_031.pdf. Cf. David O. McKay, diary, June 27, 1968, MS 668, David Oman McKay Papers, JWML.

116. Church of Jesus Christ of Latter-day Saints, *General Handbook of Instructions* (Salt Lake City: Church of Jesus Christ of Latter-day Saints, 1989), 5–1.

117. "Naming and Blessing Children," *Bulletin*, no. 3 (1989): 1.

118. Edward L. Kimball, "The History of LDS Temple Admission Standards," *Journal of Mormon History* 24 (Spring 1998): 135–176.

119. *Handbook 1: Stake Presidents and Bishops 2010* (n.p.: Church of Jesus Christ of Latter-day Saints, 2010), 140 [16.1.1].

120. Boyd K. Packer, "The Power of the Priesthood," *Ensign* (May 2010), 6–10.

121. First Presidency and Quorum of the Twelve, "The Family: A Proclamation to the World," *Ensign* (November 1995), 102.

122. Caroline Kline, "Saying Goodbye to the Final Say: The Softening and Reimagining of Mormon Male Headship Ideologies," in Mason and Turner, *Out of Obscurity*, 214–233. See, e.g., Bruce C. Hafen and Marie K. Hafen, "Crossing Thresholds and Becoming Equal Partners," *Ensign* (August 2007), 24–29; Valerie M. Hudson, "Equal Partnership in Marriage," *Ensign* (April 2013), 18–23; Aaron West, "Flora and I: Equal Partners in the Work of the Lord," *Ensign* (January 2015), 38–43.

123. Dallin H. Oaks, "Priesthood Authority in the Family and the Church," *Ensign* (November 2005), 24–27.

124. Since Oaks's sermon, church manuals have indicated that "if there is no father in the home, the mother presides over the family." See Church of Jesus Christ of Latter-day Saints, *Family: Guidebook* (Salt Lake City: Church of Jesus Christ of Latter-day Saints, 2006), 3; Church of Jesus Christ of Latter-day Saints, *Gospel Principles* (Salt Lake City: Church of Jesus Christ of Latter-day Saints, 2007), 215.

125. Accounts of participants in possession of the author.

126. Aaron Shill, "LDS Church reaffirms doctrine of marriage, updates policies on families in same-sex marriages," *Deseret News*, November 5, 2015; Spencer Hall, "LDS Church: Underage children of same-sex couples not eligible for membership," KSL.com, November 5, 2015; Sarah Pulliam Bailey, "Mormon Church to exclude children of same-sex couples from getting blessed and baptized until they are 18," *Washington Post*, November 6, 2015.

127. D. Todd Christofferson, interview, November 6, 2015, http://www.mormonnewsroom.org/article/handbook-changes-same-sex-marriages-elder-christofferson.

128. First Presidency, circular letter, November 13, 2015, https://www.lds.org/pages/church-handbook-changes?lang=eng.

129. LDS Public Affairs, "Interview with Elder Dallin H. Oaks and Elder Lance B. Wickman: 'Same-Gender Attraction,'" http://www.mormonnewsroom.org/article/interview-oaks-wickman-same-gender-attraction.

CHAPTER 4

1. Joseph Smith, sermon report, Female Relief Society of Nauvoo Minutes, April 28, 1842, in FFY, 55.

2. *Handbook 2: Administering the Church* (Salt Lake City: Church of Jesus Christ of Latter-day Saints, 2010), 174.

3. Zina D. H. Young, diary, 1886 January, 1889 January–June, May 21, 1889, digital images of holograph, MS 6240, Folder 2, CHL; "Wasatch and Utah," *Woman's Exponent* 18, no. 1 (June 1, 1889): 6. Young's blessing register for 1889–1891 indicated that she washed, anointed, and blessed "Louisa Fanny U[nder]. G[round]." for confinement alongside eleven other individuals, for whom Young performed healing rituals on May 21, 1889. Zina D. H. Young, memorandum, microfilm of holograph, MS 4780, Box 1, Folder 15, Zina Card Brown Family Collection, 1806–1972, CHL. Her diary also indicates that she performed blessings for six or seven individuals on May 22, 1889. Louisa gave birth to a son on July 14, 1889, but he died three days later.

4. Church of Jesus Christ of Latter-day Saints, *Preach My Gospel: A Guide to Missionary Service* (Salt Lake City: Church of Jesus Christ of Latter-day Saints, 2005), 33.

5. The most sophisticated and accessible study of extreme unction is Frederick S. Paxton, *Christianizing Death: The Creation of a Ritual Process in Early Medieval Europe* (Ithaca, NY: Cornell University Press, 1990). See also Achille M. Triacca, ed., *Temple of the Holy Spirit: Sickness and Death of the Christian in the Liturgy*, trans. Matthew J. O'Connel (New York: Pueblo, 1983); Antoine Chavasse, *Étude sur l'onction des infirmes dans l'Église latine du IIIᵉ au XIᵉ siècle*, Vol. 1, *Du IIIᵉ siècle à la réforme carolingienne* (Lyons, France: Librairie du Sacré-Cœur, 1942). Volume 2 of Chavasse's study was never published; however, his findings are

summarized in his "Prières pour les malades et onction sacramentelle," in *L'église en prière: Introduction à la liturgie*, edited by A. G. Martimort (Paris: Desclée & Cie, 1961), 580–594; and in Placid Murray, "The Liturgical History of Extreme Unction," *Studies in Pastoral Liturgy*, edited by Vincent Ryan (Dublin: Gill & Son for the Furrow Trust, 1963): 2:18–38.

6. Donald F. Durnbaugh, *Fruit of the Vine: A History of the Brethren, 1708–1995* (Elgin, IL: Brethren Press, 1997), 120; Church of the Brethren, *Minutes of the Annual Meetings of the Church of the Brethren: Containing All Available Minutes from 1778 to 1909* (Elgin, IL: Brethren Publishing House, 1909), 19, 30, 50, 52, 64. The Tunkers were also called the "Dunkers" and are now typically known as the Old German Baptist Brethren. That they had also anointed the area of affliction is attested by Morgan Edwards, *Customs of Primitive Churches; or a Set of Propositions Relative to the Name, Matterials, Constitution, Power, Officers, Ordinances, Rites, Business, Worship, Discipline, Government &c. of a Church; to Which Are Added Their Proofs from Scripture; and Historical Narratives of the Manner in Which Most of Them Have Been Reduced to Practice* (Philadelphia, 1768), 94.

7. See, e.g., Parley P. Pratt, *A Voice of Warning and Instruction to All People, Containing a Declaration of the Faith and Doctrine of the Church of the Latter Day Saints, Commonly Called Mormons* (New York: W. Sanford, 1837), 204, 211–212; John Hardy, *Hypocrisy Exposed, or J. V. Himes Weighed in the Balances of Truth, Honesty and Common Sense, and Found Wanting; Being a Reply to a Pamphlet Put Forth by Him, Entitled Mormon Delusions and Monstrosities* (Boston: Alber Morgan, 1842), 3, 6–7; William I. Appleby, *A Few Important Questions for the Reverend Clergy to Answer, Being a Scale to Weigh Priestcraft and Sectarianism In* (Philadelphia, Brown, Bicking & Guilbert, 1843), 10–11; John Taylor, *Truth Defended and Methodism Weighed in the Balance and Found Wanting: Being a Reply to the Third Address of the Rev. Robert Heys, Wesleyan Minister to the Wesleyan Methodist Societies in Douglas and Its Vicinity, and Also an Exposure of the Principles of Methodism* (Liverpool: J. Tompkins, 1841), 12.

8. On Mormonism as antecedent to Pentecostalism, see D. William Faupel, "What Has Pentecostalism to Do with Mormonism? The Case of John Alexander Dowie," in *New Perspectives in Mormon Studies*, edited by Quincy D. Newell and Eric F. Mason (Norman: University of Oklahoma Press, 2013).

9. Jan Shipps and John W. Welch, eds., *The Journals of William E. McLellin, 1831–1836* (Provo, Urbana, and Chicago: BYU Studies and University of Illinois Press, 1994), 45.

10. Readers should note that while cessationism was the position of Christian authorities during this time, the lived religion of Christian believers often diverged from this orthodoxy.

11. Beyond the discussion in chapter 1, these themes are traced in great detail in several papers: Stapley and Wright, "Forms and the Power," 42–87; Jonathan A. Stapley, "Last Rites and the Dynamics of Mormon Liturgy," *Brigham Young University Studies* 50, no. 2 (2011): 97–128. See also Jonathan A. Stapley and Kristine Wright, "Female Ritual Healing in Mormonism," *Journal of Mormon History* 37 (Winter 2011): 1–86;

Jonathan A. Stapley and Kristine Wright, "'They Shall Be Made Whole': A History of Baptism for Health," *Journal of Mormon History* 34 (Fall 2008): 69–112.

12. An example of the procedure can be seen in the following account by Hyrum Smith: "[I] visited Brother Blackmen he Being Sick[.] he Cald upon mySelf and Elder Theyden to pray for and lay our hands upon him[.] accordengly we did and he began to recover from that time forth." Hyrum Smith, diary, January 19, 1832, vol. 1, 14, digital copy of holograph, MSS 774, LTPSC.

13. Joseph Smith, revelation, December 7, 1830, in JSP D1, 221 [D&C 35:9]; idem, revelation, February 9, 1831, in ibid., 254 [D&C 42:44]; idem, revelation, October 29, 1831, in JSP D2, 91 [D&C 66:9].

14. Stapley and Wright, "Forms and the Power," 57.

15. Ibid., 59, 63–65; Stapley and Wright, "Female Ritual Healing in Mormonism," 4.

16. Shipps and Welch, *Journals of William E. McLellin*, 217.

17. Stapley and Wright, "Forms and the Power," 65–67; Jonathan Stapley, "'Pouring in Oil': The Development of the Modern Mormon Healing Ritual," in *By Our Rites of Worship: Latter-day Saint Views on Ritual in Scripture and Practice*, edited by Daniel L. Belnap (Provo and Salt Lake City: Deseret Book/Religious Studies Center, 2013), 284–289.

18. Joseph Smith led the promulgation of this practice by example. He baptized his wife Emma Smith for her health when she was sick, as well as a young girl in his care. See JSP J2, 161, 165; see also Lucy Walker Kimball, "Autobiography," n.d., 7, microfilm of typescript, CHL. For a complete and detailed history of baptism for health, see Stapley and Wright, "'They Shall Be Made Whole.'"

19. Stapley and Wright, "Forms and the Power," 71–80.

20. Joseph Smith, sermon, April 28, 1842, in FFY, 54–59.

21. Ibid. Two years later, when Emma Smith used her position in the Relief Society to fight Mormon polygamy, she invoked this teaching and claimed that "if thier ever was any authourity on the Earth she had it." Emma Smith, statement, March 16, 1844, in FFY, 131.

22. JSP J2, 53 [May 1, 1842].

23. Ibid., 52 [April 28, 1842].

24. FFY, 43 [March 31, 1842].

25. Ibid., 115–116 [August 13, 1843].

26. Jonathan Stapley, "Women and Mormon Authority," in *Women and Mormonism: Historical and Contemporary Perspectives*, edited by Kate Holbrook and Matthew Bowman (Salt Lake City: University of Utah Press, 2016), 101–117.

27. John Taylor, sermon, November 30, 1879, in JD, 20:359. See also idem, Relief Society meeting report, July 17, 1880, in FFY, 475–478; Franklin D. Richards, sermon, July 19, 1888, in FFY, 543–552; Ruth May Fox, diaries, March 8, 1896, microfilm of holograph, MS 6348 1–2, CHL.

28. Orson Pratt, ed., *The Doctrine and Covenants, of the Church of Jesus Christ of Latter-day Saints, Containing the Revelations Given to Joseph Smith, Jun., the Prophet, for*

the Building Up of the Kingdom of God in the Last Days (Liverpool: William Budge, 1879), 462–463 [D&C 131]. Cf. William Clayton, journal, April 1–4, 1843, in JSP J2, 403–406.

29. Almost two years earlier Taylor had spoken to a group of home missionaries and made the association between the priesthood and the marriage sealing explicitly cosmological: "In relation to a wife it may be said she holds Priesthood in connection with her husband, but not separate from him. It is because he is or will be a Priest that she is or will be a Priestess." Minutes of Home Missionary Meeting, January 30, 1884, microfilm of manuscript, LR 604 11, Salt Lake Stake, General Minutes, CHL.

30. Salt Lake Stake High Council Minutes of Trials, October 13, 1885, vol. 10, LR 604 10, CHL.

31. See, e.g., Relief Society Conference in the Logan Tabernacle, September 11, 1886, microfilm of holograph, LR 1280 14, Logan Utah Cache Stake, Relief Society Minutes and Records, CHL.

32. Joseph F. Smith, "Questions and Answers," *Improvement Era* 10 (February 1907): 308. The narrative was popular enough that even some participants in the temple liturgy in Nauvoo adopted it. See, e.g., Lucy Meserve Smith, "Reminiscences," June 12, 1889, in FFY, 215. For the persistence of the idea among Mormon schismatic groups, see Janet Bennion, *Women of Principle: Female Networking in Contemporary Mormon Polygyny* (New York: Oxford University Press, 1998), 56.

33. E. R. Snow Smith, "To the Branches of the Relief Society" [letter], September 12, 1884, in FFY, 514–516.

34. Ibid., 516, n. 256.

35. Minutes of Home Missionary Meeting, January 30, 1884.

36. Richard S. Horne, "A Remarkable Healing," *Juvenile Instructor* 30 (November 1, 1895): 660–663. Horne repeated the story twenty years later, as recorded in Anthon H. Lund, diary, September 21, 1915, MS 2737, CHL.

37. "Editorial Thoughts: Authority to Rebuke Disease," *Juvenile Instructor* 31 (January 15, 1896): 60.

38. "Editorial Thoughts: Authority to Rebuke Disease," *Juvenile Instructor* 31 (February 15, 1896): 102–103. For similar discussions involving affirmations of Aaronic Priesthood officers performing healing rituals, see "Editorial," *Deseret News*, April 8, 1901, in JH, April 8, 1901; Meeting Minutes of the First Presidency and Twelve, February 18, 1903, in JH, February 18, 1903, 4.

39. Stapley and Wright, "Female Ritual Healing in Mormonism," 51–52; Susa Young Gates, letter to Joseph F. Smith, December 11, 1888, MS 1325, Box 15, Folder 7, Joseph F. Smith Papers, CHL; Joseph F. Smith, letter to Susa Young Gates, January 8, 1889, Box 31, Folder 4 Joseph F. Smith Papers.

40. Joseph F. Smith, letter to Susa Young Gates, January 8, 1889, Box 31, Folder 4, Joseph F. Smith Papers.

41. Stapley and Wright, "Female Ritual Healing in Mormonism," 42–49.

42. Ibid., 48–50.

43. Young Women General Board minutes, September 16, 1901, microfilm of type-script, CR 13 6, CHL; see also Stapley and Wright, "Female Ritual Healing in Mormonism," 48.

44. Ibid., 53–64.

45. *Aaronic Priesthood Handbook* (Salt Lake City: Presiding Bishopric, 1941), 45. This section of the handbook was based on Joseph Keeler, *The Lesser Priesthood and Notes on Church Government, Also a Concordance of the Doctrine and Covenants for the Use of Church Schools and Priesthood Quorums* (Salt Lake City: Deseret News, 1904), 30; idem, *The Lesser Priesthood and Notes on Church Government for the Use of Church Schools and Priesthood Quorums* (Salt Lake City: Deseret News, 1929), 40.

46. James E. Talmage, letter to J. D. Montague, April 22, 1921, MS 1232, James E. Talmage Collection, CHL; David O. McKay, letter to J. B. Duncan, April 3, 1935, FPL.

47. "Ward Teachers May Administer to Sick," *Messenger*, no. 53 (September 1960): 2.

48. Stapley and Wright, "Female Ritual Healing in Mormonism," 81–82.

49. John Wesley, "The Nature, Design, and General Rules of the United Societies" and "Directions Given to the Band," in *The Bicentennial Edition of the Works of John Wesley*, edited by Rupert Eric Davies (Nashville, TN: Abingdon Press, 1976–), 9:73 and 79.

50. Ryan G. Tobler, "'Saviors on Mount Zion': Mormon Sacramentalism, Mortality, and the Baptism for the Dead," *Journal of Mormon History* 39, no. 4 (Fall 2013): 182–238.

51. Smith taught explicitly that "without the authority" held by ancient patriarchs and prophets, "the ordinances could not be administered in righteousness." Joseph Smith, "Instruction on Priesthood," October 5, 1840, handwriting of Robert B. Thompson, in JSP W.

52. Joseph Smith, et al., "Church History," *Times and Seasons* 3, no. 9 (March 1, 1842): 709. Though the language of laws and ordinances is original to this docu-ment, Smith and/or his scribes based this text on earlier documents by Orson and Parley Pratt. See JSP H1, xxxiv, 520, 540, 542.

53. I thank Kevin Barney for making me aware of this relationship.

54. *The City Charter: Laws, Ordinance, and Acts of the City Council of Nauvoo. And Also, the Ordinances of the Nauvoo Legion: From the Commencement of the City to This Date* (Nauvoo, IL: Joseph Smith, 1842), 7–8.

55. Edward Leo Lyman, *Candid Insights of a Mormon Apostle: The Diaries of Abraham H. Cannon, 1889–1895* (Salt Lake City: Signature Books, 2010), 441 [November 29, 1893].

56. Zina D. H. Young, sermon, April 6, 1889, Box 3, Folder 1, Family Collection 1806–1972.

57. Wilford Woodruff, letter to Emmeline B. Wells, April 27, 1888, in FFY, 541–542.

58. For the ongoing appellation of female healing rituals as "ordinances," see, e.g., Annie M. Cannon, "Our Girls: Officers Conference," *Young Woman's Journal* 6 (May 1895): 386; Eliza R. Snow Smith, letter to Branches of the Relief Society, September

12, 1884, Salt Lake City, reproduced in *The General Relief Society: Officers, Objects and Status* (Salt Lake City: General Officers, 1902), 26–27; First Presidency, letter to William A. Hyde, October 3, 1905, microfilm of typescript, FPL; Oakley, Idaho, 2nd Ward Relief Society, minute book, 1901–1909, 195–198, microfilm of manuscript, LR 6360 14, CHL; Anonymous, "Ye Ancient and Honorable Order of Midwifery," *Relief Society Magazine* 2 (August 1915): 347; First Presidency, letter to A. W. Horsley and Counselors, December 29, 1922, FPL; washing and anointing blessing texts, ca. 1923, CR 11 304, Folder 2, Relief Society Washing and Anointing File, CHL; First Presidency, letter to Relief Society Presidency, August 11, 1923, typescript in Salt Lake Liberty Stake, Relief Society scrapbook selections, 1915–1933, LR 4880 41, CHL; Martha A. Hickman, letter to Louise Y. Robison, November 28, 1935, MS 6020, CHL; Joseph Fielding Smith, letter, July 29, 1946, typescript on Relief Society letterhead, CR 11 304, Folder 1, Relief Society Washing and Anointing File, CHL.

59. *Handbook 1: Stake Presidents and Bishops 2010* (n.p.: Church of Jesus Christ of Latter-day Saints, 2010), 174.

60. On Priesthood Reform, see William Hartley, "The Priesthood Reform Movement, 1908–1922," *BYU Studies* 13 (Winter 1973): 137–156; William Hartley, "From Men to Boys: LDS Aaronic Priesthood Offices, 1829–1996," *Journal of Mormon History* 22 (Spring 1996): 115–117. On Priesthood Correlation, see Mathew Bowman, *The Mormon People: The Making of an American Faith* (New York: Random House, 2012), 184–215; Daymon Mickel Smith, "'The Last Shall Be First and the First Shall Be Last': Discourse and Mormon History" (Ph.D. diss., University of Pennsylvania, 2007).

61. B. H. Roberts, "Seventy's Council Table," *Improvement Era* 11, no. 10 (August 1908): 814; Mangal Dan Dipty, "My Journey as a Pioneer from India," *Ensign* (July 2016), 68. For examples of women being witnesses for temple sealings, see David O. McKay, diary, January 12, 1968, MS 668, David Oman McKay Papers, JWML.

62. Church of Jesus Christ of Latter-day Saints, *General Handbook of Instructions*, no. 21 (n.p., 1976), 47.

63. On progressivism in the church, see Bowman, *Mormon People*, chs. 6–7; idem, "Eternal Progression: Mormonism and American Progressivism," in *Mormonism and American Politics*, edited by Randall Balmer and Jana Riess (New York: Columbia University Press, 2015), 53–71.

64. Hartley, "From Men to Boys," reviews this change in great detail.

65. "Articles and Covenants," in JSP D1, 124 [D&C 20:40, 58]

66. Kristine L. Wright, "'We Baked a Lot of Bread': Reconceptualizing Mormon Women and Ritual Objects," in Holbrook and Bowman, *Women and Mormonism*, 82–100.

67. "Teachers Not Authorized to Break Bread," *Messenger*, no. 13 (January 1957), 2.

68. George Q. Cannon, "Passing the Sacrament," *Juvenile Instructor* (May 15, 1895), 317; Francis M. Lyman, "The Administration of the Sacrament in the Sunday School," in *Proceedings of the First Sunday School Convention of the Church of Jesus Christ of Latter-day Saints* (Salt Lake City: Deseret Sunday School Union, 1899), 77; "Answers

to Questions," *Juvenile Instructor* (August 15, 1901), 506; Heber J. Grant, letter to Henry Rolapp, June 28, 1928, quoted in Hartley, "From Men to Boys," 129–130.

69. "Young Women Should Not Prepare Sacrament Table," *Messenger*, no. 14 (February 1957), 2.

70. *Aaronic Priesthood Manual 2* (n.p.: Church of Jesus Christ of Latter-day Saints, 1993), 72–73.

71. First Presidency circular to stake presidents and bishops, May 2, 1946, First Presidency Circular Letters, CHL.

72. "Passing the Sacrament: Highest Authority to Be Recognized First," *Messenger*, no. 1 (January 1956), 1.

73. Church of Jesus Christ of Latter-day Saints, *General Handbook of Instructions*, no. 18 (n.p., 1960), 45.

74. For a more complete history, see Stapley, "Last Rites."

75. *The Missionary's Hand Book* (Independence, MO: Press of Zion's Printing and Publishing Company, 1937), 145.

76. *Handbook of Instructions for Stake Presidencies, Bishops and Counselors, Stake and Ward Clerks and Other Church Officers*, no. 16 (n.p., 1940), 128. This was also taught in priesthood curricula. John A. Widtsoe, *Priesthood and Church Government in the Church of Jesus Christ of Latter-day Saints* (Salt Lake City: Deseret Book Co., 1939), 360; Melchizedek Priesthood Committee of the Council of the Twelve, "Melchizedek Priesthood: Melchizedek Priesthood Outline of Study, December, 1941," *Improvement Era* 44 (November 1941): 685.

77. *The Missionary's Hand Book*, rev. ed. (Independence, MO: Press of Zion's Printing and Publishing Company, 1946), 150.

78. Anonymous, "I Want to Know," *Deseret News*, September 1, 1948, 24C. I thank Ardis E. Parshall for sharing this reference with me. See also General Priesthood Committee, *Melchizedek Priesthood Handbook* (Salt Lake City: Deseret News Press, 1948), 86; General Priesthood Committee of the Council of the Twelve, "Melchizedek Priesthood: Ordinances and Ceremonies," *Improvement Era* 51 (November 1948): 731.

79. *General Handbook of Instructions* (Salt Lake City: Church of Jesus Christ of Latter-day Saints, 1983), 79.

80. *Church Handbook of Instructions, Book 1: Stake Presidencies and Bishoprics* (Salt Lake City: Church of Jesus Christ of Latter-day Saints, 1998), 34.

81. E.g., see comments on J. Stapley, "Priesthood and Church Liturgy," *By Common Consent*, January 13, 2011, http://bycommonconsent.com/2011/01/13/priesthood-and-church-liturgy/).

82. *Handbook 2: Administering the Church* (n.p.: Church of Jesus Christ of Latter-day Saints, 2010), 177.

83. In addition to the examples presented in this section, the temple prayer circle is also another ritual as part of which Mormon women have in the past led prayers but currently are not authorized to do so.

84. Tally S. Payne, "'Our Wise and Prudent Women': Twentieth-Century Trends in Female Missionary Service," in *New Scholarship on Latter-day Saint Women in the Twentieth Century*, edited by Carol Cornwall Madsen (Provo, UT: BYU Press, 2005), 125–140; Calvin S. Kunz, "A History of Female Missionary Activity in the Church of Jesus Christ of Latter-day Saints, 1830–1898" (M.A. thesis, Brigham Young University, 1976); Kelly Lelegren, "'Real, Live Mormon Women': Understanding The Role of Early Twentieth-Century LDS Lady Missionaries" (M.A. thesis, Utah State University, 2009).

85. Jennifer Reeder and Kate Holbrook, eds., *At the Pulpit: 185 Years of Discourses by Latter-day Saint Women* (Salt Lake City: Church Historian's Press, 2017), xx, n. 33.

86. First Presidency, letter to Joseph Merrill, February 11, 1935, FPL.

87. Joseph Wirthland, Thorpe Isaacson, and Carl W. Buehner, letter, June 5, 1956, in *Messenger*, no. 6 (June 1956), 1.

88. *Priesthood Bulletin* 3, no. 3 (July–August 1967): 1.

89. *General Handbook of Instructions*, no. 20 (Salt Lake City: First Presidency of the Church of Jesus Christ of Latter-day Saints, 1968), 44.

90. "News of the Church," *Ensign* (August 1975), 90–96.

91. "Report of the Seminar for Regional Representatives," *Ensign* (November 1978), 100–101; "Pres. Kimball says gospel needed in Third World nations," *Deseret News*, September 29, 1978, A1; "LDS permit women to offer prayers," *Salt Lake Tribune*, September 30, 1978, A2; "Sisters can pray in meetings," *Church News*, October 7, 1978, 6. See also Leonard J. Arrington, diary, September 29, 1978, MCL.

92. Allison Moore Smith, "The Prayer Thing: Why Women Aren't Worthy to Open Meetings," June 18, 2007, http://mormonmomma.com/prayer-thing/; Allison Moore Smith, emails to author, November 1, 2015.

93. *Handbook 2* (2010), 97.

94. Cynthia L., "Let My People Pray: It's Time to Consider Having Women Give Opening/Closing Prayers in General Conference," *By Common Consent*, October 1, 2011, http://bycommonconsent.com/2011/10/01/let-my-people-pray-its-time-to-consider-having-women-give-openingclosing-prayers-in-general-conference/.

95. E.g., Rosalynde Welch, "Women's Voices, Women's Prayers," *Patheos Mormon*, October 5, 2011, http://www.patheos.com/Resources/Additional-Resources/Womens-Voices-Womens-Prayers-Rosalynde-Welch-10-06-2011.

96. Stapley and Wright, "Female Ritual Healing in Mormonism."

97. *The Missionary's Hand Book* (Independence, MO: Press of Zion's Printing and Publishing, 1937), 140; *The Missionary's Hand Book*, rev. ed. (Independence, MO: Press of Zion's Printing and Publishing, 1946), 145.

98. See, e.g., Thomas S. Monson, "Success Steps to the Abundant Life," *New Era* (May 1971), 2–5; "The Army of the Lord," *Ensign* (May 1979), 35–37; "The Message: Priesthood Profiles," *New Era* (June 1987), 4–8; "The Priesthood—a Sacred Gift," *Ensign* (May 2007), 57–60; "The Priesthood—a Sacred Gift," *Ensign* (May 2015), 88–90.

99. Richard Dance, notes from Elder Oaks's visit to the Renton, Washington North Stake Conference, March 7–8, 1992, typescript in my possession.

100. Daniel Tyler, patriarchal blessing for Hannah Adelia Crosby, in *John S. Crosby Family History Project*, Vol. 2: *United in All We Do, Biographical Essays, Reminiscences, and Correspondence of the Samuel Obed Crosby and John Silas Crosby Families*, edited by Jeffrey E. Crosby (n.p., 1997), 150–151.

101. Stapley and Wright, "Female Ritual Healing in Mormonism," 23, n. 69.

102. Cannonville Relief Society Record, 1898–1907, 126–130, microfilm of manuscript, LR 1371 22, CHL; Escalante Ward Relief Society minutes and records, 1876–1920, Vol. 5: 1897–1907, 236–240, microfilm of manuscript, LR 2691 14, CHL; Tropic Ward Relief Society minutes and records, 1894–1958, Vol. 2: 1894–1912, 246–249, microfilm of manuscript, LR 9290 14, CHL.

103. Oakley, Idaho, Second Ward Relief Society, Minute Book, 1901–9, 195–198, LR 6360 14, CHL; Relief Society General Board, Office Minutes, August 7, 1923, typescript, Box 1, Folder 2, Washing and Anointing Blessing Texts, ca. 1923, Relief Society Washing and Anointing File.

104. Panguitch Stake, mimeograph washing and anointing text, Box 1, Folder 2, Relief Society Washing and Anointing File.

105. The 1910 Census indicated that Garfield County had 677 dwellings and a population of 3,660, or approximately 5.4 people per dwelling. That same census indicated that Tropic town had a population of 358, which would indicate approximately 66 dwellings. Department of Commerce, *Thirteenth Census of the United States Taken in the Year 1910*, Vol. 3: *Population 1910, Reports by States, with Statistics for Counties, Cities and Other Civil Division, Nebraska—Wyoming, Alaska, Hawaii, and Porto Rico* (Washington, D.C.: Government Printing Office, 1913), 873, 883.

CHAPTER 5

1. Report of Joseph Smith's teachings, in William Clayton, journal, April 1–4, 1843, in JSP J2, 404.

2. George Laub's account may be drawn from contemporaneous notes from Nauvoo. Reminiscences and journal, microfilm of holograph, MS 9628, 25–26, CHL. See also Joseph W. Musser, journal, May 24, 1900, microfilm of holograph, MS 1862, CHL. Note that many other church leaders taught that the woman whom Saul visited was indeed a witch.

3. A. Karl Larson and Katherine Miles Larson, eds., *Diary of Charles Lowell Walker*, 2 vols. (Logan: Utah State University Press, 1980), 2:603.

4. Joseph Smith, *The Holy Scriptures, Translated and Corrected by the Spirit of Revelation* (Philadelphia: Church of Jesus Christ of Latter-day Saints, 1867), 344.

5. 1 Samuel 28:9–13 (King James Version). Additions to the text in Joseph Smith's revision are indicated by italics, deletions by strikethrough. Edits are based on "Old Testament Manuscript 2," in *Joseph Smith's New Translation of the Bible: Original*

Manuscripts, edited by Scott H. Faulring, Kent P. Jackson, and Robert J. Mathews (Provo, UT: BYU Religious Studies Center, 2004), 713.

6. This motif is frequent in the Book of Mormon. See 2 Nephi 3:19–20; 2 Nephi 33:13; Ether 8:24; Mormon 8:23; Moroni 10:27. See Samuel Morris Brown, *In Heaven as It Is on Earth: Joseph Smith and the Early Mormon Conquest of Death* (New York: Oxford University Press, 2012), 122–123.

7. On cunning-folk and charmers, see Owen Davies, *Popular Magic: Cunning-folk in English History* (London: Hambledon Continuum, 2003); Hans de Waardt, "From Cunning Man to Natural Healer," and Willem de Blécourt, "Cunning Women, from Healers to Fortune Tellers," both in *Curing and Insuring: Essays on Illness in Past Times*, edited by Hans Binneveld and Rudolf Dekker (Larenseweg: Verloren, 1993), 33–42, 43–56; Jonathan Roper, ed., *Charms and Charming in Europe* (New York: Palgrave MacMillan, 2004); Jonathan Roper, *English Verbal Charms* (Helsinki: Suomalainen Tiedeakatemia, 2005). On the broader context of "occult" or natural philosophy, see Paul Kléber Monod, *Solomon's Secret Arts: The Occult in the Age of Enlightenment* (New Haven, CT: Yale University Press, 2013). Religious studies scholars have challenged and complicated the utility of the term "magic" in the study of religion. See, e.g., Jonathan Z. Smith, "Trading Places," in *Relating Religion: Essays in the Study of Religion* (Chicago: University of Chicago Press, 2004), 215–229; Wouter J. Hanegraaff, *Esotericism and the Academy: Rejected Knowledge in Western Culture* (Cambridge: Cambridge University Press, 2012), esp. 164–176.

8. Confrontations with devils or evil spirits, including formal exorcisms, are common in early Mormon records. See Stephen C. Taysom, "'Satan Mourns Naked Upon the Earth': Locating Mormon Possession and Exorcism Rituals in the American Religious Landscape, 1830–1977," *Religion and American Culture* 27, no. 1 (Winter 2017): 57–94. While some Mormons certainly believed in witches, I have never seen a witch or witchcraft documented in any Mormon records.

9. Owen Davies, "Cunning-Folk in the Medical Market-Place During the Nineteenth Century," *Medical History* 43 (1999): 73.

10. Michael Hubbard MacKay and Nicholas J. Frederick, *Joseph Smith's Seer Stones* (Provo and Salt Lake City: Religious Studies Center and Deseret Book, 2016); Brown, *In Heaven as It Is*, 69–87; Mark Ashurst-McGee, "A Pathway to Prophethood: Joseph Smith Junior as Rodsman, Village Seer, and Judeo-Christian Prophet" (M.A. thesis, Utah State University, 2000); D. Michael Quinn, *Early Mormonism and the Magic World View*, 2nd rev. ed. (Salt Lake City: Signature Books, 1998).

11. Brown, *In Heaven as It Is*, 82–83, 136.

12. Oliver Boardman Huntington, diary, October 21, 1846, Book 3, 1846, 50–59, digital images of holograph, MSS 162, LTPSC; shorthand transcription courtesy LaJean Purcell Carruth.

13. While some Andertons converted in Preston, Huntington refers to Margaret Anderton as a "woman" and not as a "sister."

14. Editor, "Blessing of Children," *Millennial Star* 24 (February 15, 1862): 107.

15. Brown, *In Heaven as It Is*, 136, 185, 194.

16. See Robin Scott Jensen, "'Rely Upon the Things Which Are Written': Text, Context, and the Creation of Mormon Revelatory Records" (MLIS thesis, University of Wisconsin–Milwaukee, 2009), 151–172.

17. Joseph Fielding, journal, September 2, 1841, digital images of holograph, MS 1567, Folder 2, Volume 4, Images 85–87, CHL; Laurel Thatcher Ulrich, *A House Full of Females: Plural Marriage and Women's Rights in Early Mormonism, 1835–1870* (New York: Alfred A. Knopf, 2017), 41–45.

18. T. Ward, "Special General Conference," *Millennial Star* 7 (January 1, 1846): 9.

19. Cynthia Doxey, "The Church in Britain and the 1851 Religious Census," *Mormon Historical Studies* 4 (2003): 107–138.

20. Stephen J. Fleming, "The Religious Heritage of the British Northwest and the Rise of Mormonism," *Church History* 77 (March 2008): 73–104.

21. In the nineteenth century over ninety thousand converts departed from Liverpool in England and immigrated to the Great Basin. Fred E. Woods, "The Tide of Mormon Migration Flowing Through the Port of Liverpool, England," *International Journal of Mormon Studies* 1 (2008): 60–86.

22. Alfred Cordon, diary, March 27, 1841, microfilm of manuscript, MS 1831, CHL.

23. Wandle Mace, "Autobiography," 48–49, microfilm of manuscript, MS 1189, CHL.

24. Reginald Scot, *The Discovery of Witchcraft* (London: A. Clark, 1665), 344–346, 354–355, 360–362; Francis Barrett, *The Magus, or Celestial Intelligencer* (London: Lackston, Allen, and Co., 1801), 135–139. Robert Priddle notes that while much of *The Magus* was culled from previously published grimoires, its section on creating seer stones was not. Robert A. Priddle, "More Cunning Than Folk: An Analysis of Francis Barrett's *The Magus* as Indicative of a Transitional Period of English Magic" (M.A. thesis, University of Ottawa, 2012).

25. See Joseph Smith, revelation, August 30, 1831, and "The Vision," in JSP D2, 50, 191 [D&C 63:17, 76:103]. These texts are allusions to Revelation 21:8 and 22:15.

26. Cordon, diary, March 27, 1841. The subsequent day, the Staffordshire Conference "unanimously carried that no such thing as Magic, Fortunetelling, Witchcraft or any such devices should be allowed in the Church. And that fellowship would be withdrawn from any who used or caused to be used any of the aforesaid things." Ibid., March 28, 1841. In 1850 Cordon warned the English church against "Planet rulers, Glass or crystal peepers, and fortune tellers." Ibid., January 13, 1850.

27. The concern over evil spirits communicating through seer stones and deceiving the user was commonly addressed in consecration rituals for the stones. William W. Phelps in his 1854 *Almanac* later reproduced a sixteenth-century legal indictment against those who "use invocation, or conjuration, of any evil spirit, or shall consult, covenant with, entertain, imploy, feed or reward an evil spirit." W. W. Phelps, "Extracts," in *Deseret Almanac* (Salt Lake City: W. Richards, 1854), 16.

28. John Stockdale, "Conference Minutes," *Millennial Star* 10 (March 15, 1848): 92.

29. Donald G. Godfrey and Rebecca S. Martineau-McCarty, eds., *An Uncommon Common Pioneer: The Journals of James Henry Martineau, 1828–1918* (Provo, UT: Religious Studies Center, Brigham Young University, 2008), 15.

30. John Sanderson, et al., letter to Brigham Young, December 24, 1854, Box 23, Folder 16, BYOF. Besides those mentioned elsewhere in this chapter, John J. Hayes (born in 1825 in Ireland) was another documented student of Sanderson. Eleanor Jane Hayes, "Biography of John Joseph Hayes," http://hayesjhfo.org/materials/biographies/JJHBiobyEJHWeb.pdf.

31. Bliss J. Brimley, *The Book of Thomas Job* (n.p., 1988), 93.

32. Thomas Job, "Autobiography," in Brimley, *Book of Thomas Job*, 29, 117; Quinn, *Early Mormonism*, 280–281.

33. Priddle, "More Cunning Than Folk"; Owen Davies, *Grimoires: A History of Magic Books* (Oxford: Oxford University Press, 2009), 135–138. One of Sanderson's students in Utah created a manuscript comprising most of *The Magus* and a section on geomancy from Robert Cross Smith, *The Astrologer of the Nineteenth Century* (London: Knight and Lacey, 1825). William K. Barton, journal, 1855–1887, Image 132, digital images of holograph, MS 26472, Box 1, Folder 1, William K. Barton Collection, 1855–1887, CHL; William K. Barton, "The Magus," manuscript, ca. 1856, Box 1, Folder 2, William K. Barton Collection, 1855–1887, CHL. The section on geomancy likely came from Thomas Job, who mentions both geomancy and possessing writings from Smith [Raphael] in his autobiography.

34. Job was excommunicated for apostasy in 1863 and joined the Reorganized Church in 1864. Brimley, *Book of Thomas Job*, 152. In the late 1860s Sanderson vocally dissented from church leaders but died before any discipline could be imposed. D. Robert Carter, "Mysterious fires plagued Springville Hotel," *Daily Herald* [Provo, UT], April 1, 2006, B2.

35. Register of the John Steele Collection, 1847–1936, Vault MSS 528, LTPSC.

36. John Steele, journal, digital images of holograph, MS 1847, Folder 2, Volume 1, Images 206–221, CHL; John Steele Papers, MSS 528, Box 3, Folder 10, LTPSC. Cf. Scot, *Discovery of Witchcraft*, book 15, ch. 16, 243; Barrett, *Magus*, book 2, 107. On the Paracelsian charm, see Davies, *Popular Magic*, 150–153.

37. Angels were sometimes the focus of crystal or stone divination. Owen Davies, "Angels in Elite and Popular Magic, 1650–1790," in *Angels in the Early Modern World*, edited by Peter Marshall and Alexandra Walsham (Cambridge: Cambridge University Press, 2006), 297–319; Monod, *Solomon's Secret Arts*, 35, 63–64, 71.

38. Owen Davies, "French Charmers and Their Healing Charms," in Roper, *Charms and Charming in Europe*, 108.

39. Godfrey and Martineau-McCarty, *Uncommon Common Pioneer*, 15, 29, 37. Martineau apparently maintained some interest in astrology and in 1860 visited Thomas Job, who by then had left the Utah church. Ibid., 112. William Barton, another of Sanderson's students, similarly visited Young to get "some of the Planets Right Ascentions and diclenation." Barton, journal, March 22, 1858, Image 135.

40. Orson Pratt, *Prophetic Almanac for 1846* (New York: New York Messenger Office, 1845), 2.

41. James B. Allen, *No Toil Nor Labor Fear: The Story of William Clayton* (Provo, UT: Brigham Young University Press, 2002), 328–338; Quinn, *Early Mormonism*,

277–291. To an individual seeking to create an astrology school in 1861, Young responded that "it would not do to favor Astrology." Brigham Young, office journal, December 30, 1861, Box 72, Folder 5, BYOF. See also Heber Ferrin, letter to Brigham Young, December 29, 1875, Box 35, Folder 15, BYOF; and Brigham Young, letter to Heber Ferrin, January 6, 1876, Box 10, Volume 14, 104, BYOF.

42. Editor, "Astrology and Magic," *Millennial Star* 10 (February 15, 1848): 50–52; Orson Hyde, letter to Daniel H. Wells, October 4, 1855, Box 39, Folder 22, BYOF. See also Larson and Larson, *Diary of Charles Lowell Walker*, 1:419.

43. Allen, *No Toil Nor Labor Fear*, 328–338.

44. Jane Fisher, letter to Joseph F. Smith, May 11, 1857, digital images of holograph, MS 1325, Box 9, Folder 5, Images 32–35, Joseph F. Smith Papers, CHL.

45. Barton, journal, 1855–1887, Image 149. Barton later remarked that "during the Winter of 1870 & 71 I was ingaged in several debates and gave a lecture on Astronomy and a many of its absurdities which was noticed in the Deseret News." Ibid., Image 163.

46. Kenney, *Wilford Woodruff's Journal*, 6:393–394; cf. Church Historian's Office Journal, February 3, 1868, digital copy of manuscript, CR 100 1, CHL.

47. George Q. Cannon, ed., "Astrology and Its Evils," *Deseret News*, February 5, 1868, 412. See also A. Milton Musser, "Correspondence," *Deseret News*, March 25, 1868, 49.

48. J.E.T. [James E. Talmage], "My Study of Astrology," *Contributor* 14 (November 1892): 33–36.

49. Kenney, *Wilford Woodruff's Journal*, 2:144.

50. Susan Juster, *Doomsayers: Anglo-American Prophecy in the Age of Revolution* (Philadelphia: University of Pennsylvania Press), 57–85.

51. John H. Wigger, *Taking Heaven by Storm: Methodism and the Rise of Popular Christianity in America* (Urbana and Chicago: University of Illinois Press, 2001), 231, n. 9.

52. Besides the examples and analysis presented in this chapter, see also Quinn, *Early Mormonism*, 247–255; Ian F. Barber, "Mormon Women as 'Natural Seers,'" in *Women and Authority: Re-emerging Mormon Feminism*, edited by Maxine Hanks (Salt Lake City: Signature Books, 1992), 167–184.

53. JSP J2, 324, 404. This teaching was later canonized with the 1879 edition of the Doctrine and Covenants. Orson Pratt, ed., *The Doctrine and Covenants* (Liverpool: William Budge, 1879), 460–462 [D&C 130]. See also Ashurst-McGee, "Pathway to Prophethood," 188–190, 270.

54. For an early example of this teaching's integration into Latter-day Saint belief, see Isaac Morley, blessing on Lorenzo Snow, December 19, 1843, MS 1330, Folder 1, digital Images 152–160, Lorenzo Snow journal and letterbook, 1836–1845 and 1872, CHL.

55. Council Minutes, September 30, 1855, digital images of manuscript, CR 100 318, Box 3, Folder 7, Image 44, Historian's Office General Church Minutes, 1839–1877, CHL.

56. J. Cecil Alter, ed., "Journal of Priddy Meeks," *Utah Historical Quarterly* 10 (1942): 179–180.

57. Joseph Fish, autobiography, ch. 22, microfilm of typescript, MS 649, CHL.

58. Martha Ann Smith, letter to Joseph F. Smith, July 29, 1856, Box 8, Folder 31, Image 13, Joseph F. Smith Papers. See also Jane Fisher, letter to Joseph F. Smith, July 20, 1856, Box 9, Folder 2, Image 32, Joseph F. Smith Papers; Jane Fisher, letter to Joseph F. Smith, May 11, 1857, Box 9, Folder 5, Images 32–35, Joseph F. Smith Papers.

59. Brigham Young, office journal, May 7, 1860.

60. Godfrey and Martineau-McCarty, *Uncommon Common Pioneer*, 298.

61. "Astrology and kindred topics. Evils that should be avoided by the people," *Deseret News*, March 18, 1885, 143.

62. Godfrey and Martineau-McCarty, *Uncommon Common Pioneer*, 96.

63. George F. Gibbs, letter to Orson D. Romney, June 20, 1911, FPL.

64. Council Minutes, September 30, 1855, digital images of manuscript, CR 100 318, Box 3, Folder 7, Image 44, Historians Office General Church Minutes, 1839–1877, CHL.

65. Brigham Young, office journal, December 23, 1860; Brigham Young, sermon, July 26, 1857, in JD, 5:77. See also John Taylor's comments as recorded in Kenney, *Wilford Woodruff's Journal*, 5:549–550 [February 11, 1861].

66. Salt Lake School of the Prophets, minutes, June 9, 1873, digital images of manuscript, CR 390 7, Box 1, Folder 5, CHL. In discussing the failure of apostles to be "seers" despite having the privilege of becoming "prophets, seers, and revelators," Orson Pratt stated that the "fault is in ourselves." Orson Pratt, "Discourse," May 11, 1878, in JD, 25:145.

67. Jensen, "'Rely Upon the Things,'" 151–172.

68. Josiah E. Hickman, Journal A, December 25, 1890, holograph in private possession, digital images of entry in author's possession.

69. Christian Anderson, journal, December 16, 1890, microfilm of holograph, MS 15793, CHL.

70. Ibid., December 9, 1890, and December 16, 1890.

71. Hickman, Journal A, December 25, 1890.

72. Mary Ellen H. Kimball, journal, May 8, 1858, microfilm of holograph, MS 4218 2, CHL. The seer stone in question belonged to Edwin Rushton. See also ibid., July 22, 1858.

73. "Astrology and kindred topics," 143.

74. Wilford Woodruff, letter to John T. Ballantyne, August 20, 1888, FPL.

75. Ibid.

76. James E. Talmage, diary, February 21, 1893, vol. 6, 175, 178, holograph, MSS 229, Box 2, Folder 2, LTPSC.

77. "The Seer-stone of Edwin Rushton," typescript, MS 24401, Folder 1, Edwin Rushton Family Collection, CHL. A photograph of Rushton's seer stone is available as PH 60, CHL.

78. Talmage, diary, February 21, 1893, and February 22, 1893, 175–185.

79. See chapters 1 and 4.

80. Jonathan Stapley, "Pouring in Oil: The Development of the Modern Mormon Healing Ritual," in *By Our Rites of Worship: Latter-day Saint Views on Ritual in Scripture and Practice*, edited by Daniel L. Belnap (Provo and Salt Lake City: Deseret Book/Religious Studies Center, 2013), 283–316.

81. Oliver Cowdery to Dr. S. Avord [Samson Avard], December 15, 1835, Oliver Cowdery Letter Book, Henry E. Huntington Library, San Marino, CA. On Frederick G. Williams's medical practice, see Frederick G. Williams, "The Medical Practice of Dr. Frederick G. Williams," *BYU Studies Quarterly* 51, no. 1 (2012): 153–169; idem, *The Life of Dr. Frederick G. Williams: Counselor to the Prophet Joseph Smith* (Provo, UT: BYU Studies, 2012).

82. See Stapley, "Pouring in Oil," for a detailed discussion of the interplay in Mormonism between the healing liturgy and professional medicine.

83. de Waardt, "From Cunning Man," 41.

84. Godfrey and Martineau-McCarty, *Uncommon Common Pioneer*, 162.

85. Brigham Young, office journal, May 7, 1860. On bosom serpentry, see Wayland D. Hand, *Magical Medicine: The Folkloric Component of Medicine in the Folk Belief, Custom, and Ritual of the Peoples of Europe and America* (Los Angeles: University of California Press, 1979), 251–260; Richard C. Poulsen, "Bosom Serpentry among the Puritans and Mormons," *Journal of the Folklore Institute* 16, no. 3 (1979): 176–189.

86. John Steele, journal, Images 206–221, Box 3, Folder 10, John Steele Papers.

87. Williams, "Medical Practice," 158–159.

88. Young later returned the amulet to Watt. Ronald G. Watt, *The Mormon Passage of George D. Watt: First British Convert, Scribe for Zion* (Logan: Utah State University Press, 2009), 125–126, 268.

89. Brigham Young, account book, 1856–1877, January 5, 1858; May 23, 1859; June 2, 1859; November 13, 1861; May 16, 1868; July 11, 1868; and February 3, 1870, all in Vault MSS 155, LTPSC. See also Quinn, *Early Mormonism*, 271.

90. See Stapley and Wright, "Female Ritual Healing in Mormonism," 29–31.

91. Zina D. H. Young, loose sheets, digital images of holograph, MS 4780, Box 3, Folder 11, Image 23, Zina Card Brown Family Collection 1806–1972, CHL. Cf. Henry Swainson Cowper, *Hawkshead: Its History, Archaeology, Industries, Folklore, Dialect, Etc., Etc.* (London: Bemrose & Sons, 1899), 314–315; Davies, "Healing Charms in Use," 23. Young's charm is consistent with Smallwood's observation that later charms often included misreadings of archaic terms. T. M. Smallwood, "The Transmission of Charms in English, Medieval and Modern," in Roper, *Charms and Charming in Europe*, 21–22. See also Roper, *English Verbal Charms*, 170–174.

92. Zina D. H. Young, diaries, digital images of holograph, Box 1, Folders 9, Images 24 and 26, Zina Card Brown Family Collection 1806–1972. Brigham Young similarly recommended the use of the "fat lying near the anus of" a pig to cure hemorrhoids. Brigham Young, office journal, March 2, 1860.

93. Zina D. H. Young, loose sheets, Box 3, Folder 11, Image 23, Zina Card Brown Family Collection 1806–1972.

94. Roper, *English Verbal Charms*, 109–110.

95. Heber C. Kimball, March 15, 1857, in JD, 4:294. For an introduction to the healing canes fashioned from Joseph and Hyrum Smith's coffins, see Steven G. Barnett, "Canes of the Restoration," in "The Historian's Corner," edited by James B. Allen, *BYU Studies* 21, no. 2 (1981): 205–211. The case of the coffin canes is interesting but does not readily conform to the traditional folk remedies associated with funereal items. See, e.g., "Superstitious Cures," *Atkinson's Casket* (June 1833), 264. See also Hand, *Magical Medicine*, 12–13, 69–80; and entries related to coffin rings in the *Online Archive of American Folk Medicine*, http://www.folkmed.ucla.edu/.

96. Charles Kelly, ed., *The Journal of John D. Lee, 1846–47 and 1859* (Salt Lake City: University of Utah Press, 1984), 67.

97. John Albiston, letter, April 30, 1848, in *Millennial Star* 10 (May 15, 1848): 158. Note that during this period, "stick" was a common synonym for cane. See, e.g., "Sticks," *Chamber's Edinburgh Journal* (September 18, 1841), 277–278.

98. Wayland D. Hand and Jeannine E. Talley, eds., *Popular Beliefs and Superstitions from Utah* (Salt Lake City: University of Utah Press, 1984), xxvi, xxxvii. See also Hand, *Magical Medicine*, 321–330. Smallwood has documented a case of a British immigrant passing verbal charms to American grandchildren. Smallwood, "Transmission of Charms," 22–23.

99. Claire Noall, "Superstitions, Customs, and Prescriptions of Mormon Midwives," *California Folklore Quarterly* 3 (April 1944): 103–104; see also Richard C. Poulsen, "Some Botanic Cures in Mormon Folk Medicine: An Analysis," *Utah Historical Quarterly* 44 (Fall 1976): 378–388.

100. Stapley, "'Pouring in Oil.'"

101. Claire M. Cassidy, "Social and Cultural Factors in Medicine," in *Fundamentals of Complementary and Alternative Medicine*, 5th ed., edited by Marc S. Micozzi (St. Louis: Elsevier Saunders, 2015), 60–61; Ronnie Moore and Stuart McClean, "Folk Healing and a Post-scientific World," in *Folk Healing and Health Care Practices in Britain and Ireland: Stethoscopes, Wands and Crystals*, edited by Ronnie Moore and Stuart McClean (Oxford: Berghahn Books, 2010). Candy Gunther Brown, *The Healing Gods: Complementary and Alternative Medicine in Christian America* (New York: Oxford University Press, 2013); Kate Shellnut, "The Proverbs 31 Woman Has a Facebook Page," *Christianity Today* (December 2015), 34–41.

102. Bruce H. Lipton, *The Biology of Belief: Unleashing the Power of Consciousness, Matter, and Miracles* (Santa Rosa, CA: Mountain of Love, 2005). John A. Ives and Wayne B. Jones, "Energy Medicine," in Micozzi, *Fundamentals of Complementary and Alternative Medicine*, 197–212. Cf. the magnetic healing of eighteenth-century Britain. Monod, *Solomon's Secret Arts*, 304–313.

103. Jonathan Stapley, oral interview, April 23, 2014.

104. See, e.g., Janae Francis, "Christ-centered healing conference June 15–17 in Ogden," *Standard Examiner*, June 11, 2016, http://www.standard.net/Faith/2016/06/11/Christ-centered-healing-conference-draws-many-for-alternative-approaches;

Daniel Woodruff, "The business behind Christ-centered energy healing," *KUTV*, September 21, 2016 http://kutv.com/news/local/the-business-behind-christ-centered-energy-healing.

105. Brady McCombs, "LDS Church dismisses 'blood moon' worries," *Deseret News*, September 26, 2015.

106. Church of Jesus Christ of Latter-day Saints, Seminaries and Institutes, "Spurious Materials in Circulation," August 31, 2015, https://si.lds.org/bc/seminary/content/binary-content/binary-content/news-tim-gurr/publication_caution---a_greater_tomorrow_my_journey_beyond_the_veil_04-statements-in-circulation3831.pdf.

107. Church of Jesus Christ of Latter-day Saints Newsroom, "Church Responds to Inquiries about Preparedness," http://www.mormonnewsroom.org/article/church-responds-to-inquiries-about-preparedness.

108. Woodruff, "Business behind Christ-centered energy healing."

109. David Elton Gay, "On the Christianity of Incantations," in Roper, *Charms and Charming in Europe*, 3, 34–35, 40, 43.

110. Roper, *English Verbal Charms*, 16, 80; de Waardt, "From Cunning Man to Natural Healer"; Davies, *Popular Magic*, 78, 82, 94.

111. Davies, *Popular Magic*, 61–62.

CONCLUSION

1. Bruce R. McConkie, *Conference Report* (April 1949), 90.

2. "History," ca. June 1839–1841 [Draft 2 and 3], in JSP H1, 214–215.

3. John Wesley, "The Nature, Design, and General Rules of the United Societies," in *The Bicentennial Edition of the Works of John Wesley*, edited by Rupert Eric Davies (Nashville, TN: Abingdon Press, 1976–), 9:69.

4. Christopher C. Jones, "The Power and Form of Godliness: Methodist Conversion Narratives and Joseph Smith's First Vision," *Journal of Mormon History* 37, no. 2 (Spring 2011): 87–94.

5. Joseph Smith, revelation, September 22–23, 1832, in JSP D2, 295 [D&C 84:19–22].

6. Bruce R. McConkie, *Conference Report* (April 1949), 90.

7. David F. Holland, "Revelation and the Open Canon in Mormonism," in *The Oxford Handbook of Mormonism*, edited by Terryl L. Givens and Philip L. Barlow (New York: Oxford University Press, 2015), 149–163.

8. Joseph Cardinal Ratzinger, "Preface," in Alcuin Reid, *The Organic Development of the Liturgy* (San Francisco: Ignatius Press, 2005), 9–13.

Index

Note: Page numbers followed by the letters "f" or "n" indicate material found in figures or footnotes, respectively.